BACKROADS & BYWAYS
OF
COLORADO

BACKROADS & BYWAYS OF COLORADO

Drives, Daytrips & Weekend Excursions

Drea Knufken
& John Daters

SECOND EDITION

THE COUNTRYMAN PRESS
WOODSTOCK, VERMONT

Interior photographs by Drea Knufken unless otherwise specified
Frontispiece photo: Trail Ridge Road, Rocky Mountain National Park, by Seth K. Hughes
Maps by Erin Greb Cartography, © The Countryman Press
Book design by Susan Livingston
Composition by Chelsea Cloeter

Published by The Countryman Press,
P.O. Box 748, Woodstock, VT 05091

Distributed by W. W. Norton & Company, Inc.,
500 Fifth Avenue, New York, NY 10110

Printed in the United States of America

10 9 8 7 6 5 4 3 2 1

Backroads & Byways of Colorado
978-1-58157-161-5

MY THANKS TO: *Kim Grant for giving me this opportunity years ago. Everyone at Countryman Press, especially Kermit and Lisa, for being so helpful along the way. The many Coloradans I met during my travels who shared a passion and devotion to this state. And Beth, my partner, my rock, who reminds me every day that beauty and love are simple and always available.*   —D.K.

THIS BOOK IS DEDICATED TO BETH, *whom I love without reservation. Without you, this edition would never have been finished.*   —J.D.

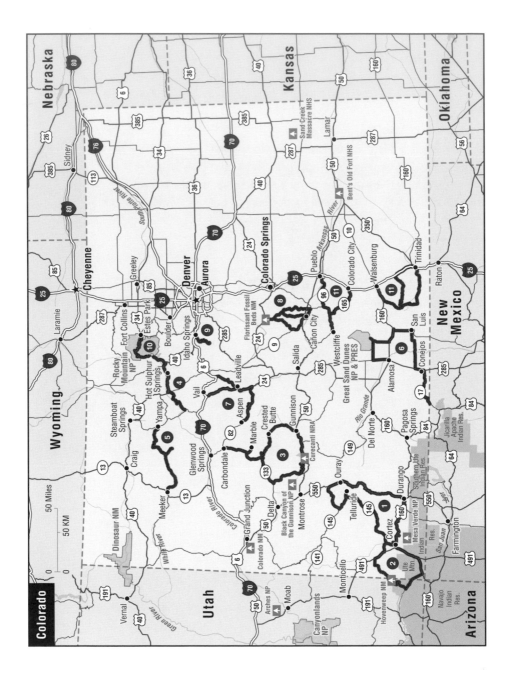

CONTENTS

INTRODUCTION

Colorado's wide-open skies, rich history, and fluorescent peaks under high-altitude sunrises have held people captive from as early as the Ice Age. Archaeological digs just outside of Fort Collins, conducted in 1932, found some of the state's earliest human residents to no doubt marvel at the region's landscapes. Scientific findings from the digs place the state's first human inhabitants at roughly 9000 B.C. Decades later, more similarly aged sites were uncovered along the Front Range. While the area between Fort Collins and Pueblo uncovered some of the earliest people, perhaps the best understood prehistoric settlers came years later in southwest Colorado. These native people settled in the region around 1500 B.C. Sites found near modern-day Mesa Verde uncovered a wealth and variety of well-crafted woven artifacts—leading scientists to dub this culture "Basketmakers." For the most part, these early residents were hunter-gatherers with relatively rudimentary farming and ranching techniques. However, some time between A.D. 1 and 750, the Basketmakers began to show evidence of well-established farming techniques and the construction of architecturally improved dwellings—evidenced by pit houses. With less time devoted to basic survival needs, these technological progressions allowed for an increase in leisure time among the community, allowing them to achieve such innovations as utilitarian and artistically rendered pottery. It's believed that this turning point in technological progression actually evidences the coming of a new age within this society. These original settlers had progressed beyond simple basketmakers to become a significantly distinct people. We know the name for this new culture through not their own language, but that of their future neighbors, the Navajo. The Navajo christened these people *Anasazi,* a word meaning "the ancestors of our enemies" or "ancient people who are not us." Through oral histories and genealogical studies, today's Pueblo have been found to be the most closely related descendents of the Anasazi. While the name *Anasazi* is still prevalent, today's descents prefer their forbearers be referred to as "Ancestral Puebloans," as the Navajo name is considered mildly derogatory—and besides, being named by a nonrelated tribe may also be construed as a cultural embarrassment. During their height, it's estimated that thousands of Ancestral Puebloan families may have lived in today's southwest Colorado.

Unfortunately, the Ancestral Puebloans were victims of circumstance and their own success. Through farming, these native people pulled all the nutrients from the soil, making crops continually harder to grow. Coupled with unseasonal droughts and environment- and population-related natural resource decline, the first settlers of today's Colorado were forced to migrate to what is now Arizona and New Mexico. The Pueblo in both of those states can trace their roots to Ancestral Puebloans, who first staked a claim in Colorado.

Not too long after their departure, the stalwart and nomadic Ute and Navajo frequented the area, leaving behind evidence of their transitory visits with temporary shelters, long-since abandoned. Centuries later, in 1776, the Spanish friars Dominguez and Escalante would be the first non–American Indians to explore and record the area's various archaeological sites, geological features, and natural resources. Today's visitors to the region are treated to this exceptional historical record by the Anasazi Heritage Center and Canyons of the Ancients National Monument, both operated by the Bureau of Land Management. Perhaps the best-known location showcasing much of the region's early history is Mesa Verde National Park—one of the state's most-visited national parks, as well as among the nation's most well known.

Centuries after the Anasazi left, around A.D. 1500, the nomadic Ute moved into the southern Rockies. Plains American Indians later settled in eastern Colorado, the Arapaho and Cheyenne in the northeastern plains, the Shoshoni in the northwestern part of the state, and the Comanche and Kiowa in the southeastern plains. The tribes comprised a diverse demographic that traded, communicated, bonded, and fought—sometimes migrating to new territories, other times defending home turfs.

This thriving American Indian world started to change when European explorers arrived in the area in the mid-1500s. They were searching for something: The Spanish sought gold, the Pacific Ocean, and mythical cities; the French came looking for new territory. The last people to scout the territory were also its final settlers. In 1803 the brand-new United States claimed rights to eastern Colorado through the Louisiana Purchase. Newly minted American lieutenants and majors arrived with the intent to claim the land. They renamed the landscape in their own language, prospected for resources, and took ownership of American Indian territories.

Local American Indian tribes had mixed reactions to the new settlers. Some fought hard to protect their land. Others cooperated with the settlers, hoping to gain advantage over feuding tribes. Still others had mixed reactions, alternately fighting and cooperating with the settlers. One visionary Ute, Chief Ouray, saw that the turmoil could have no positive outcome for his people. He advocated diplomacy and peaceful resolution on both sides. Unfortunately, despite his courage, a peaceful outcome never happened. One of Colorado's most beautiful mountain towns is his namesake.

As the conflict between the American Indians and the U.S. continued to boil, settlers kept pouring into Colorado. In the mid-1800s, new kinds of pioneers were attracted to the area: the fur trader, the merchant, and the mountain man. These men were the cowboys of yore, the roughnecks who swung saloon doors and carbine rifles with equal ease. Many of the state's rivers and natural features are named after these maverick adventurers: the St. Vrain River, the town of Kit Carson, and Wooten Road.

Meanwhile, the U.S. government, continually striving to establish wider boundaries, concluded the Mexican Cession of 1848, when a large portion of what is now the U.S. Southwest was ceded to the U.S. as part of a Mexican-American war treaty. As a result, Colorado's boundaries were drawn along longitudinal and latitudinal lines. This enigmatic frontier state, where roughnecks and merchants searched for trading opportunities, where American Indians defended land, and through which pioneers traveled, was drawn into a simple rectangle.

New settlers soon discovered the rich minerals embedded in the surrounding Rockies, and the first mines were dug. Not long after that, the first nugget of gold was torn from the Rockies' rich innards. Arguably, the man to first discover gold in the area was A. D. Green Russell, who found gold in the silty South Platte River in 1858, precipitating a mass of enthusiastic wealth-seekers from the East, who pioneered into Colorado chanting "Pikes Peak or Bust!"

So many gold diggers poured in that townships sprung up like mushrooms near what are now Denver, Boulder, and Fort Collins. These sites served as bases from where gold-hungry men traveled in droves to the rivers, ready to strike their fortunes with pans and picks. More gold was soon discovered deeper in the Rocky Mountains, from Chicago Creek (near modern-day Georgetown) to Black Hawk.

Men were finding gold everywhere, and rapidly growing towns were a result. The state's first newspaper, the *Rocky Mountain News,* and its first school soon appeared, as did local governments. Meanwhile, because of the influx of settlers and a series of treaties with the U.S. government, American Indians had all but been brokered out of power.

In 1876 Colorado became the 38th state of the Union. It was named Colorado, or "colored red" in Spanish, for the thick, red waters of the Colorado River. Because its statehood was granted one hundred years after the signing of the Declaration of Independence, it was also nicknamed the Centennial State. By then, the state's many settlers had built a new economy based around tanning, farming, mining, ranching, and tending to the civic needs of their towns. In 1888 the last of the Ute were moved to reservations outside of the state. Around the same time, the ancient cliff dwellings that the Anasazi had abandoned so long before were found by two cowboys who came upon them while searching for lost cattle.

Colorado was a state on the rise, and the discovery of silver added to its burgeoning economy. Due to this massive injection of valuable ore, the state's people began expanding its infrastructure, beginning with its now-historic railroads—the first of which was the Pikes Peak cog railroad completed in 1891, followed by the Moffat railroad over the Continental Divide. This easy access to pristine Colorado caught more than the eye of the explorer and prospector; some of the nation's earliest conservationists quickly grasped the unique, natural beauty of this new state. Not long after, people voted to keep the state's beauty intact by ordaining Colorado's first national forest reserve, White River National Forest, near modern-day Meeker.

In the 1920s, Colorado began to build its many quality highways along heavily traveled routes. By this time, the boom-or-bust gold rush had created a few booming towns, like Georgetown, and more than a few ghost towns. After the gold rush stabilized, the state's natural assets became its new draw. Word spread about Colorado's many marvelous ski and tourism opportunities, convincing even more people to move into the state. In the 1950s, the government built the Eisenhower Tunnel through the Continental Divide west of Denver, making it easy to access western Colorado's ski slopes.

Since the mid-20th century, a new lifestyle has emerged around Colorado's natural bounty. Its ski slopes, the towering Rockies, its forests, and its now-fertile prairies now draw settlers of a new kind—people from around the globe seeking a way of life centered on quality rather than speed, nature and fresh air rather than the bustle of a metropolis.

At the same time, those initial settlers of Colorado, the Ute and other Native American tribes, are reclaiming their territory. Today, this takes the form of casinos, tourist establishments, shares in oil and gas, and various other business investments. Because of their shrewd investments, the Ute are one of the wealthiest tribes in the region. Though the contrast between the petroglyphs their ancestors left and the high-tech slot machines they run today is stark, many of their traditions remain intact.

The people inhabiting Colorado are now an eclectic mix of everything from old-time ranchers to techies to professional athletes. What binds people together is a connection to the land, not too dissimilar from that connection of the American Indians before them. The state continues to draw pioneers and mavericks in every form, from business entrepreneurs to permaculture farmers.

CULTURE

Drive down any of Colorado's byways and you'll see that Colorado's Wild West past is still very much a part of the present. Many of the roadside souvenir shops dotting the state's byways look almost exactly like outposts from days of yore—or maybe what Hollywood would have us believe they looked like. Wheelbarrows and crates filled with geodes and crystals often sit outside these wooden pioneer houses with their creaky floors and general-store smell. Finds ranging from American Indian war bonnets to Rockies-themed snow globes might line the wooden shelves inside these outposts. Common Colorado souvenirs include carved antlers, leather goods like belts and moccasins, wood carvings, jams and jellies, columbine seeds, and trinkets. High-quality Western-wear stores that sell cowboy hats, boots, and bolo ties also abound.

Art buffs, take note: Colorado is also famous for its Southwestern and Native American art. During the times of Spanish exploration, American Indians learned advanced silversmithing techniques, and have since been mastering the art of metallurgy. Beadwork, traditional since pre-Columbian times, is also very advanced in both form and intricacy. Jewelry made from local silver and turquoise—such as carved-stone animals, beadwork, and sand paintings—is common.

You can often judge the authenticity of a piece by observing its quality: no scratches, loose hinges, or stone settings, and attention to detail. Authentic pieces take time to make, and the cost may reflect this. Most important, ask where the jewelry was made, and by whom. The best work will usually be made by local artists. Purchasing their work will ensure the survival of their strong traditions as well as move money away from the imposters. Be wary of purchasing items like dream catchers, round leather-and-string ornaments that are often hung from ceilings or rearview mirrors, and peace pipes; although they may look attractive on your mantel, these objects are considered sacred by many groups. Buyers are advised against their purchase. Think of it as the cultural equivalent of wearing Catholic rosaries as fad jewelry without knowing their meaning.

Finally, a mention about Colorado food: The state has a sensational range of microbrewed beers, local chocolate, and, of course, wild game and buffalo products, such as sausage and jerky. With its over 3 million head of cattle, the state is a carnivore's paradise. Truly the best meal you can find here is a burger and microbrewed beer. Yet a fair number of Colorado residents are vegetarian, so you'll find surprisingly good veggie fare all over the state. Other specialties include chili, jams and jellies, trail mix, and dried soups. Finally, there's nothing quite like picking a fresh, plump Colorado peach off a tree on the Western Slope in the heat of August.

GEOGRAPHY

To the east rises a prairie sun, lighting the fields of Western ranchland in golden hues. One hundred years ago, before cattle grazed and cowboys rode rows of lonely fence lines, covered wagons could be seen traversing the roadless terrain, buckboards creaking with pioneers perched upon them, looking west. Today, the major roadways of I-70 and I-76 cut through much the same pioneer routes in the high plains of eastern Colorado, offering modern travelers exponentially more comfort and speed.

Contrary to popular belief, Colorado is not uniformly mountainous. In fact, to the east of the Rockies the state is ice-rink flat, with prairie stretching far enough to create a horizon-bending effect. While flat, the plains are still lofty; the plains bottom out in elevation higher than most U.S. cities, the lowest elevation measuring in on the extreme eastern border near the town of Wray at 3,500 feet. While a third of Colorado is composed of plains, the rest of the landscape is composed of granite and sandstone.

The Rockies announce their presence with pomp, rising thousands of verti-

COLORADO QUICK FACTS

Nickname: Centennial State
  Having been inducted into the Union in 1876, one hundred years after the Constitution was signed, the state's founders saw fit to tip their hats to this historic fact by nicknaming the state the Centennial State.

State flower: White and lavender columbine

State mammal: Bighorn sheep

State bird: Lark bunting

State fish: Greenback cutthroat trout

State capital: Denver

Population: 5,029,196 (2010 U.S. Census)

Area: 104,247 square miles

State song: "Where the Columbines Grow" by A. J. Fynn (1915) and "Rocky Mountain High" by John Denver and Mike Taylor (1973)

Motto: "Nil Sine Numine" (Nothing without Providence)

Time zone: Mountain

Daylight savings: Yes

Bordering states: Arizona, Utah, Wyoming, Nebraska, Kansas, Oklahoma, New Mexico

Abbreviated timeline:

- *9000 B.C.: Colorado's first human inhabitants*
- *A.D. 1–750: Anasazi are established in the Four Corners Region of Colorado.*
- *1541: Spanish conquistador, Coronado, traverses southeastern Colorado.*
- *1803: Land that includes modern-day Colorado is purchased from Napoleon Bonaparte of France in the Louisiana Purchase.*
- *1806: Zebulon Pike becomes the first American to officially explore the area.*
- *1859: Gold rush begins in and around the Colorado Rockies, and settlement begins in earnest.*
- *1861: Colorado becomes a U.S. territory.*
- *1879: Colorado is inducted into the Union—exactly one hundred years after the signing of the Declaration of Independence—becoming the 38th state.*

cal feet into the sky in a matter of a few miles. The eastern side of the Continental Divide isn't a gentle upslope to pinnacles of granite. Instead, it is a gnashing collision of tectonic plates, which forced immeasurable amounts of mass to rise quickly. In fact, from Denver, situated at the cusp of the plains and Rocky Mountains, a short one-hour drive takes travelers to the highest paved road in North America: Mount Evans Road. Here, in the Colorado Rockies, postcard-perfect snapshots are captured, and renowned professional and amateur photographers the world 'round capture raw, powerful shots of nature.

> ### CAR KIT CHECKLIST
>
> - 2 liters of water per person
> - Nonperishable food
> - Spare tire/Fix-a-Flat (tire inflator and sealant)
> - Cell phone and charger
> - Blanket
> - Flashlight
> - Coolant
> - Full gas can (kept in trunk)
> - Flares
> - Medical kit
> - Change of clothes

The section of the Rockies surrounding the Continental Divide contains the peaks of the highest mountains in the continental U.S. This is where quintessential Colorado lives. The majority of Colorado's 25 ski resorts are found in these areas, as are river headwaters, mining towns, and the state's ubiquitous high-mountain passes.

West of the Continental Divide, inverse of its eastern counterpart, the land slowly tapers down to lower elevations, and is aptly named the Western Slope. Rivers on this side of the divide spill over the landscape and flow toward the Pacific Ocean—the iconic Colorado River being just one among many. These rivers have carved their fingerprints into red sandstone and granite as they make their way west. Gorges and canyons, nearly of the Grand Canyon variety, have been gouged out of this terrain—chief among them being the Black Canyon of the Gunnison and the Black Ridge Canyons. So deep, sheer, and well visited are these cuts in the earth that each has been given special consideration: Black Canyon is a national park and the Black Ridge Canyons a designated wilderness area.

To the southern terminus of the state's Western Slope lies the Four Corners Region, home to ancient civilizations and arid, cavernous landscapes.

RECREATION

Trunks and roof racks only hold so much, so how do you know what to bring along on an extended car trip? This question is even trickier when you consider the wealth of pursuits Colorado's varied terrain has to offer. After all, Colorado is peppered with rivers, mountains, deserts, sand dunes, gorges, and anything else that nature has a mind to throw into the mix. Such simple questions like whether to pack a fly-rod or lure-rod, an inflatable raft or beach chair, hiking shoes or flip-flops become matters of debate as car space is finite. If you've got a specific area of interest, pack for that; if you're eclectic in taste, flip through this guide and get a taste for what each area has to offer, then pack accordingly. We'll try and help you out along the way.

PREPARING FOR YOUR TRIP

ALTITUDE

How it affects your car: The effects of altitude on your car are minimal, especially in newer vehicles. Your gas mileage may get slightly worse, though nothing you'd notice unless you kept detailed books on your fuel economy. The most common problem with driving at altitude is vapor lock, a relatively common problem among later-model cars. Vapor lock occurs when the air pressure in your gas tank has to equalize to the pressure of higher altitudes, making it hard for the proper amount of gas to reach your engine. Newer cars, or even just newer gas caps, are able to equalize the pressure more readily. If you're at altitude and your car won't start, or sputters and dies while you still have gas in the tank, chances are vapor lock is the culprit. Luckily, it's one of the easiest things to remedy. Get your car out of traffic, then unscrew your gas cap. This will allow exterior air pressure into the tank, equalizing it. You may have to wait a bit before your car will start up again, but once it does, it should be smooth driving for the rest of the route.

How it affects you: Altitude will affect travelers much more readily than it will an automobile. Sometimes these effects are welcome. Case in point: Alcohol's effects on the body are more potent at altitude. However, other physiological effects certainly aren't welcome, the most notorious being altitude sickness. For a full medical explanation of altitude sickness and a professional opinion on how to counter it, consult your local physician. We make no claim to be medical experts, though we will enlighten you to a few effects and remedies. No one knows what predisposes one person to altitude sickness and not another. Even top-tier athletes experience altitude sickness, while the least fit of us may feel fine. So, even if you consider yourself in good health, it won't guarantee that you'll dodge the effects of altitude. The main symptoms of altitude sickness include dizziness, headache, vomiting, lack of appetite, fatigue, and general malaise. Various degrees of these symptoms may occur. Some people encounter all and more of these symptoms, whereas others experience only a few. The only true remedy for altitude sickness is to descend in elevation. Slowly introducing yourself to increasingly higher elevations may help the body acclimatize. Before rising dramatically in elevation, try spending a few days at a high elevation, but slightly lower than your final elevation goal. Staying well hydrated and limiting alcohol intake may also be effective in staving off symptoms. If you feel really ill, seek professional help immediately.

COLORADO DRIVING TIPS

In the snow: Driving in snow can be intimidating, especially for people from a snow-free state. In severe weather or on heavily snow-covered roads, snow tires or chains are encouraged, and sometimes mandatory. You can purchase chains at most gas and service stations. Snow tires take a bit more preplanning, as you'll have to connect with a tire store.

If you find yourself in a skid, be sure to let up on the accelerator and turn in the direction of the skid, as this will help you gain control—while a hard habit to break, do not slam on the brakes, as this will make matters much worse. When following another car, add a few extra feet between you and it, just in case one of you loses control. And with any type of adverse driving conditions, if you feel uncomfortable, pull over and call someone or wait for conditions to improve. Remember, tow trucks don't just haul away broken cars; they are also much better equipped for snowy conditions and have been known to get even the best drivers out of sticky situations.

On dirt roads: By nature, dirt roads are bumpy and often deserted. While it may be tempting to lay heavy on the gas, try to refrain, especially on turns. A driver's biggest enemy here isn't other drivers, it's the road itself. The top level of dirt is often loosely packed, and when making a sharp turn at high speed, it can feel like you're driving on ball bearings instead of solid ground. Taking it slow is certainly the best way to drive on a dirt road.

Four-wheel drive: If you find a sign or map that says four-wheel-drive vehicles are required for sections of road, take it as gospel. It's more than a liability issue, as some roads are not maintained in Colorado, and often double as waterways in the wetter months, which makes for some treacherous driving conditions. While most of the scenic byways do not require extensive off-road skills, the use of four-wheel drive may still be needed. All-wheel drive, while handy in slick conditions, can't take the place of four-wheel drive on poorly maintained roads.

WEATHER WARNINGS

Snow: Some roads in Colorado are closed from Labor Day through Memorial Day, some scenic byways included. This is for safety reasons, as not all of the roads in the state are plowed or salted year-round. The interstates and other main arteries are always open, but some of the back roads or county roads may be impassible due to current or anticipated snowy conditions. To be sure your desired route is 100-percent open, check with the Colorado Department of Transportation (www.cotrip.org, 303-639-1111 or just 511 when in the state).

Summer thunderstorms: It's a well-known meteorological fact that mountains tend to create their own weather patterns, making forecasts hard to predict. One thing you can be certain of is late-afternoon thunderstorms. Heavy rains, and sometimes lightning, can roll in and out fast. If you ever feel uncomfortable driving in slick conditions, pull over and wait for the weather to pass. There's a saying in Colorado, "If you don't like the weather, wait 20 minutes."

WESTERN SLOPE

Four Corners Monument

Graveyard, downtown Silverton *Seth K. Hughes*

1 San Juan Skyway

Estimated length: 233 miles

Estimated time: 6 hours to drive, or take two or more days to fully experience the byway

Highlights: Ride the Durango & Silverton Narrow Gauge Railroad; photograph some of Colorado's most stunning mountain passes; rent a jeep and conquer Ophir Pass north of Silverton; soak in the Ouray Hot Springs; shop, dine, and enjoy a summer festival in downtown Telluride.

Getting there: From the east, get on I-25 and head west on US 160 until you hit Durango. From I-70 near Denver, take US 285 south, then US 160 west to Durango. From I-70 at Grand Junction, take US 50 south, then US 550 south to Durango. This trip is easily combined with either Trail of the Ancients or the West Elk Loop because of proximity to both.

San Juan Skyway has some of the most striking mountain views in all of Colorado. The San Juans boast a variety of features, from the craggy 12,968-foot peak of Engineer Mountain to the sheer cliffs on the way to Ouray, with dramatic old mine sites along the way. Alpine lakes, quaking aspens, and wildflowers accent the scene, making for breathtaking views that span most of your drive.

Note that once you leave Durango, you will encounter a number of steep sections of road that don't have a guardrail. If you're driving a large vehicle, please take your time navigating. If you or some of your passengers are sensitive to altitude and/or afraid of heights, note that this road will test you a little bit. Rest assured, it will be worth it.

History: The San Juan Skyway boasts a rich history, from the nomadic hunter-gatherers who traveled in the area until about 7500 B.C. to the nature lovers, athletes, and movie stars who call it home today. Until the 13th century, Ancestral Puebloans, best known for the cliff dwellings they built here and in the Four Corners Region, lived here. You can still see some of their petroglyphs in places like Indian Creek, Durango, and Mesa Verde.

After the Ancestral Puebloans left under circumstances that some deem mysterious, bands of nomadic Ute made the San Juans their home, foraging and hunting in the area. You'll also see some Spanish-influenced architecture in the southwestern section of the byway, where the famous Dominguez-Escalante expedition passed through in the late 1700s.

In the late 19th century, rumors of fortune in the San Juan Mountains spurred a massive influx of miners. Toll roads were opened to transport gold and silver from the high mountains, further opening the region for mining and commerce. The Ute, meanwhile, continued to lose land.

One of the 19th century's great peacemakers, Chief Ouray ("The Arrow") of the Uncompahgre Ute, represented this area in negotiations with the federal government. In 1868, Ouray negotiated the Great Ute Treaty, which allotted the Ute 6 million acres of land in the San Juans. When miners flooded into the area, breaking the law, Ouray convinced the Ute that the issue could not be resolved with violence. After signing another treaty that Uncle Sam also ended up reneging on, the tensions reached a boiling point within the Ute, with events like the 1879 Meeker Massacre (see the Flat Tops Wilderness chapter) emblematic of the times. A true pacifist, Ouray, working in concert with his wife, Chipeta, fought for a peaceful solution until the end of his life. The Ute were eventually forced onto reservations, which you can see today both east of Durango and in the Four Corners Region. As you drive the San Juan Skyway, imagine what it would be like if Ouray's vision of peaceful coexistance, well ahead of its time, had come to fruition.

Back in the late 1800s, miners quickly discovered that the Red Mountain Mining District around Silverton and Telluride contained deep and abundant mines, and the Wild West as we know it from movies truly took hold here. You can still see the dramatic tailings and sunset colors of the old strip mines today; there's word that some of the mines may become active again. You can ride a mine train into Silverton's Old Hundred gold mine, exploring a real gold mine and viewing the refurbished boardinghouse where miners used to live.

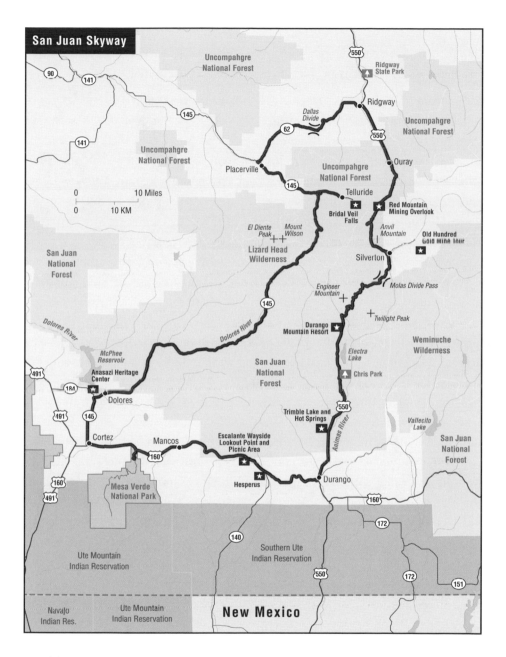

After mining companies hit the limits of their extraction capabilities, the towns lining the San Juan Skyway found a new payload in the form of tourism. Silverton, Telluride, and an area outside of Durango called Wolf Creek boast some of Colorado's best powder skiing. Mesa Verde sees millions of visitors a year, and

Telluride, tucked away into a scenic box canyon, is an annual destination vacation spot for Tom Cruise and Oprah Winfrey, among others. Once you drive this byway, you'll know why so many people choose to return time and again.

Mile Marker 33 (US 550)—Durango: A college town at heart, Durango is a destination location in itself. Lewis College, one of the last liberal arts colleges left in the state, lends Durango a hip, young appeal. You'll find lots of cutting-edge art galleries here, from Southwestern art to photography, as well as CD stores, hip clothing boutiques, and outdoor outfitters. Breweries, coffee, and good eats abound. Live bands and theater shows will keep you entertained into the night; if you need to nod off early because you're with young kids or mature adults, be sure to either watch the immaculately maintained Durango & Silverton Narrow Gauge Railroad leave, or jump aboard. It's a living piece of history that will be a highlight of your trip. Saloons, 1900s-style boutiques, knickknack shops, and the ghostly whistle of the narrow-gauge railroad add to the historical feel.

If you're a fan of the outdoors, you'll find plenty of opportunities for recreation here, from rafting to mountain biking to fishing. The combination of nearby desert and mountains makes it easy to find warmth in the winter and cool in the summer. Everything is accessible, from snow sports to summer four-wheeling excursions. You can rent bikes, four-wheel-drive vehicles, kayaks, and any other equipment under the sun, as well as take guided outdoor tours. Ask for more information at the **Durango Area Tourism Office** on 11 South Camino del Rio Road.

For the ultimate historical experience, stay at the **Strater Hotel.** The distinctive red-and-white hotel is hard to miss when you first turn on Main Avenue from the highway. Conveniently located just steps away from the best Main Avenue has to offer, as well as the narrow-gauge railroad, the Strater's rooms come equipped with antique furniture from the Old West, cleaned and maintained to the highest standard. The adjacent **Diamond Belle Saloon,** with its cocktail waitresses dressed as flappers, will give you a frontier ambiance and dining experience. It's no wonder this place is listed as a National Historic Hotel of America.

Dining options abound in Durango, enough to suit any mood. The hip **Sushitarian** on 601 East Second Avenue has a killer happy-hour special that includes lip-smacking yam sushi rolls. For something more upscale, try the tourist-friendly **Mahogany Grill** on 699 Main Avenue. Ask the waiter about the regular entertainment there. Favorites include spinach and cheese ravioli and pistachio-encrusted halibut.

Durango & Silverton Narrow Gauge Railroad in front of Strater Hotel

For family entertainment, hit up the **Diamond Circle Melodrama Vaudeville** on Seventh and Main Streets, just a couple of shops down from the Strater. They have vaudeville dancing, singing, and comedy most weekday nights, with weekday matinees in summertime. Their logo: "Cheer the hero! Boo the villain!"

Head up US 550 north out of Durango. Look for signs for **Vallecito Lake.** This 8,000-foot-high lake is a summer paradise with ample water recreation opportunities and is flanked by restaurants, stores, campgrounds, and RV parks. Besides that, you can rent all-terrain vehicles (ATVs) and horses, as well as hike the surrounding San Juan National Forest and Weminuche Wilderness. Lake access is free, and is 22 miles away from the signs on US 550. Notice the clear, tree-flanked Animas River as you cross it on your way out of town.

The **Animas Museum,** located in a 1904 schoolhouse at the corner of 31st Street and West Second Avenue, offers the chance to immerse yourself in Durango history through interactive exhibits, a photo archive, and a massive research library. Starting your trip here will add depth to everything else you see in this National Historic Town.

At Mile Marker 30, Trimble Lake and Hot Springs are at the intersection of CO 252 and US 550. After this, you'll pass through a couple of suburban areas and RV parks. There's a fountain with an informational kiosk on the right at Mile Marker 36, the first of several informational overlooks. About 2 miles later, notice the border of the **San Juan National Forest.** The forest flaunts its full glory around 10 miles later, when you'll find yourself climbing through densely wooded areas complemented by rocky mesas and verdant pine trees. Nearby Chris Park and Haviland Lake at Mile Marker 42 offer accessible camping and hiking, cycling, and fishing opportunities.

The road continues its climb into aspen groves, high mountain valleys, and the trademark red mesas of southwestern Colorado. In summer, this is wildflower country. You'll see a palette of colors, from the lavender-and-white columbine to the fiery oranges of Indian paintbrush, on both sides of the road, especially in July. A pointy, bald mountain pokes its peak above the horizon as you climb. This is the 12,968-foot **Engineer Mountain,** a steeply triangular edifice that will accompany you for a few miles yet. More distant members of the San Juan Mountains become visible to your right as dark, rugged peaks.

At Mile Marker 45, you'll hit the hamlet of Needles, with a café and country store. Notice that the San Juans look even more dramatic as you continue on your way. At Mile Marker 49, you'll hit the **Durango Mountain Resort,** also known as Purgatory. This is a favorite vacation spot for skiers in winter, and is known for its downhill mountain biking in summer. There's a livery stable across from the resort where you can ride scenic trails on the mountainside. About 0.5 mile later, there's Hermosa Park Road, which leads to some good, steep hiking. It's the first of many national forest access roads that lead to places for riding, camping, hiking, snowmobiling, and other starting points.

You'll dive into a pine-filled valley next, with the bald shock of Engineer now in the forefront. Roll down your window in this valley: You may be able to smell the coal exhaust from the narrow-gauge railroad. After the road pivots around Engineer, you'll hit Coalbank Pass slightly after Mile Marker 56. It's a good place for a bathroom break and a picnic. Stretch your legs along its short interpretive walk, which tells you more about the one hundred avalanche passes crossing the

Molas Lake

next stretch of road—between Coalbank Pass and Ouray. (That's right: You're about to drive the most avalanche-prone major road in America.) Additional interpretive signs describe the history of the highway, which has gone through incarnations as a series of Ute game trails, a Spanish horse trail, a trail for white prospectors and their animal pack trains, a four-hour drive along Lime Creek Canyon (from the 1920s to the 1940s), to, finally, the scenic one-hour drive it is today. The signs will also tell you more about the high-mountain wildlife here, which includes tiny redbacked voles and elusive boreal owls.

After you descend Coalbank Pass, look out for a hulking, brooding mountain to your right. That's the aptly named **Twilight Peak,** whose deeply shadowed crags could easily backdrop a horror flick. The road, believe it or not, gets even narrower and more winding. Keep your eyes on the road: The guardrail appears in only parts of the road. At Mile Marker 59, notice Lime Creek Road, the old way of getting through these mountains. You can still drive it if you have a four-wheel-drive vehicle; others choose to hike or mountain bike this road. It's still a good way to see the Las Animas Valley.

After Lime Creek Road, you'll ascend in the direction of Molas Pass, a gas-eating stretch with a death-defying drop-off to your right. Just before Mile Marker 63, Andrews Lake offers a fishing, hiking, and picnic reprieve. Keep driving and you'll hit Molas Pass. Pull over for an expansive mountain lookout and abundant photo opportunities. To your right, the Weminuche Wilderness dapples the fronts of West Needle Mountain, Electric Mountain, and others with aspen, pine, and wildflowers. Lakes, such as Little Molas Lake to your left, provide an ideal photo foreground. Interpretive signs tell you more about the panorama in front of you, and why the air you're breathing here is some of the cleanest in the United States.

Back on the road, the San Juans continue to cradle high-mountain valleys, a color palette of red rock mixed with steely gray, and mildly curving hogbacks in the valleys. At Mile Marker 65, you can explore the valley in more depth by hiking the Molas Trail or fishing Molas Lake, where you can also camp.

Mile Marker 66 (US 550)—Silverton: A few switchbacks later, at Mile Marker 66, the historic (some say haunted) town of Silverton opens up in a yawning valley beneath you. Notice the mountains streaked with mine tailings, or mining waste products, in sunset colors. Inside these mines, extensive networks of platforms, some as high as 10,000 feet, tell the story of the huge mining industry that supported this town for years. At Mile Marker 70, you'll hit the town itself, located

One of Silverton's many antiques

at an elevation of more than 9,000 feet. Follow the road straight into Silverton rather than turning left toward Ouray.

Silverton hasn't changed much in appearance since the late 1870s, when it was founded as a mining town. Back then, it was a rapidly growing, gritty little town filled with miners and other hardy souls. While isolated in its early days, after Stony Pass Road and the railroad reached it, Silverton grew to a bustling town of several thousand. Silver and gold mines dotted the mountains; miners generally lived near their places of work in boardinghouses and, it's reputed, only came to town to cause trouble.

After several boom and bust cycles, Silverton, once known as the Silver Queen of Colorado, is now a National Historic Landmark proud of its rough-and-tumble history. This five-hundred-person town caters to tourists and outdoorspeople. Like many historic Colorado towns, the best way to explore Silverton is by foot.

Silverton has a nice visitors center to your right before you hit the main street. Stop here for more information on whatever you might seek, be it four-wheeling, mine tours, walking tours, history, or food. In winter, you'll find skiing if you go straight through town; ask at the visitors center for more information.

Running the Durango & Silverton Narrow Gauge Railroad

Old buildings look like they must have at the turn of the 20th century; the past is still alive in the spirits that move about this place. Park your car and walk around town, or take a guided historical walking tour, which the folks at the visitors center can tell you more about. Stop off for a longneck at the **Miner's Tavern** on 1069 Greene Street. It's best described as an authentic dive bar. If that's not your pace, **The Pickle Barrel** on 1304 Greene Street offers tasty food for the whole family for a decent price.

The narrow-gauge railroad goes

The Durango & Silverton Narrow Gauge Railroad

San Juan Skyway, just south of Ouray

almost into the center of town. It's a popular way to visit Silverton without having to drive from Durango. If you want to stay longer than the two hours the train ride allots you, there are plenty of motels, historic hotels, and bed & breakfasts to check out around town. The **Bent Elbow** on 1114 Blair Street feels like miners still occupy it, thick with Old West intrigue. The **Teller House,** which is on the National Register of Historic Places, is a Victorian-style bed & breakfast. It's located on 1250 Greene Street.

The **Old Hundred Gold Mine Tour,** which is a little out of Silverton on County Route 4-A (CR 4-A; take CR 2 to CR 4, then swing a left on CR 4-A), is a must-do family experience. The one-hour guided tour includes a ride into the mine in a miner's train, a walk of the old gold vein, and a mining equipment demo. It's rounded off with an opportunity to pan for gold, silver, and gemstones.

On your way out of Silverton, drive up **Anvil Mountain** just before Mile

Marker 71 to your right, to the Christ of the Mines Shrine, built during the mining era to invoke God's blessing on San Juan's mining industry. You can get there
by driving up Shrine Road or walking up 10th Street. If you time it right, you can
see the narrow-gauge train emerging through the valley into Silverton from here,
a great photo if you have a powerful telephoto lens.

If you're in a four-wheel-drive vehicle, don't miss **Ophir Pass** to your right at
Mile Marker 75. It's known as one of the easiest trails in the San Juans and makes
for a good four-wheeling opportunity. The first of several old, inactive mines reveals itself at Mile Marker 77. Here, the road winds up toward Red Mountain Pass.
Old mines pop up everywhere you look, but again, don't look too hard, as there's
no guardrail. ATVers will find lots of opportunities toward the top of Red Mountain Pass.

On your way back down the pass, you'll drive some switchbacks that coil back
upon themselves so exactly that, though you're descending, you're not getting
much bang for your mileage buck. In the middle of these switchbacks is the **Red
Mountain Mining Overlook** just before Mile Marker 82, with a set of interpretive signs that you really should read to appreciate this area more. They detail
the six towns, with a combined population of more than two thousand, that used
to be right here in the Red Mountain Mining District. These now-busted towns
(Albany, Ironton, Gustan, Red Mountain Town [Rogersville], Red Mountain City
[Congress], and Chattanooga) covered 8 square miles in front of the overlook.
They used to buzz with prospectors, miners, cooks, saloon patrons, prostitutes,
and all the other colorful characters that made up an Old West mining town.

That's not all. You can see the headframe of the famous **Yankee Girl Mine**
here, which followed a $12 million vein of silver 1,200 vertical feet straight down—
one of the biggest silver ore concentrations in the nation. Nearby **Idarado Mine**
burrows all the way to Telluride. If you come back in 10 years, you might not see
as many tailing piles: There's a restoration project underway that is turning tailing piles into alpine fields. A couple of miles from the lookout, between Mile
Markers 85 and 86, you'll see more evidence of mining in the bright orange rock
lining Red Mountain Creek, which runs through Ironton Park Recreation Area.
The scenic theme for this part of the journey is more cliffs and fewer trees. Indeed, it looks a lot like the Alps around Switzerland, which is exactly what the
folks in Ouray want you to think. **Alpine Loop** and **Engineer Mountain Trail**,
both popular four-wheel-drive destinations, end up at Mile Marker 89. Sheer cliffs

dominate both the right and left sides of the road, making for an exhilarating portion of the drive. **Bear Creek Trailhead** at Mile Marker 91 is the first of many hiking opportunities that Ouray prides itself on.

Mile Marker 92 (US 550) — Ouray: Swing a left at the Uncompahgre National Forest Amphitheatre if you have the energy to view more scenery before hitting town. This is Ouray Ice Park, where ice climbers flock to claw their way up frozen waterfalls in winter. In summer, Box Canyon is still a striking sight. Farther toward the right, **Cañon Falls** is worth the $3 admission price. Back in the mid-20th century, Cañon Falls was a major attraction with an electric sign. These days, it's a bird sanctuary that's still a huge tourist draw.

As you descend into Ouray, you'll see a lot of Swiss chalet–style homes. This town is indeed the "Switzerland of America," as many signs around town proclaim. This little mountain town was the inspiration for the town of Galt's Gulch in Ayn Rand's *Atlas Shrugged*. High mountains flank the town on all sides, notably Mount Abrams on the southern side of town, and the Amphitheater on the eastern side.

Back in the mining days, Ouray had more horses and mules than people. Part of the reason for this was that it served as a transportation center for nearby Ironton, the Sneffels district, and Imogene Basin, located to the south and west. Shortly after inception in 1875, people discovered ore in nearby Box Canyon, a find that attracted more than 2,600 people by 1880.

The town was lucky enough not to burn down at any point in its history, as many of its neighbors did. Today, this National Historic District contains a number of original old buildings, such as the **Beaumont Hotel** and the Ouray City Hall, that are the same as they were at the turn of the 20th century. Head to St. Joseph's Miners Hospital, home of the **Ouray County Historical Society and Museum,** for more information and a walking map.

Ouray has a couple of claims to fame outside of its stunning mountain location. The Ouray County Courthouse appeared in the 1968 John Wayne movie *True Grit*. Ice climbers flock to Ouray Ice Park, a famous ice-climbing park, in winter. The ice park is a combination of natural and artificial frozen waterfalls. Nearby Box Canyon contains more than a mile of frozen waterfalls, both natural and constructed. There's now an annual ice festival in the Ouray Ice Park that attracts exhibitors, instructors, and elite international ice climbers.

The variety of historic and Swiss-themed buildings down Main Street offer

View from near the box canyon entrance, Ouray

Ouray Hot Springs

restaurants, galleries, a general store, hotels, and knickknack shops. Notable among the town's shops is a gallery named **Skol Studio and Design** on 812 Main Street. It's run by a couple: He does the metalwork, while she curates a rotating art show. Their shop displays an eye-catching combination of media, some of it modern, some of it classic, like mountain photographs. Main Street is touristy, but the dramatic outdoor scenery that towers over the town offers plenty of opportunities for solitude.

Recreation, especially hiking and four-wheeling, is a huge reason to stick around Ouray for a couple of days. Nearby county roads offer unparalleled four-wheel-drive and ATV opportunities. There are also enough hiking trails to keep you busy and gasping for breath for months. Aspen groves, steep cliffs, eye-popping views, and old mines define much of the hiking around here. For history buffs, the **Ouray County Historical Society and Museum** at 420 Sixth Avenue has three floors, 27 rooms, and 37 exhibits, including a gem collection, simulated mine, displays on ranch history, and much more. They also have guided walking tours of Main Street.

At the north end of town, follow US 550 to Mile Marker 94, location of the much-loved **Ouray Hot Springs Park.** Admission to these healing waters is $10, but most hotels offer their guests discounts. The Ute revered these waters for their restorative qualities; soak up the minerals and views for a few hours and you'll know why. A long hike or jeep tour, followed by a soak in the hot springs and delicious dinner downtown, makes an overnight stay in Ouray worth it. The town's visitors center is also located near the hot springs, should you want to load up on information about more area attractions on your way in or out. Also at the north end of town is **Cascade Falls,** another must-see waterfall.

As you enter Main Street from the south, you'll see a cluster of midrange hotels, some with their own small hot springs. The **Ouray Chalet Inn** is a great place to beef up your intimate knowledge of the town. Owners Lora Slawitschka and Steve Turk are full of Ouray lore, and know the town like the backs of their hands. She's also a talented photographer with work on display in the lobby. The nearby **Ouray Victorian Inn** offers clean, comfortable beds, breakfast, and, if you're located at the west wing, the sound of the rushing creek through your hotel window. Campers will enjoy the fantastic views at the **Amphitheater Campground** (look for signs to your right as you make the final downhill turn into town, uphill from the Box Canyon climbing area).

Ouray boasts several delicious eateries. The high-end Italian at the **Bon Ton** in the **St. Elmo Hotel** on 426 Main Street is absolutely worth the price. For dessert, or an earlier treat, try **Mouses Chocolates** on 520 Main Street. They make their own chocolate, mostly truffles, from raw materials imported from Belgium. If it's cold out, you can't beat their hot chocolate. After exiting Ouray, around Mile Marker 96 of US 550, the landscape mellows. You cross Dexter Creek, then Cutler Creek, into a land of sprawling ranchland and medium-sized mesas.

Mile Marker 102 (junction of US 550 and CO 62)—Ridgway: The first thing you'll notice in Ridgway is the railroad museum to your left. This historical town has the slow, earthy feel of a ranching town. Rollans Park, with its bridge over the gray-blue Uncompahgre River, has a walking path that runs alongside the river. It precedes a small main street (Sherman) that includes a smattering of bookstores, cafés, and accommodations. John Wayne buffs might experience déjà vu

Ridgway

here—part of *True Grit,* his breakthrough movie that was later remade by the Coen brothers, was filmed here. Ridgway fills up with second- and third-home owners during summer months. The rest of the year it's a quiet town of roughly five hundred. Nearby **Ridgway State Park,** located 5 miles north of town, is a good place to park the RV, pull out the boat, and take a leisurely day off. There's also hiking nearby.

On the way out of town on CO 62 you drive up for a couple of miles past a sizable hogback on your left. Watch for speed traps, as speed requirements change rapidly through town. The road then curves around to reveal the San Juans once again. From here, they look dark and distant, a single line of jagged peaks first in front of you, then to your left. Before you know it, you dive back into the San Juans again. National forest access roads appear amid increasingly large aspen groves set into a series of hogbacks. Gray dirt turns to pine duff as you swing a left onto CO 145, following signs to Telluride.

At Mile Marker 84, you enter the small town of Placerville. It has a few amenities, including a general store, motorcycle rentals, the **Blue Jay Lodge and Café,** and camping at the San Miguel County Park. As you keep driving, you'll see red cliffs just like the ones north of Ouray. Indeed, you're looping back to Telluride, a not-too-distant line of latitude from Ouray. Breeze through Sawpit, a small town nestled next to the river at Mile Marker 80, with food, fuel, and a small general store. Red cliffs stretch upward to your right, to a pullout just after town where you can horseback ride, bike, or hike.

A couple of forest access roads later, stop off at Keystone Overlook, just past the boundary to the **Uncompahgre National Forest.** Here, you can see both the Telluride ski resort and remnants of the Rio Grande Southern Railroad alongside the San Miguel River. Interpretive signs explain the history of the railroad, which ran from Durango to Ridgway from 1890 to the early 1950s, as well as the history of the river, which was used for hydraulic mining, and the lynx habitat here.

Mile Marker 77 (CO 145) — Telluride: Past Keystone Overlook, you'll start seeing mountain condos at the foot of the ski resort. This is the first sign of the energetic, festival-filled, and culture-rich town of Telluride. The mountains surrounding Telluride and Mountain Village comprise the biggest concentration of "Fourteeners" (mountains measuring 14,000 vertical feet or higher) in North America, including Canada. Go straight toward Colorado Avenue (rather than right, where the byway goes) and park as soon as you can.

This former silver-mining camp of about two thousand people sits in a box canyon flanked by dramatic green and cliffed mountains. Its companion town, Mountain Village, is a gondola ride over the ridge. The town's isolation is part of its beauty. The route you took into town is one of three ways; the other two are known to be treacherous four-wheel-drive roads.

Telluride has quite a history. Like many mining towns, it was founded in the late 1800s after the discovery of gold and silver ore. When the Rio Grande Southern Railroad came to Telluride, the town boomed. The mines themselves were located in the hills above Telluride. Owners of lode-bearing mines, such as the Smuggler-Union, the Sheridan, and the Tomboy, became fabulously wealthy, building the elaborate Victorians in town that still stand today.

A fatal labor dispute in 1904 marked the beginning of the end of mining in Telluride. The town was in a holding pattern until the 1970s, when the first ski lifts opened up. Telluride then became known as a counterculture getaway, with media coverage of the "bad boy of Colorado" putting Telluride on the national radar. These days, it's cleaned up its act and remains a high-end, if less party-addled, ski resort. If you go in summer, don't be surprised if you run into a major festival—they seem to happen every weekend here from June through September, with national names in film, bluegrass, jazz, adventure sports, and more visiting. Festivals are so pervasive that Telluride even has one weekend devoted to a festival called the "Un-Festival."

The best way to see this ski town is by walking and exploring the shops, brightly colored Victorian houses, European-style cafés, boutiques, galleries, and venues scattered throughout town. Load up on info bits at the information center at the head of West Colorado Avenue. This main street is of varied construction and looks as though it runs straight into the valley, where **Bridal Veil Falls** spill thousands of feet from high mountains. One stunning and unique characteristic of this town are its gardens. From front yards to public spaces, the town erupts in poppies, columbine, tulips, and other colorful flora in spring and summertime.

If you're in the mood for a couple of days of culture, music, recreation, and good food, do stay in Telluride. It's a place of pampering, as the **New Sheridan Hotel** on 231 West Colorado Avenue can prove. With its art gallery, Victorian-themed rooms, rooftop hot tubs, and library, this place will meet your high-end needs. If you're on a budget, there's a campground at the **Town Park and Campground** at 500 East Colorado Avenue. It's first come, first served, with 28 vehicle sites and 5 primitive sites. If you're staying in town, try an evening or morning walk along the **San Miguel River Trail**, a local favorite that runs through town. Interpretive signs along the way explain the area's history and geography.

If you're historically minded, check out the **Telluride Historical Museum** on 201 West Gregory Avenue. It offers a comprehensive, hands-on look at Telluride, from its American Indian roots all the way to its current resort days. There are also sections on immigration, mountain health, geology and nature, the railroad, and local technology, such as the tram. The **Nugget Theatre** on 207 West Colorado Avenue is a classic place to see new movies, with the "best popcorn in the West."

Downtown Telluride during the annual Mountain Film Festival *Seth K. Hughes*

Food-wise, Telluride is good. Very good. Standing out amid some of the higher-end selections, **La Cocina de Luz** serves southern Mexican cuisine that's organic, healthy, and tasty. For a smaller bite, try **Baked in Telluride,** which produces some of the town's best baked goods, fresh every morning.

Two classic Telluride experiences, besides skiing and summer music festivals, are the tram and Bridal Veil Falls. The free tram runs up the scenic ski resort to **Ski Mountain,** which you can explore by foot. Bridal Veil Falls, always visible in the background, is the highest in Colorado. The house that sits on top of the falls is called the Generator House. Owned by Eric Jacobson, the Generator House now provides roughly 1/4 of Telluride's electricity. In the mining days, the house powered the nearby Smuggler-Union Mine; these days, its AC generator remains intact and Jacobson and his family have to ride an aerial tramway to get home.

Head out of Telluride and turn left on CO 145 toward Rico. Here, the road quickly ascends to timberline and through large aspen groves. You'll start seeing Fourteeners to your left, such as Wilson Peak. Just past the Alta Lake and Sunshine Campground at Mile Marker 64, there's a scenic overlook with information on the Rio Grande Southern Railroad and the Ames Power Plant.

You'll swing by some abandoned mining buildings, then reach the hamlet of Matterhorn at Mile Marker 62, where you can hike and RV camp. Notice the scenic and, in summer, wildflower-flanked lake 1 mile after Matterhorn. It's a good photo opportunity. Next, you climb to Lizard Head Pass at 10,222 feet at Mile Marker 60, where there's a lookout point filled with interpretive signs. Notice the sheep pen in front of the interpretive sign, a sign of days past and present. Many aspen still bear carvings from American Indian and Mexican sheepherders; these carvings were made between the 1920s and 1960s, when sheep and cattle were still herded by shepherds from high- to low-country grazing lands. They're now put on trains.

This is also the gateway to the **Lizard Head Wilderness,** a roughly 41,000-acre wilderness area hugging a series of high mountains, including two Fourteeners, **El Diente** and **Mount Wilson.** The wilderness area is named after the 13,113-foot Lizard Head Peak. You can mountain bike, hike, horseback ride, and camp here. Be aware that "leave no trace" rules apply. These rules require you to pack out all of your garbage, camp at least 200 feet from lakes and streams, and avoid altering the landscape in any way. (For a detailed list of "leave no trace" rules, visit www.lnt.org/learn/7-principles.) No motorized vehicles are allowed.

Pass the more than 13,000-foot Sheep Mountain on your left, underlined by the zigzagging Coal Creek. You traverse a high-mountain meadow, located just slightly below timberline, before descending back into a valley. If you want to enjoy this area longer, several campgrounds beckon along the way.

After the National Forest Information Center at Mile Marker 49, you'll enter the town of Rico, which doesn't span much beyond its main street. A mine to your right has an interpretive sign explaining its use. Other than that, there's a liquor store, candle shop, town park, and a couple of accommodations. There's also gas at the tail end of town.

You pass a couple of national forest access roads to cross the Dolores River and descend into Red Rock Canyon country. The Priest Gulch Trailhead, at Mile Marker 36, also marks the last campground for a little while. Mile Marker 34, with

Bear Creek Trailhead, is the last mountain-hiking opportunity until you get back to Durango. From here on out, it's all grazing land, then scrub, and then, eventually, desert.

Mile Marker 12 (CO 145)—Dolores: The town of Dolores is all ranchland, big yards, fishing, and river trails. There's gas, motels and inns, a couple of restaurants, and a railroad museum with the *Galloping Goose* #5 on display. The *Goose* is a Buick motor–powered rail bus that carried mail, passengers, and freight from 1933 to 1959.

Cross the wide and calm Dolores River, then take a right at Mile Marker 8 to the **Anasazi Heritage Center** on CO 184. This brilliant, hands-on museum is an absolute must-see, whether the words Ancestral Puebloan strike a chord with you or not. The center lies 1 mile in and costs $3 to get in, unless you have a national parks pass or are under 18, in which case it's free.

The first thing you see is an old ruin, with barely a foundation left. This is

The *Galloping Goose* in Dolores

Dominguez Pueblo, likely the first Ancestral Puebloan ruin you'll see on your journey. When you walk into the visitors center, you'll be warmly greeted and given an overview of the museum's content.

They have a library with millions of artifacts. Due to space constraints, they only exhibit hundreds of artifacts at a time. Researchers examine artifacts along with museum visitors. The staff has ensured that exhibits are as hands-on as possible, making them easy for researchers to study and visitors to play with. You can be your own archaeologist here. The center provides microscopes to examine pottery, woven items, and other artifacts; there's also an exhibit on archaeological tools of the trade. You'll find pots, woven sandals, stone and bone tools, jewelry, and more on display. Additional exhibits cover digs from the 1800s to today, as well as information on the timber, train, and water industries.

A politically loaded 90-minute movie explains more about the history of the archaeology behind sites such as Canyons of the Ancients and Mesa Verde. When you've had your fill of exhibits, you can plan your next activity using the wealth of information on nearby attractions. You can also pick up some Anasazi- and Southwestern-themed souvenirs at the museum's gift shop, which is fully wheelchair accessible. Weather permitting, you may want to take a stroll up to **Escalante Pueblo,** a short walk from the museum, or have a picnic at one of the museum's shaded tables.

Take a left back onto CO 145. Notice **Sleeping Ute Mountain** to your right. This landmark will accompany you for a good part of your journey.

Mile Marker 2 (CO 145)—Cortez: Cortez is one of the biggest towns on your entire drive. Its long Main Street includes a host of hotels, gas stations, restaurants, grocery stores, and other places to buy amenities. It's the only good place for miles to stock up on gas, water, and food for the rest of your drive, especially if you're exploring the remote Canyons of the Ancients from here.

Stay here a night to get some rest before your trek to Mesa Verde. The **Holiday Inn Express** is possibly the most high-end hotel with that name in the American West. With its Southwestern styling; clean, quite luxurious rooms; and the most expansive continental breakfasts you're likely to get anywhere, the Holiday Inn Express is one of the best deals in town. Do stay here if you get the chance. Otherwise, there are plenty of good accommodations just down the road, many with familiar names. You'll also find campgrounds and RV hook-ups around town.

For food, try one of the many Mexican places around town for locally made

Cortez Cultural Center

tamales and a *cerveza*. **Koko's Friendly Pub**, the restaurant and pub next to the Holiday Inn Express, has American pub fare and a variety of drinks, as well as darts and sports entertainment. There are also several delicious restaurants around town featuring local, farm-fresh cuisine. Notable among them is **The Farm Bistro**, located on 34 W. Main Street.

The **Colorado Welcome Center** on the corner of Mildred and Main Streets is a good place to find information about nearby activities and attractions, including the nearby Canyons of the Ancients. Head to the **Cortez Cultural Center** for even more exhibits on archaeology and the Ancestral Puebloans. The cultural center is housed in a building constructed in 1909, adding an additional layer of history to its interpretive and cultural exhibits. It also has an extensive video collection and occasional live dancers, workshops, and rotating exhibits.

As you leave town in the direction of Mesa Verde, notice **Totin Reservoir** to your left. Shortly thereafter is the Montezuma County Fairground and Racetrack.

Cliffs and mountains stretch to medium heights to your right, interspersed with scrub fields and low-lying mesas, behind which larger hills boast pinkish sandstone exposures. Beneath this land, there may still lie thousands of Ancestral Puebloan ruins. A few miles later, you come upon **Mesa Verde National Park**, one of the Southwest's trademark experiences.

Mile Marker 48 (US 160)—Mesa Verde National Park: If you spend the day in Mesa Verde (see Trail of the Ancients chapter), it's almost guaranteed you'll be tired. It would be advisable to stay in nearby Cortez or Mancos; however, some hardy souls choose to drive all the way back to Durango, where the byway finishes. To do this, take a right out of Mesa Verde, where you'll see more mesas, trees, and scrub. You'll soon hit the Mancos Valley at Mile Marker 54, whose official slogan is "Between Mesa Verde and Mountains." The thing that they don't mention is the many Native American trading posts and gift shops in and around town; this is an ideal place to pick up folk art, ceramics, jewelry, or a life-sized chainsaw carving of a Ute chief.

Overall, Mancos is a Southwestern-style ranching and farming community.

In the late 1800s, a conscientious East Coast journalist named Virginia McClurg saw the vandalism and theft that was going on unchecked at Mesa Verde. She decided to make it her life's work to save the cliff-top dwellings and artifacts there. At first the government ignored her, but after President Theodore Roosevelt supported the cause, she was able to push the U.S. Congress into designating Mesa Verde a national park in 1906, the first to be dedicated to human, as opposed to natural, artifacts.

There's a range of hotel and motel accommodations. For more information, take a right at the first stoplight to the **Visitor Center and Pioneer Museum.** Mancos State Park, a 338-acre playground centered around the 7,800-foot-high **Mancos Lake,** is down this same road. Mancos offers gas and groceries in case you need to stock up. On your way out, you cross the **Mancos River,** over a bucolic bridge that seems to mark the end of anything related to flatlands and the beginning of a long, winding trip back up into the San Juan Mountains. This is the last piece of road before again hitting Durango; it's also a last gasp at the high-elevation beauty that defines most of the San Juan Skyway. The **Echo Basin Ranch** area, often used as an RV retreat, kids' camp, and outdoor family playground, is at Mile Marker 58 to your left.

About 3 miles later, you descend into the green La Plata County, where national forest access roads provide the opportunity to dive into the wild every few miles. The **Target Tree Campground,** at Mile Marker 63, includes a fully equipped campground with RV hook-ups. The Ute used to harvest sap and bark from trees in the area, as well as use them for target practice—you can still see scarred trees here today. It also offers hiking trails and interpretive historical signs.

At Mile Marker 66.5, the **Escalante Wayside Lookout Point and Picnic Area** is a good place to read about the history of the area—interpretive signs explain more. About 3 miles later, you'll begin heading down the hill again. Notice **Hesperus,** or "Durango's Other Ski Area," shortly after Mile Marker 71. This small resort offers lift tickets for the unheard-of price of $30.

You'll bottom out in the canyon at around Mile Marker 78. The road swerves its way around hogbacks and buttes. Look for the red barn house near the Dry Fork forest access road to your left. You'll soon pass a sign for West Durango, amid familiar-looking pine stands, aspen groves, and mountains. Before you know it, you'll be back in Durango, full circle after the adventure that brought you through haunted hotels, the Switzerland of America, the state's most musical ski resort, ancient ruins, the heat of the Southwestern desert, and back into the high mountains again.

IN THE AREA

DURANGO

Accommodations

Strater Hotel, 699 Main Ave. Call 970-247-4431.

Attractions and Recreation

Animas Museum, 3065 West Second Ave. Call 970-259-2402.

Diamond Circle Melodrama Vaudeville, 699 Main Ave. Call 970-375-7160.

Durango Mountain Resort, 327 South Camino Del Rio. Call 970-385-8901.

Dining/Drinks

Diamond Belle Saloon, 699 Main Ave. Call 970-375-7150.

Mahogany Grill, 699 Main Ave. Call 970-247-4433.

Sushitarian, 601 East Second Ave. Call 970-382-0001.

SILVERTON

Accommodations

Bent Elbow, 1114 Blair St. Call 970-387-5775.

Teller House, 1250 Greene St. Call 970-387-5423.

Attractions and Recreation

Old Hundred Gold Mine Tour, 721 CR 4-A. Call 970-387-5444.

Dining/Drinks

Miner's Tavern, 1069 Greene St. Call 970-387-9885.

The Pickle Barrel, 1304 Greene St. Call 970-387-5713.

OURAY

Accommodations

Amphitheater Campground, US 550 S. Call 1-877-444-6777.

Beaumont Hotel, 505 Main St. Call 970-325-7000.

Ouray Chalet Inn, 510 Main St. Call 1-800-924-2538.

Ouray Victorian Inn, 50 Third Ave. Call 970-325-7222.

St. Elmo Hotel, 426 Main St. Call 970-325-4951.

Attractions and Recreation

Ouray County Historical Society and Museum, 420 Sixth Ave. Call 970-325-4576.

Ouray Hot Springs Park, 1200 Main St. Call 970-325-7065.

Skol Studio and Design, 812 Main St. Call 970-325-7290.

Dining/Drinks

Bon Ton, 426 Main St. Call 970-325-4951.

Mouses Chocolates, 520 Main St. Call 970-325-7285.

PLACERVILLE

Dining/Drinks

Blue Jay Lodge and Café, 22332 CO 145. Call 970-728-0830.

TELLURIDE

Accommodations

New Sheridan Hotel, 231 W. Colorado Ave. Call 970-728-4351.

Town Park and Campground, 500 E. Colorado Ave. Call 970-728-2174.

Attractions and Recreation

Telluride Historical Museum, 201 W. Gregory Ave. Call 970-728-3344.

Nugget Theatre, 207 W. Colorado Ave. Call 970-728-7507.

Dining/Drinks

Baked in Telluride, 127 S. First St. Call 970-728-4775.

La Cocina de Luz, 123 E. Colorado Ave. Call 970-728-9355.

DOLORES

Attractions and Recreation

Anasazi Heritage Center, 27501 CO 184. Call 970-882-4811.

CORTEZ

Accommodations

Holiday Inn Express, 2121 E. Main St. Call 1-800-626-5652.

Attractions and Recreation

Colorado Welcome Center, corner of Mildred St. and Main St. Call 970-565-4048.

Cortez Cultural Center, 25 N. Market St. Call 970-565-1151.

Dining/Drinks

The Farm Bistro, 34 W. Main St. Call 970-565-3834.

Koko's Friendly Pub, 2121 E. Main St. Call 970-565-6000.

MANCOS

Accommodations

Target Tree Campground, 7 miles east of Mancos, on the north side of US 160. Call 970-882-7296.

Attractions and Recreation

Hesperus, US 160. Call 970-259-3711.

Visitor Center and Pioneer Museum, 101 E. Bauer St. Call 970-533-7434.

Echo Basin Ranch, 43747 CR M. Call 970-533-7000.

Ancient masonry at Hovenweep National Monument

2 Trail of the Ancients

Estimated length: 114 miles

Estimated time: 3–4 hours (depending on whether you drive to the Four Corners Region)

Highlights: Take the Cliff House and Balcony House tours at Mesa Verde National Park; hike around the ancient ruins at Hovenweep; view dwellings in a raw, untouched setting at Ute Mountain Tribal Park; immerse yourself in history at the Anasazi Heritage Center; take a picture of yourself in four states at once.

Getting there: From Durango, travel west on US 160 to where it intersects with CO 145. From the Utah border, travel south on US 491 and then east on US 160. From the Four Corners Region, travel north on US 491/160 and then east on US 160. Follow CO 145 north. Note that this byway is full of spur roads, different ways of going to the same place, and different parks that you may or may not choose to visit. We offer you a simple loop route that includes the best sites in and very near Colorado; please bring an additional road atlas with you as you travel this area so that you can choose exactly the route you want to take.

The Trail of the Ancients winds through one of the most historically fascinating stretches of land in the nation. Almost everyone who visits the breathtaking cliffside dwellings at Mesa Verde comes out stunned by the civilization's artifacts; beauty; and rapid, mysterious disappearance.

History: The cliff dwellings at Mesa Verde were first explored by Anglo-Saxon Americans in 1874, and have been the subject of research and fascination ever since. Various artifacts—including cliff dwellings, pottery, petroglyphs, tools, and

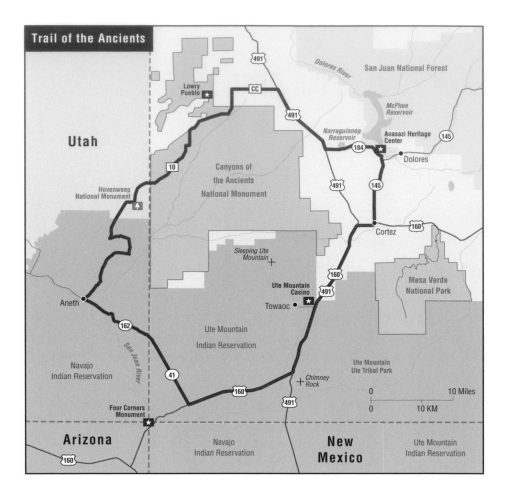

Trail of the Ancients

San Juan National Forest

Dolores River

Lowry Pueblo ★

CC

491

491

McPhee Reservoir

Utah

Narraguinnep Reservoir

184

Anasazi Heritage Center ★

145

Dolores

10

Canyons of the Ancients National Monument

491

145

Hovenweep National Monument ↟

Cortez

160

Sleeping Ute Mountain +

160

Mesa Verde National Park

Ute Mountain Casino ■

491

Aneth ●

Towaoc ● ★

162

Ute Mountain Indian Reservation

San Juan River

Ute Mountain Ute Tribal Park

Navajo Indian Reservation

41

Chimney Rock +

0   10 Miles

160

0   10 KM

Four Corners Monument ★

491

Arizona

160

Navajo Indian Reservation

New Mexico

Ute Mountain Indian Reservation

even food—were discovered on the site, leading to much speculation about the mysterious predecessor to the modern Pueblo.

After settling in Mesa Verde around A.D. 550, the first Ancestral Puebloans lived in pithouses on top of the mesas, where they farmed, made pottery, and hunted with bows and arrows. These initial settlers, now known as the Basketmakers, thrived in Mesa Verde, eventually building mud houses and, by A.D. 1000, stone buildings to house their growing population. Two hundred years later, the Ancestral Puebloans grew so large in number that they began constructing their homes in the sides of the cliffs below the mesa top. Researchers still don't know exactly why the inhabitants chose to move down into cliffs, where they had to climb rock walls and ladders to enter and exit; theories range from defense to weather protection to the tops of the mesas being needed for more farmland.

The Ancestral Puebloans' spectacular cliff dwellings, which you can still explore today, are sandstone living and storage structures built artfully into the cliff walls, with kivas dug in below. People would hunt and farm on the plateau, and return into their cliff cities for their day-to-day activities. The cliff-dwelling era, however, only lasted about one hundred years. Nobody knows for sure why the Ancestral Puebloans lived in their cliff cities for about three generations, then left en masse for different locations. Drought, deforestation, and political upheaval are but a few theories.

Years later, the nomadic Ute populated the Four Corners Region. More nomadic than their predecessors, they migrated seasonally and hunted and gathered in the region. Interestingly enough, they feared the abandoned cliff dwellings at the mesa tops. The Navajo or "Dine" people arrived after the Ute, and some still live on a Navajo reservation in the area today, as do the Ute on their respective reservation.

Today, some modern Puebloan groups hold the cliff dwellers and Mesa Verde sacred, as these people were their ancestors. Visitors can still see Ancestral Puebloan dwellings at Mesa Verde National Park, Canyon de Chelly National Monument, Bandelier National Monument, Chaco Culture Historical Park, and Hovenweep National Monument. But Mesa Verde, where the cliff dwellings remain well preserved and can be visited by foot (for now, as some sites, including the famous Cliff Palace, are seeing major erosion from water damage), remains the most spectacular site.

2 Miles into CO 184—Anasazi Heritage Center: Leave the town of Cortez on CO 145 north. Turn left onto CO 184, following a sign to the **Anasazi Heritage Center.** It's 1 mile in on your right. The museum, with its hands-on archaeological exhibits, is a must-see. The center costs $3 to get in, but is free with a parks pass or for those under 18. In front of the center is **Dominguez Pueblo,** a crumbled ruin with informational signs detailing its history. The hundreds of artifacts on display are only a fraction of the millions in the museum's collection. The hands-on exhibits include microscope stations, a weaving loom, jewelry that you can pick up and touch, exhibits on how pots and tools are made, and much more. They also play an interesting movie about the history of the area's archaeology digs. Be sure to get a map for the Canyons of the Ancients at the center. The roads you're about to drive are not marked well and it's easy to get lost, but the maps point out what roads you need to follow.

McPhee Reservoir

When you've had your fill of exhibits, you can plan your next activity with the wealth of information on other attractions here. You can also pick up some Ancestral Puebloan– and Southwestern-themed souvenirs at their gift shop. It's fully wheelchair accessible. Weather permitting, you may want to take a stroll up to **Escalante Pueblo,** a short walk from the museum, or have a picnic at one of the museum's shaded tables.

On your way out, you can take a dip, catch fish, boat, and camp at **McPhee Reservoir.** The entrance is at Mile Marker 4. After you cross over the dam on the left side of the reservoir, take a right at the junction of CO 184 toward Dove Creek, at Mile Marker 0. You'll pass through miles and miles of flat farmland area. Farmers on this land contributed many of the pottery shards, arrowheads, and other artifacts that now belong to the Anasazi Heritage Center. What's more, there may be ancient pueblos still buried miles beneath the surface of the land. The surface looks innocuous, but the vast majority of ruins in this area haven't been dug up, so they could be located anywhere.

Montezuma County Road CC (CR CC)—Trail of the Ancients and Hovenweep National Monument: Notice the sign for Hovenweep to the left at Mile Marker 45. Don't follow this road. Instead, take a left on Montezuma CR CC, where there's a brown TRAIL OF THE ANCIENTS sign. You're now entering **Canyons of the Ancients National Monument,** a loose amalgamation of ruins with no headquarters or visitors center. You soon hit a stop sign intersection with CR 10. A sign points straight toward Lowry Ruins, a slight detour where you can see what were once astounding, full-color murals inside these self-guided ruins. Don't miss the beautiful and well-preserved Grand Kiva, which is a short detour from the main building. To follow the rest of the byway, turn right on CR 10 if you're backtracking from the Lowry Ruins, or take a left if you want to skip Lowry. This road will take

Great Kiva at Lowry Ruins

Hovenweep National Monument

you to **Hovenweep National Monument.** You're now driving some fun rollers in the Great Sage Valley. Between here, Montezuma Valley, and Mesa Verde, there are about 45,000 ruins. More people lived in the valley in those days than today (about 20,000 now). It was an ancient metropolis, and most of it remains buried in the earth.

This is cattle country, so please watch out for loose ruminants on the road. You're also likely to see hawks and turkey vultures scouring the fields for rodents. The second cattle guard on the road to Hovenweep roughly marks the Utah border. Shortly thereafter is Hovenweep National Monument, which contains six ruins on 784 peaceful desert acres. Take a left at the sign, which leads up CR 213 to the adobe visitors center, some bathrooms, and (in the summer) a nice expanse of shade near the bathrooms. Pay your entry fee at the visitors center.

The 31-site camping here is mostly for tents, with a couple of RV spots. The campground includes tent pads, shaded picnic tables, and canyon views. Note that the ruins here are best accessed by foot; there's little to see by car. If it's not too hot out, take the **Square Tower Group** self-guided trail and see a number of ruins in 2 relatively easy miles of hiking. Notice also how wild this place still is: jackrabbits, lizards, butterflies, nighthawks, coyotes, and others share this peaceful, mysterious land. Rangers can tell you about longer hikes that lead to places like **Holly Ruin,** a rarely seen—and supposedly haunted—ruin 12 miles from the campground.

Notice **Sleeping Ute Mountain** to your left. Legend has it that this is a sleeping Ute chief who will wake up someday and give the native people back their land. The big protrusion is his nose, and his arms are folded over his chest. For now, he's the penultimate Four Corners landmark, visible from most places in the region. See how often you can see him from your car window.

Leaving Hovenweep, CR 2422 dead-ends at Mile Marker 0. Depending on the nature of your road trip, you have a couple of options here: Go left toward Cortez or go right toward Blanding and explore the vast Utah side of the Trail of the Ancients. The latter includes Natural Bridges National Monument; the Monument Valley; Glen Canyon; the towns of Bluff, Blanding, and Monticello; and more. Here, we focus on Colorado, so we will guide you to take a left, back toward Cortez.

CR 2416—Aneth: At the stop sign at Mile Marker 65, take a right toward Aneth, on CR 2416. The scenery around Aneth sprawls in postcard-quality panoramas typical of the Colorado Plateau, with grazing horses, sprawling ranchland, and dust-capped mesas. You'll see spectacular canyon views on your way to Aneth, sheer rock walls that fade out into the horizon. Toward the latter half of this portion of the drive, keep an eye out for impossibly bright-red rock ledges jutting out toward the road. Turn left and cross McElmo Creek toward the end of CR 2416. You'll cross a cattle guard back into Colorado and Ute tribal land. At the junction with US 160, take a left back toward Cortez. If you go right, you can detour into the Four Corners.

US 160—Four Corners Detour: Turn right on US 160 and follow it through sparse desert to the **Four Corners Monument,** which will greet you with a sign and a trailer where you can pay your admission fee, which was $3 (cash-only) at time of writing. Park anywhere in the gravel lot and walk into the monument, where you will see a bronze disc marking the spot where the borders of Colorado, Utah,

New Mexico, and Arizona intersect. A favorite pose can be captured by getting on all fours, with one arm and one leg in each state. Once you're finished here, backtrack on the highway to Cortez.

Junction of US 491 and US 160—Ute Mountain Tribal Park: At the junction of US 491 and US 160, you'll see the Ute Mountain Visitors Center. This is the gateway to the **Ute Mountain Tribal Park,** where Weminuche Ute guides lead tours of the ancient cliff dwellings on this 125,000-acre tract of land. Book your half- or full-day tour in advance—the visitors center has odd hours. It's an excellent way to see a more raw, authentic (you sometimes hike on ancient pottery shards) side of the Ancestral Puebloan civilization. If wild horses descended from the Dominguez-Escalante mission, untouched red buttes, and deeply knowledgeable Native American guides are your pace, make this place a priority.

The Ute Mountain Tribal Park is an American Indian reservation belonging to the Ute Mountain band of the Utes, one of seven tribes that comprise the Ute Indian Nation. The land here is gritty and dry, with only a few hardy trees and shrubs able to eke out an existence on the nearly bone-dry land. While stark, dry, and sunny, the area carries a proud, raw beauty. Monolithic buttes reach skyward in absurdly straight fashion; ridges that cut across the horizon are low and sharp, then disappear abruptly back into the earth.

Not only is the area known for such uninhibited rawness, it is well known to be a hotbed of Ancestral Puebloan and Ute ancestral sites. While the better-known Mesa Verde National Park is home to some of the best preserved and advertised cliff- and pit-dwelling sites of prehistoric people, the Ute Mountain Tribal Park's sites outnumber Mesa Verde's at least ten to one. And while no official count has been made of cliff dwellings, towers, kivas, and pit houses, the general consensus is that the Ute Mountain Tribal Park holds more than 100,000 distinct sites.

In fact, the deposit of artifacts is so dense, that when touring the park, visitors often crunch Ancestral Puebloan pottery with every footfall.

Although visitors are welcome, they are not free to roam the territory by themselves. All access to the tribal park is made through reservations with a trained Ute guide. Call the visitors center to make reservations at 1-800-847-3751. Don't count on just checking in with the visitors center on-site, as it's open only when expecting a tour.

The next signs of civilization you'll see are in the tiny town of Towaoc, really

Cliff Palace, Mesa Verde

just a holding place for a gas station and the giant, Ute-run **Ute Mountain Casino.** This large, boxlike structure is constantly humming with people courting Lady Luck. This gambling hall is the largest in the Four Corners Region, and the first Native American gaming operation in the state of Colorado. If you are looking for a mini-Vegas, however, you won't find it here. It's just the one casino, shows are limited, and there is no alcohol admitted on the premises. But, if you're a slot jockey, or just want to see one in its natural habitat, you can bet on being happy here.

This route continues back toward Cortez. Chapter 1 contains more information on Cortez, at Mile Marker 2.

Mile Marker 48 (CO 145)—Mesa Verde National Park: Tune to AM radio 1610 in the park's vicinity for more information. After you turn right into the park and pay your fee, it's still 15 miles to the visitors center. The road winds deep into cliff country as you start driving. A few steep climbs later, you'll see Knife Edge Road, the first of several overlooks. This was the park's first vehicular entry road, from Mancos. In the early 1900s, it cost $1 to get in. Back then, the drive usually took four hours on a precarious cliffside road in a Studebaker. Times have changed. It's now one of the park's many hiking routes. Farther up the road, other lookouts lead to short hikes and last chances at getting some quiet before entering the Far View Visitors Center, just past the **Far View Motor Lodge and Dining,** as well as the campgrounds.

The visitors center should be your first stop at the park. Besides the usual books and exhibits, you can buy guided tours of mesa dwellings here. At $3 each, the tours are an affordable way to see the bigger and better-preserved dwellings in the park. Note that tours book out hours ahead of time, a good reason to come early if you're visiting during high tourist season. Also remember that each dwelling is a sacred place to hundreds of people. Treat it like you would a cathedral or other holy place from your own tradition.

Richard Wetherill, a rancher and trader who was the first Anglo-American to extensively explore the ruins in 1888, named the inhabitants of the ruins "Anaas·zÌ." In Navajo, which Wetherill spoke, the word means enemy ancestors. Subsequent archaeologists kept the name because of its convenience as a classification, though the word, which does not mean "The Ancients" as is popularly portrayed and does not have any relation to Pueblo languages, is a misnomer.

Don't miss the **Cliff Palace,** which is the city structure you see in most Mesa Verde postcards. It's extraordinarily well preserved, with intact doorways, kivas, stairs, ladders, and walls. There are a couple of steep climbs and descents on the informative guided tour, but most people can handle them. This is less the case with the **Balcony House,** an Indiana Jones–like site nestled into cliffs at the end of a couple of very steep ladders. Both locations require tour tickets, which you get in the visitors center.

Make the Cliff Palace your main event, and supplement it with tours such as the Balcony House or Long House. Even if you're not usually inclined toward guided tours, the men and women working at Mesa Verde

Balcony House, Mesa Verde

make them very much worth your while. Some tours, like **Wetherill Mesa,** are self-guided and therefore less crowded; information is available at the visitors center. Please remember to walk as though on feathers, don't lean on ancient structures, and leave the place looking like you never visited. The stone that the ruins are made of is ancient and sensitive to corrosion from everything from finger oils to shoe scuffs.

Get the most out of Mesa Verde by doing a couple of guided tours in the morning, then, if you have any energy left, spending the afternoon exploring quieter places like Wetherill Mesa—or saving that for the next day. If the heat or crowds start feeling intense, take a break at the **Far View Terrace,** where you can get grub and gifts. It can get painfully crowded here during summer and fall. Please keep that in mind when planning your trip: your timing (leave in the early morning) and your provisions are critical. Stocking up on a picnic lunch and more

Kiva in Balcony House, Mesa Verde

water than you think you need is a good start. Wear sturdy hiking shoes, apply sun protection, and have a backpack to hold water for the trail. With the more than 7,000-foot elevation and the heat, many visitors start feeling dizzy if they come unprepared. Also, come with a full tank of gas: the drive from the visitors center to the dwellings is another 25 minutes, one way.

Now that you've seen the Colorado section of the Trail of the Ancients, consider the hundreds of miles in Utah and Arizona that you still have left to explore, either on this road trip or another one. The mystery and beauty left by the Ancestral Puebloans is worth experiencing time and again.

IN THE AREA

Accommodations

Far View Motor Lodge and Dining, Mesa Verde National Park 81330. Call 970-529-4465.

Attractions and Recreation

Anasazi Heritage Center, 27501 CO 184, Dolores 81323. Call 970-882-5600.

Four Corners Monument. Call 928-871-6647. www.navajonationparks.org/htm/fourcorners.htm.

Hovenweep National Monument. Call 970-562-4282. www.nps.gov/hove/index.htm.

Mesa Verde National Park. Call 970-529-4465. www.nps.gov/meve/index.htm.

Ute Mountain Casino. Call 970-565-8800. www.utemountaincasino.com.

Ute Mountain Tribal Park. Call 970-565-3751 ext. 330. www.utemountainute.com/tribalpark.htm.

Dining/Drinks

Far View Terrace, Mesa Verde National Park 81330. Call 970-529-4465.

Roadside waterfall, CO 133

3 West Elk Loop

Estimated length: 205 miles

Estimated time: 8–10 hours

Highlights: Watch golden eagles ride thermals in the Black Canyon of the Gunnison; drive Kebler Pass in the fall, when the aspen leaves are golden; mountain bike or hike around Crested Butte during wildflower season; touch building-sized hunks of marble in the Marble Millsite Park; snack on juicy, fresh-picked peaches and cherries in Paonia.

Getting there: From I-70 heading west from Denver, get off at the easternmost Glenwood Springs exit. From I-70 heading east from Grand Junction, do the same. Follow CO 82 to Carbondale, then follow the signs to CO 133. Start on CO 133 at Carbondale.

This byway follows CO 133 south from the town of Carbondale to the Paonia Reservoir. Here, the byway begins a loop that eventually meets back at the reservoir. Stay on CO 133 and travel west through the town of Paonia to the town of Hotchkiss. From there, meander along CO 92 south until it joins up with US 50, about 52 miles away. Follow US 50 for 28 miles until it reaches the town of Gunnison. From Gunnison, jump on CO 135 northward through the town of Almont to the town of Crested Butte. From Crested Butte, travel west again over a dirt and gravel section of road for 31 miles over Kebler Pass, rejoining CO 133 again at the Paonia Reservoir.

From mountaintop aspen groves to cherry blossom–filled fields, West Elk Loop covers an abundant and varied landscape as it travels through the Crystal River Valley. Not only does this make for excellent sightseeing but it opens

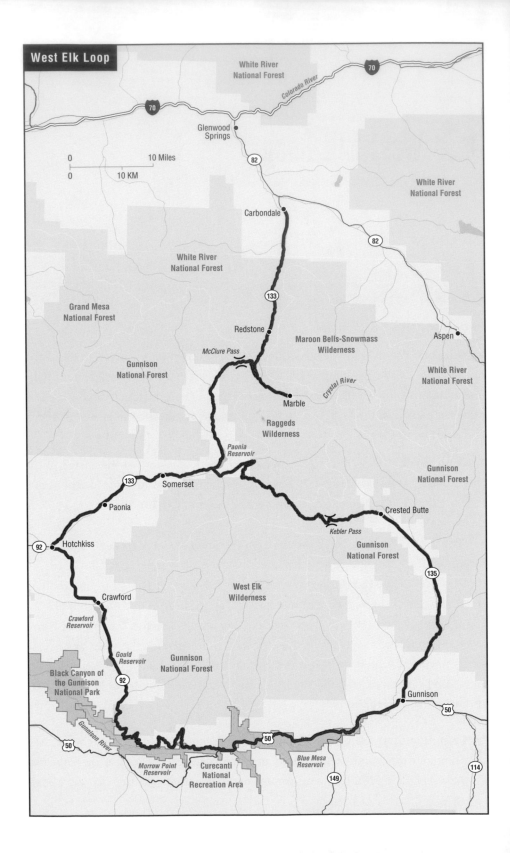

up a nearly endless variety of recreation opportunities. There's a state park or national forest at nearly every bend. Paonia and Crawford State Parks offer easy spots for camping, bird-watching, and picnicking. A few miles south of Carbondale, the route reveals three stunning national forests: White River, Grand Mesa, and Gunnison. The 2.3-million-acre White River National Forest boasts first-class ski resorts like Vail and Aspen, climbing meccas like Rifle, and enough wilderness expanse in which to spend years getting lost. The Black Canyon of the Gunnison, Colorado's deepest canyon, could swallow the Empire State Building. Visitors can gape down at the roaring Gunnison River from the tops of 1,000-foot canyon walls. Three dammed lakes—Blue Mesa, East Portal, and Morrow Point Reservoirs—define the Curecanti National Recreation Area, a haven for fishers, boaters, and kayakers. Farther northeast, the Gunnison National Forest is a vast area known for its aspen-covered hiking routes, excellent hunting, and generally abundant recreational opportunities. As in all the other parks in the area, visitors can camp here.

History: The Crystal River Valley is one of the most fertile places in Colorado. Early hunter-gatherers from the Ancestral Puebloans to the Ute set up camp here to hunt, fish, and gather the abundant resources of the land. As more and more pioneers settled in Ute territory in the mid-1800s, first by foot, horse, and cart, then by Union Pacific Railroad, tension between the Ute and settlers heated up, reflecting a wider pattern of settler American Indian relations across the West. After the Ute were corralled into reservations, despite the best efforts of the visionary Chief Ouray (see the San Juan Skyway chapter), settlers populated the area, first attempting to mine the area without fruitful results, then as ranchers and farmers. A smattering of small towns, each with a unique identity, established themselves in the area.

In towns such as Gunnison, Crested Butte, and Paonia, a rich history of ranching and farming still results in a mouthwatering summer bounty of peaches, cherries, and other fruits, as well as some mighty tasty steaks. At the same time, the discoveries of oil shale and coal gave the Western Slope a new economic edge. The town of Redstone, founded by fuel tycoon John Osgood, became a home to coal miners who worked west of town. Visitors can still see rows of coke ovens, which were used to burn volatile elements off coal, at nearby Segundo. Somerset and Carbondale were also big coal-mining towns. In Carbondale, a fatal mine explosion in 1981 killed 15 people and heralded the downfall of nearly a century of coal mining.

The town of Marble took a rather individualistic approach to resource extraction by becoming a national capital of marble mining in the early 1900s. The Lincoln Memorial in Washington, D.C., and the Tomb of the Unknown Soldier contain some marble from this town.

These days, Aspen homesteaders, urban escapees, retirees, and New Age hippies find themselves drawn to the fascinating towns around the West Elk Loop. Some come to farm and ranch; others set up shops, cafés, and national companies, such as the Chaco footwear company in Paonia. Still, the old days are never far away: An increasing demand for coal in the northeastern United States has caused coal trains to run through the area at such a frequent rate that residents sometimes have to crawl under them to get to their cars in the morning.

In sum, the area is a fascinating combination of beauty, rich history, and unique, quirky small towns. The grit of the mines remains a stark contrast to the fertile, mountain-flanked natural beauty of the Crystal River Valley—and is also one of its enduring appeals.

Mile Marker 1 (CO 133)—Carbondale: We begin the West Elk Loop at the eastern edge of Carbondale, with a view of Mount Sopris ahead of you and a brightly colored stack of red rocks in your rearview mirror. If you need supplies for the long trip, this is a good place to stock up—it's a decently sized town containing everything from bike shops to Laundromats.

The town was once much smaller, as the folks at the scarecrow-decorated **Carbondale Historical Society** at 500 Weant Boulevard will tell you. The old jail in the museum's front yard recalls the time when Carbondale's first settlers came all the way from Pennsylvania. The name of the town they'd emigrated from? Carbondale. Nobody initially found minerals in Carbondale, so the settlers focused on growing produce, especially potatoes, for miners in nearby Aspen, which was undergoing a silver boom. The town became the only stage stop on the 40-mile run from Aspen to Glenwood Springs. It catered to travelers accordingly, and by 1906, the town was a lively rest stop with an impressive 13 saloons.

That all changed when Idaho became a center of industrial agriculture. Potato harvesting activity moved up north. As a result, the town's economy relied more heavily on local ranchers who supplied cattle to other towns around the Crystal River. In the mid-1800s, prospectors discovered coal in Carbondale. The high-grade coal here powered the town's economy until the late 1980s. With its high methane content, Carbondale coal was as hazardous as it was precious, and in 1991 the mines shut down for good.

Since then, Carbondale has catered to Aspen tourists and people building second homes in the Aspen area. The town nestles in the shadow of Mount Sopris, the 12,660-foot giant marking the beginning of West Elk Loop. Carbondale is known as an adventure town, with white-water kayaking, climbing, and even skateboarding a short drive away. A pleasing bike path meanders along the byway and into town.

Like Aspen, Carbondale offers an impressive variety of galleries, restaurants, and nightlife—with a down-to-earth attitude. A smattering of art galleries adds a unique flavor to the town. Mary Matchael has been running the **Crystal Glass Studio** since 1972. Her work includes fused-glass chandeliers, large windows with sandblasted aspen leaf patterns, stained glass, glass wall displays, and much more. Ask the store manager for a tour of her studio, where you can see the glass furnaces, sculpting tools, and variety of paints that make the magic in Mary's work. She also did the window at the Redstone Church in downtown Redstone.

Stock up on roadside memorabilia at Marty Garfinkel's **Roadside Gallery** at 320 Main Street. He's been traveling across the country by car and taking pictures for over 20 years. You'll find photos of classic cars, signs, and other artifacts of the American road, as well as an astounding selection of black-and-white motorcycle rally photos from a couple of decades ago.

Carbondale's Main Street is a bustling Colorado town center with a theater, galleries, bookstores, and a variety of eateries. **Restaurant Six89,** on 689 Main Street, offers a stellar gourmet prix fixe menu. For something simpler, try **Fatbelly Burgers** on 220 Main Street.

Like many Colorado towns, Carbondale promotes sustainability. The biggest straw-bale structure in the country is located here. It's a Waldorf school at 16543 CO 82. People from around the country bring their kids here to get a top-tier education.

There's not much here in the way of historical museums unless you happen to be in town on a weekend or on a weekday between 1 and 3 PM. That's when the **Mount Sopris Historical Museum,** a two-story log cabin filled with artifacts tracing Carbondale's history from potato farmers to cowboys, is open. They've kept a rather eclectic variety of historical finds, like an early-20th-century mercantile store ledger and letters found in the pockets of an old army uniform.

Lodging runs the gamut from campgrounds to bed & breakfasts, such as the **Ambiance Inn B&B,** to modern chain hotels. The nearest campground is the Crystal River Resort at Mile Marker 62. The campgrounds include RV hook-ups, cabins, and tent spots, some of which are directly in front of the river. Familiar establishments like the Comfort Inn and Days Inn are also visible.

Just out of Carbondale, you'll enter the **White River National Forest.** Keep an eye on the river as you drive—this bubbling body of water has old bridges, interesting rock formations, and a variety of good places to picnic as you continue your drive. Slabs of marble will start appearing soon after the sign for White River, an indicator of things to come. The road at this point almost feels like a tranquil swim as it winds softly parallel to the river. At Mile Marker 53, you'll see Redstone's north entrance. Keep driving—a fascinating historical artifact is just 1 mile away. At Mile Marker 54, across from Redstone's south entrance, a long row of brick structures resembling beehives crouches in at the base of the hill. These are old coke ovens where 95 men used to load, coke, rake, and ship coal to John Osgood's steel mill in Pueblo. These men all lived across the river in Redstone.

Mile Marker 54 (CO 133)—Redstone: In the early 1900s, John Osgood, a wealthy coal baron, gazed upon the expanse of cliff-sheltered land that would eventually become Redstone. He decided that it was the perfect location to build a utopian community. For Osgood, that meant commissioning chalet-style homes and the 22-acre Redstone Inn for coal miners working at the nearby Colorado Fuel & Iron Company. If the miners had it good, Osgood had it even better—he owned and lived in the **Cleveholm Manor,** also known as the Redstone Castle, a 42-room Tudor mansion, constructed for himself at the edge of town. At time of writing, the manor was undergoing renovations in order to transform into a super-high-end spa hotel. If you want to relax and fish in Redstone, rustic-style, consider staying in a cabin at the peaceful **Avalanche Ranch.**

The first building you'll notice as you drive into town is the **Redstone Inn.** As a National Historic Hotel of America, the inn resonates with history. Old pictures complement original furniture to transport visitors back in time. It's worth a walk-through even if you're not staying. If you do choose to stay overnight, a four-star resort with a pool, hot tub, tennis court, and private fishing lake awaits.

Swing a left onto Main Street and discover its quaint, peaceful beauty. Red-

Coke ovens, Redstone

stone is a National Historic District with an enchanting main street that makes visitors drift into another time. Antique stores, a country store, galleries, restaurants, and a smattering of accommodations make an enchanting walk for fans of history and Victorian architecture. The tiny Redstone Museum provides more details on Osgood's utopia, while Bruno Moegli's riverside marble sculpture garden at 363 Redstone Boulevard lures viewers into an artistic interpretation of nature in its full glory. **Tiffany of Redstone,** identifiable by the three metal stars on the south side of its wall, sells antiques and collectibles, including a variety of Tiffany lamps.

Another option for overnighting is the **Redstone Campground,** with RV and tent camping and hot showers. As you leave Redstone and make your way toward Marble, make a photo stop at **Hayes Creek Falls.** Located at Mile Marker 50, these medium-sized falls offer a taste of the majestic natural beauty to come on

Sculpture garden, Redstone

the tour. There's also an option to take a steep hike farther up the falls. You'll notice that the road gradually begins its climb toward McClure Pass here. The first aspen groves come into sight on the roadside, and more peaks become visible as you ascend.

Mile Marker 47 (CO 133)—Marble: At Mile Marker 47, swing a left and head 5 miles out to the hamlet of Marble. This intersection is roughly the same place at which Crystal River prospectors fastidiously searched for gold and silver for 20 years—until they found huge marble deposits just 5 miles away. You'll know you're in the town when the road turns to gravel. Notice the thin air here: The town is located at roughly 8,000 feet. Two towering mountains come into plain view here: the Fourteener on the left is North Maroon Peak; the one to its right is Maroon Peak. These are arguably the two most photographed mountains in Colorado.

Relatively sleepy Marble lives up to its name. Not much is visible here, save for a few houses and dirt roads. The town's claim to fame is its marble mining. Its Yule Marble Quarry and Crystal Mill produced pieces of fine marble used in the Lincoln Memorial in 1916 and a 100-ton slab used in the Tomb of the Unknown Soldier. The folks at the **Marble Historical Society & Museum,** which is usually open in the summer months, will be happy to tell you a detailed history of this quarry town.

Visitors can tour the Yule Marble Quarry finishing mill in downtown Marble at the Millsite Park. This is the park where quarrymen used to mine and process

Marble

the marble. Exploring the park is a dramatic experience. This formerly active industrial site now more closely resembles a Mayan ruin than a working mill, with marble towers and old workshops jutting out from a foundation containing rusted sheets of metal and overgrown with leafy, twisting plants. The park is filled with the ruins of components of the Colorado Yule Marble Company, which was founded in 1905. Massive marble slabs stand in chunky stacks to the west, each with its weight (often in the neighborhood of 50,000 pounds) and destination scrawled on it in blue spray paint. It takes some imagination to picture what these haphazard remnants once were: an avalanche retaining wall 70 feet tall made of marble, used to protect the mill building from snowslides; gang saws for cutting marble blocks; marble firewalls built after an early small fire threatened the building; a mill for hand finishing and carving; an overhead crane for lifting marble; a shop for rubbing beds where sand was rubbed on marble; a diamond drill; and more. A map at the entrance explains each structure, though now they're much harder to recognize.

Hiking, horseback, and, in winter, Nordic skiing and snowshoeing trails run from town up into the Maroon Bells–Snowmass and the Raggeds Wilderness Areas. If you choose to camp here—be forewarned, this place won't exactly invite you in to stay overnight, due to it being a tiny town—RVs are welcome at **Bogan Flats Campground** along County Road 3 (CR 3) about midway between CO 133 and the town of Marble.

From Marble, you'll climb higher and higher through aspen groves, up toward noble-looking mountains. The river becomes a silver snake miles below as you reach the 8,755-foot summit of McClure Pass. Take the turn off just to the left of the MCCLURE PASS sign for an up-close and personal aspen grove experience. If you're a true nature lover, camp here for up to 14 days. In the fall, this is prime aspen-viewing territory.

Mile Marker 19 (CO 133)—Somerset: Somerset is one of the most prominent coal-mining towns in Crystal River Valley. A train comes through the center of town several times a day to collect coal for a number of power plants in the West. Workers still commute daily from nearby towns such as Paonia and Hotchkiss. The coal mine truly defines the town; there aren't any tourist amenities here, save for the town restaurant.

Just before Mile Marker 28, you'll see a sign for Paonia State Park and, shortly after that, Paonia Reservoir. These two areas comprise a North Fork Valley recreation paradise offering boating, fishing, camping, waterskiing, and picnicking.

Mile Marker 10 (CO 133)—Paonia: Home to some of the best peaches in the state, Paonia is a small, homey agricultural and coal-mining town in the fertile North Fork Valley of the Gunnison. Ute inhabited the area until 1880, when the infamous Meeker Massacre prompted the government to force them onto reservations. White settlers built up the town soon afterward, naming it Paonia after the many peony flowers in the area.

Though many residents are employed at coal mines in nearby Somerset, Paonia's main claim to fame is its agricultural bounty. Cherries, peaches, and apples are abundant here in summer. The region also produces some of Colorado's finest wines, with clarets that are gaining national renown.

Besides attending farmer's markets here in summer, visitors can hike, bike, and walk the town, which is currently an eclectic mixture of farmers, ranchers, miners, retirees, and hippies. The town is proud to be politically progressive and, perhaps because a number of Paonia inhabitants consider themselves escapees from the more urban Front Range, the dearth of stoplights and fast-food restaurants is also a bragging point. It's home to the Chaco sandal factory, which produces summer footwear for a notable proportion of the state's population, and the *High Country News,* a well-known nonprofit publication covering culture and sustainability in the West. Paonia is also home to several summer festivals, among them Cherry Days and an annual BMW rally.

For excellent burritos, settle into a booth at **Sol Margaritas** on Grand and Third. They serve a variety of Mexican beers and margaritas to complement the tasty food. **The Diner,** located just down the street, offers a classic small-town dining experience, with vintage movie posters. Food is all-American fare like malts, milkshakes, and burgers.

For those who want to stay a couple days in this slow-paced town, there's camping at the nearby **Paonia Reservoir and Paonia State Park.** There are also a couple of B&B options. One is the **Bross Hotel Bed & Breakfast,** which is located in a refurbished early-1900s building downtown. The other, the **Fresh & Wyld Farmhouse Inn,** is a seven-bedroom farmhouse with farm-fresh cuisine to match, and the perfect getaway for those who want a dose of natural farm life during their Paonia stay.

Mile Marker 2 (CO 133)—Hotchkiss: A few vineyard-filled miles south of Paonia lies Hotchkiss. One of its claims to fame is its fish hatchery, located 2 miles
past town on the 3100 Road to Lazear. Colorado's rivers, lakes, and streams are
often so full of sporting fish that anglers can stand just feet away from each other
and still catch enough trout for dinner. Many of these fish are hatched not in the
wild but at the **Hotchkiss National Fish Hatchery** 3 miles south of town.

The hatchery is a good education destination for families or those interested
in the environment. There's a display explaining how they hatch fish, why they
raise trout here, how they raise the trout, trout health, and more. One of two state
fish hatcheries (the other is located in Leadville), the Hotchkiss hatchery stocks
more than 70 different locations in Colorado and New Mexico. Visitor tours explaining the processes of hatching and stocking are offered seven days a week.

Apart from the hatchery, the town itself has many familiar amenities, including motels, coffee shops, cowboy collectibles shops, and antique stores. The
Creamery Arts Center is a community arts center with galleries displaying the
work of more than one hundred artists. The **Hotchkiss-Crawford Historical Society Museum,** open on afternoons only from Friday through Sunday, offers a
flavor of the Old West side of the town, with a chuck wagon, saddles, and antique
clothes worn by the first settlers in the North Fork Valley.

The **Leroux Creek Inn** on 3100 Road is a 47-acre adobe retreat and winery
catering to those who want to enjoy the bountiful countryside here. Hotchkiss
also boasts seven restaurants to grab a meal at. The **North Fork Valley Restaurant** on Bridge Street hosts live bands on the weekends and is a popular gathering spot for locals and tourists alike. Try their Navajo tacos.

Mile Marker 63 (CO 92)—Crawford: As the loop heads out of Paonia, it gets
more rural and bucolic. You'll start seeing a lot of cows, tractors, and big pickup
trucks. The last of the dramatic mountains from McClure Pass flatten out. The
landscape folds into rolling, grassy hills not unlike parts of the Midwest. As you
approach the town of Crawford, chances are you'll see more than a few real-life
cowboys. Home to spur-wearing ranchers, cattle drives still take place through
the middle of town. Nestled near sheer canyons, wide mesas, and unexpected
rock outcroppings, this cowboy town is a good place to take it easy and watch
life roll, walk, and gallop by.

This slow pace has attracted many artists, among them musician Joe Cocker,
who lives here permanently. Browse the **Crawford Country Store & Motel** on

313 CO 92, the town's general store. The **Bee Yard Gardens** on 711 CO 92 is a huge, comprehensive nursery at the beginning of town. The **North Rim Glass Studio** at 191 CO 92 shapes world-renowned pieces and has an extensive gift store. If you get hungry here, grab a rancher-sized steak at the **Branding Iron Steakhouse,** also located on the main street through town. If you're here in July, hit the Render the Rock Festival at stunning Needle Rock, where artists gather to draw, paint, and sculpt Needle Rock in every imaginable medium.

At 1 mile south of town lies **Crawford State Park** and lake. The lake is a serene, spacious fishing spot popular among locals. Nearby Crawford State Park contains a couple of reservoirs with lots of fishing, a waterskiing beach, accessible walking paths, and a couple of campgrounds. Both are good for RVs and leisurely fishing vacations. **Clear Fork and Iron Creek Campgrounds** contain fire pits, tent and RV camping, and sit on a wide open space looking out on the lake. The lake offers boating, Jet-Skiing, fishing, kayaking, and more.

Mile Marker 59 (CO 92)—Black Canyon of the Gunnison National Park. **North Rim:** There are 14 miles of sheer 1,000-foot cliff walls that define this national park, which squares off a section of a 53-mile-long gorge. The fish-filled Gunnison looks like a narrow stream as it roars below, carving ever deeper into the canyons that it started forming millennia ago. The Painted Wall, Colorado's highest cliff, stands an impressive 2,250 feet high—1,000 feet higher than the Empire State Building.

The steep walls of the canyon range in depth from 1,750 to 2,700 feet. The Gunnison River's steep gradient, with an average fall of 95 feet per mile, cut the deep, narrow grooves that formed the canyon. The Gunnison River flows at 12,000 cubic feet per second—that's 2.75-million horsepower—not bad for a river.

Visitors will find juniper, pinyon, and scrub oak forests to hike through at the rim. Those brave enough to venture to the gorge will find a vastly different riparian ecosystem, complete with 5-foot-high poison ivy. It's a good idea to cover your limbs while exploring the vast canyon. Mule deer and a variety of birds, including peregrine falcons and golden eagles nesting on cliff ledges, are the most bountiful animal sightings here. Note that the bottom of the gorge is a wilderness area. Permits are required to enter that area, and "leave no trace" ethics should be followed. Water and backcountry/climbing permits are available at the ranger's station. The campground at the more remote North Rim is first-come, first-served car camping and is not RV compatible.

Black Canyon of the Gunnison and the Gunnison River

South Rim: Note that there's no bridge between the remote North Rim and the much more accessible South Rim. To get from the North Rim to the South Rim takes around two to three hours of driving, either along the byway through the **Curecanti National Recreation Area,** or back through Hotchkiss and past the relatively sizeable town of Montrose. You can camp both at the North and South Rims; the North Rim has more primitive facilities and is closed in winter. If you prefer to overnight in a hotel, Montrose has several chain options like the Comfort Inn. The campsite at the South Rim has handicapped accessibility and is RV compatible.

Stop by the visitors center at the South Rim to learn more about recreation opportunities, which include camping, hiking (both on trails and, for the more adventurous, into the wilderness of the inner canyon), fishing, rafting, advanced climbing, horseback riding, and more. A scenic drive around the South Rim is the best way to get an overview of the park.

By driving the South Rim, you'll cover all 12 of the canyon's viewpoints, located between the park entrance and the end of the road at High Point. It's a slow and view-saturated 6-mile drive. You'll see astounding finlike rock formations in the canyon. These towers are known as pegmatite dikes. Their namesake is a type of rock that erodes much more slowly than other rocks. Thus, the rocks around the pegmatite erode, while the pegmatite remains standing in the form of a narrow stack. You can also drive down to the river from the South Rim, a steep, brake-burning descent that ends at **Crystal Dam,** a reservoir capable of releasing 42,000 cubic feet of water per second. Anglers will find Gold Medal Waters here, which are fishing areas designated by the Colorado Wildlife Commission as outstanding waters to fish for large trout.

Mile Marker 1 (CO 92)—Curecanti National Recreation Area: Close to the South Rim lies Cimarron Lake. If you take a slight detour to nearby Cimarron, you can see Locomotive #278, which stands atop the last remaining trestle on the Gunnison Railroad route.

Southeast of the Black Canyon of the Gunnison lies the **Curecanti National Recreation Area.** This fishing and outdoor mecca is defined by three stunning lakes: Blue Mesa Reservoir to the east, Morrow Point Lake in the middle, and Crystal Lake on the western edge. Each lake is separated by a dam along the Gunnison River.

Blue Mesa Reservoir floats into view soon after Cimarron. At 20 miles long and with 96 miles of shoreline, Blue Mesa Reservoir is the largest body of water in Colorado. It has two marinas, numerous boat launch sites, and abundant camping. Several hikes round out the experience here. The easiest is Neversink, a 1.5-mile round-trip that's fully accessible. The hardest hike is from the stunning viewpoint at Hermit's Rest. That hike is 6 miles round-trip, and gains more than 1,000 feet of elevation. Visitors can fish for rainbow, brook, brown, and lake trout, as well as Kokanee salmon.

Look up from the parking lot of Blue Mesa Reservoir and you'll see dramatic brown rock outcroppings. These are the **Dillon Pinnacles,** formed by volcanic ash and debris over an extended period of time. Heading back to the north side of the water, the road that follows is utterly hypnotic. Aspen and pine groves make for a verdant green blanket across the **Gunnison Gorge,** while the rugged San Juans rise dramatically in the background. The aspens turn golden in the fall, adding a dizzying element of color. The tallest peak to the south is **Uncompahgre Peak.** At 14,309 feet, it's the sixth tallest in Colorado.

At Mile Marker 55, the trail/overlook at Hermit's Rest is a don't-miss. More than 1,000 feet below, the reservoir looks more like a fjord. Steadfast hikers can take the 1.5-mile trip down to the old boat-docking area (which no longer contains a dock, but canoers do occasionally moor here), then brave the sweaty three-hour climb back up. You can also camp on the shore.

Mile Marker 160 (US 50)—Gunnison: Continue along US 50 and, to the north, you'll see the vast expanse of national forest that encompasses the Grand Mesa, Uncompahgre, and Gunnison National Forests (known affectionately as GMUG by some rangers). You'll also enter Gunnison, a town rich in Old West history. The town of Gunnison, like the national forest and river, is named after John W. Gunnison, a mid-1800s U.S. Army surveyor on an expedition to find a suitable Rocky Mountain pass for the transcontinental railroad. The town's location along the railroad helped it thrive as a regional supply center for cattle in the 1800s. For a while, the town was doing so well that planners were convinced it would eventually become the capital of Colorado. They built the town's streets wide to accommodate for what they saw as an inevitable and dramatic population boom. The boom never happened. The town remains small to this day, and the streets disproportionately wide.

Gunnison boasts some other historical tidbits. The mountain with the "W" on it (for Western State College) has some 8,000-year-old paleolithic remains inside

Black Canyon of the Gunnison *Seth K. Hughes*

of it, which archaeologists are still digging up. Before the white settlers came, American Indians lived in the area. Many of their ancient remains are still buried in the mountain.

Brothers Wyatt and Warren Earp camped on the outskirts of Gunnison after they left Tombstone in 1882. Several years later, Wyatt returned to Gunnison with Josie Marcus, his companion, and settled there. The town also escaped the Spanish influenza pandemic that killed hundreds of others in the area in 1918 by barricading all highways near county lines. Train passengers were warned that, if they exited the train in Gunnison, they'd be arrested and quarantined for five days. The barricades and threats worked: As a result, nobody in Gunnison died of influenza during the epidemic.

Yet another of Gunnison's claims to fame is climatic: Because of its location at the bottom of several valleys, the town averages 7 degrees Fahrenheit in January, making it one of the coldest winter climates in Colorado. Gunnison's predominant role today, however, is as a gateway ski town to Crested Butte's famously utopian terrain. The variety of accommodations, especially medium-sized hotels and motels, reflects this. Outside of the frigid winter months, Gunnison is a bustling tourist town full of shops, eateries, and friendly locals. Western State College, the first college on the Western Slope, lends a youthful spunk to the town, with all the cafés, pubs, and vintage stores typical of a college town, while Gunnison's cowboy history lends the town an arid, Western feel. You can also rent transportation here, be it a car, snowmobile, bike, plane, or anything in between.

In the summer, Gunnison is a hunter's paradise. Several outfitters, such as the **Lazy F Bar Ranch,** offer big-game hunting retreats. Seasons include bear, elk, and mule deer, which Gunnison is historically famous for. Elk and deer seasons generally run from August through September; black bear season is in September. Archers and rifle hunters especially will find many opportunities here. Hunting licenses are required.

Other nearby recreation opportunities include road and mountain biking, hiking, fishing, kayaking, and four-wheeling. **Hartman Rocks,** with ancient rock formations that some scientists say were formed by a meteor more than 300 million years ago, has an extensive trail system renowned for its dirt sports. Hikers, mountain bikers, and off-road motorcyclists will find days of exploration here.

History buffs will savor the sizable **Pioneer Museum** on the east side of town at 803 East Tomichi Avenue. The museum has 12 buildings, including Gunnison's first post office, the Denver and Rio Grande Narrow Gauge Railroad (lifted from its now-defunct tracks through the Alpine Tunnel of the Black Canyon of the Gunnison), and an early 1900s rural schoolhouse. Additional exhibits include antique wagons and cars, a fully equipped dairy barn, arrowhead collections, and more.

For hotel accommodations at relatively reasonable rates, try the **Water Wheel Inn**, located 2 miles west of town on US 50. Owner Dr. Jim can tell you all about local bike riding and dining opportunities. Gunnison is also a good place to shop. You'll find furniture, antiques, outdoor gear, jewelry, bikes, skis, DVDs, and almost anything else under the sun right on Main Street.

Mile Marker 26 (CO 135)—Crested Butte: Crested Butte started out as a vacation spot for the Ute, and, after a stint as a mining town, came almost full circle to become one of Colorado's favorite ski resorts. In the mid-1800s, white settlers began displacing the Ute, who used Crested Butte as a summer residence. Settlers

Crested Butte

soon discovered silver and coal in the area; as a result, the town's charming **Victorian Old Town** was built, as were several mining towns in surrounding areas, many of which are now ghost towns.

Because Crested Butte also had a handful of ranches and acted as a supply town to neighboring regions, it narrowly survived the ensuing silver bust and closure of its coal mines. The town stayed in stealth mode until the mid-1960s, when **Mount Crested Butte,** the town's ski area, opened. Tourists flooded in, reviving the town's economy and laying the groundwork for the festive, outdoorsy town it is today. The quaint downtown also offers galleries, salons, trinket shops, bike shops, and more.

Crested Butte is now known as a skiing and mountain biking mecca. It's home to the **Mountain Bike Hall of Fame,** as well as the annual Fat Tire Bike Week, a mountain biking celebration and ride held in late June of every year. Aside from mountain biking, the town has a festival almost every month, the Wildflower Festival a notable among them.

For a taste of heritage, check out the **Crested Butte Mountain Heritage Museum** at 331 Elk Avenue. The museum chronicles the history of Crested Butte from its inception as a mining town to its present status as an outdoor tourists' Eden. Visitors will find a variety of exhibits, including black-and-white mid-1800s portraits of famous visitors, the Crested Butte Mountain Resort's first gondola, merchandise originally sold in the Crested Butte hardware store (where the museum is now), a life-sized mining diorama, and more. The museum also houses the Mountain Bike Hall of Fame. Opened in 1988, the Mountain Bike Hall of Fame displays vintage bikes and components, old photos, press clippings from historic races, and a slew of additional memorabilia.

As in most ski towns, dining and lodging options abound. Quaint downtown B&Bs add flavor to the clusters of slope-side resorts and condominiums up the hill at Mount Crested Butte. You won't find the spunk of Crested Butte proper at the Mount Crested Butte resort town, but you will find the basic amenities present in most North American ski towns: liquor stores, restaurants, and a slew of hotels and condos. The **Crested Butte Retreat** on Mount Crested Butte is a true standout among the many lodging options on the mountain. This classy and lavish high-end Colorado mountain lodge offers tasteful rooms, a spa, and the kind of resort lodging that makes you linger in your room long after the lifts open.

For a personal touch, try some of Crested Butte's B&Bs, notably **The Ruby of**

Lake Irwin, near Crested Butte

Crested Butte and the **Purple Mountain Lodge.** Budget travelers might try the **Crested Butte International Lodge and Hostel** at 615 Teocalli Avenue, which has private rooms as well as bunk beds. Clean, comfortable, and with space to cook in, it offers a communal experience. The hostel is set up with a lounge and shared kitchen typical of all hostels. It's very clean, charges $5 for a shower, has key-carded doors, and is spacious enough to almost feel like a hotel.

In terms of its appearance, there's a stun factor in Crested Butte that is hard to pinpoint at first. The town's beauty is so postcard-perfect that it takes a few looks to let it all sink in. The town is surrounded by mountain landmarks each so unique that individually they still take your breath away. In addition to nearly 360-degree mountain views, the town is complemented by its towering scenery rather than overwhelmed by it. It's the stuff of Colorado tourism posters.

Another noteworthy aspect of this town is its truly cosmopolitan dining. You

Kebler Pass in the fall *Seth K. Hughes*

can find good eats here, from sushi that's flown in from Hawaii every day to savory Italian. (Be sure to make reservations before you dine out.) For breakfast, try the unbeatable stuffed blueberry pancakes at **McGill's** at 228 Elk Avenue. The **Ginger Café** at 425 Elk Avenue offers divine Thai and Indian food cooked up by a skilled chef from, strangely enough, Omaha, Nebraska. The fresh Thai spring rolls and ginger crème brûlée are to die for. **Marchitelli's Gourmet Noodle** at 411 Third Street serves quality Italian foods, complemented by a sizeable selection of wines. Don't dine there without sampling a salad with their homemade balsamic vinaigrette. For wifi access, good shots, and an independent café ambiance, head to the **Buckaroo Beanery** right next to the Phillips 66 gas station.

Crested Butte is a classic Colorado small town. Almost every building boasts a fresh coat of paint and a tin roof; town regulations prohibit the garish plastic or neon signs you might see in larger cities, giving the town a clean, artistic feel. Most townsfolk ride around on "townies," or refurbished 1970s-style cruiser bikes. Old buildings aren't demolished here; rather, they're refurbished and sometimes repurposed.

For mountain bikers, the single-tracks here are legendary. Rent a new-model bike at **Big Al's** and get a taste for local trails by heading up Maroon Avenue to The Woods, then hitting the Upper and Lower Loops, which are only mildly technical and filled with flowers in summertime. Another alternative is Tony's Ride on the west side of town. For something longer, try the 401 Ride, a Crested Butte half-day classic that boasts waist-high wildflowers.

Day trips abound from Crested Butte. One popular day trip is up the mountain to Gothic, a former ghost town that now has a biological research station where people research everything from insects to aspen/woodland ecosystems.

Mile Marker 31 (CR 12)—Kebler Pass: The last portion of the West Elk journey is **Kebler Pass,** known by many to be one of the most astounding places in the country to see the aspens turn gold in fall. The aspen grove here, which stretches into Aspen and Carbondale, is the largest in Colorado. Needless to say, when the aspens turn color on Kebler Pass, it's a powerful experience. This unpaved road, if followed to its terminus, ends up at the Paonia Reservoir and is considered a scenic back-way of getting from Crested Butte to the Paonia area.

The pass starts around Mile Marker 31 out of Crested Butte. The road soon goes to gravel, but it's smooth enough for even big RVs to pass through. Various hiking trails and campgrounds pepper the way to the summit: **Splain's Gulch** is located at Mile Marker 27. Shortly thereafter, a dirt road leads to Lake Irwin, a cold lake that is full of fish and reflects high mountain peaks. Other hiking trails include Dark Canyon, Cliff Creek, and Lost Lake.

Driving through the aspen grove at around 10,000 feet is humbling. Initially, its silence is reminiscent of a cathedral of sorts; however, if you sit for a while, you'll find it teeming with life. Field mice and insects skirt the thick leaf cover on the ground while birds converse overhead; when winds rustle through, the aspen tops sway in circular waves. The sheer volume of aspen trees here is enough to make a person forget to blink.

The aspen grove stretches for miles through a gradual ascent and descent. Eventually, the aspens give way to pine and other trees. The road or, as many would have it, the journey ends with a couple of ranches and a good view of the dam at Paonia Reservoir. The majestic drive through Kebler Pass is the ideal culmination to your scenic drive through the Western Slope. This drive is sure to leave you with memories—if not hundreds of photographs—of some of Colorado's most beautiful landscapes.

IN THE AREA

CARBONDALE

Accommodations

Ambiance Inn B&B, 66 N. Second St. Call 970-963-3597.

Attractions and Recreation

Carbondale Historical Society, 500 Weant Blvd. Call 970-963-7041.

Crystal Glass Studio, 50 Weant Blvd. Call 970-963-3227.

Mount Sopris Historical Museum, 500 Weant Blvd. Call 970-963-7041.

Roadside Gallery, 320 Main St. Call 970-963-9333.

Dining/Drinks

Fatbelly Burgers, 220 Main St. Call 970-963-1569.

Restaurant Six89, 689 Main St. Call 970-963-6890.

REDSTONE

Accommodations

Avalanche Ranch, 12863 CO 133. Call 1-877-963-9339.

Redstone Campground, 13 miles south of Carbondale on CO 133. Call 1-877-444-6777.

Redstone Inn, 82 Redstone Blvd. Call 970-963-2526.

Attractions and Recreation

Cleveholm Manor, 58 Redstone Blvd. Call 970-963-9656.

Tiffany of Redstone, 225 Redstone Blvd. Call 970-963-1769.

Marble

Accommodations

Bogan Flats Campground, 1.5 miles down Gunnison CR 3 near Marble. Call 1-800-280-2267.

Attractions and Recreation

Marble Historical Society & Museum, 412 W. Main St. Call 970-963-9815.

PAONIA

Accommodations

Bross Hotel Bed & Breakfast, 312 Onarga Ave. Call 970-527-6776.

Fresh & Wyld Farmhouse Inn, 1978 Harding Rd. Call 970-527-4374.

Paonia Reservoir and Paonia State Park. Call 970-921-5721. www.parks.state.co.us/parks/paonia /pages/paoniastateparkhome.aspx.

Dining/Drinks

The Diner, 203 Grand Ave. Call 970-527-4773.

Sol Margaritas, 240 Grand Ave. Call 970-527-4187.

HOTCHKISS

Accommodations

Leroux Creek Inn, 12388 3100 Rd. Call 970-872-4746.

Attractions and Recreation

Creamery Arts Center, 165 W. Bridge St. Call 970-872-4848.

Hotchkiss-Crawford Historical Society Museum, 180 S. Second St. Call 970-872-3780.

Hotchkiss National Fish Hatchery, 8342 Hatchery Rd. Call 970-872-3170.

Dining/Drinks

North Fork Valley Restaurant, 140 W. Bridge St. Call 970-872-4215.

CRAWFORD

Accommodations

Clear Fork and Iron Creek Campgrounds, 40468 CO 92. Call 970-921-5721.

Attractions and Recreation

Bee Yard Gardens, 711 CO 92. Call 970-921-4335.

Crawford Country Store & Motel, 313 CO 92. Call 970-921-5061.

Crawford State Park, 40468 CO 92. Call 970-921-5721.

North Rim Glass Studio, 191 CO 92. Call 970-921-4527.

Dining/Drinks

Branding Iron Steakhouse, 356 CO 92. Call 970-921-4386.

GUNNISON

Accommodations

Water Wheel Inn, 37478 US 50. Call 970-641-1650.

Attractions and Recreation

Lazy F Bar Ranch, P.O. Box 383, Gunnison 81230. Call 970-641-0193.

Pioneer Museum, 803 E. Tomichi Avenue. Call 970-641-4530.

CRESTED BUTTE

Accommodations

Crested Butte International Lodge and Hostel, 615 Teocalli Ave. Call 970-349-0588.

Crested Butte Retreat, 39 Whetstone Rd. Call 970-349-1658.

Purple Mountain Lodge, 714 Gothic Ave. Call 970-349-5888.

The Ruby of Crested Butte, 624 Gothic Ave. Call 970-349-1338.

Attractions and Recreation

Big Al's, 207 Elk Ave. Call 970-349-0515.

Crested Butte Mountain Heritage Museum, 331 Elk Ave. Call 970-349-1880.

Mountain Bike Hall of Fame, 331 Elk Ave. Call 970-349-6817.

Dining/Drinks

Buckaroo Beanery, 601 Sixth St. Call 970-349-5252.

Ginger Café, 425 Elk Ave. Call 970-349-7291.

Marchitelli's Gourmet Noodle, 411 Third St. Call 970-349-7401.

McGill's, 228 Elk Ave. Call 970-349-5240.

CONTINENTAL DIVIDE

View from Ripple Creek Overlook

Lake Granby

4 Colorado River Headwaters Scenic and Historic Byway

Estimated length: 80 miles

Estimated time: 2 hours

Highlights: Enjoy the many activities available in charming Grand Lake; fly-fish the Colorado River as it winds its way west; camp and take a boat out on Lake Granby or Grand Lake; hike the high-elevation trails winding out of Monarch Lake; enjoy deep relaxation at Hot Sulphur Springs.

Getting there: From Denver, take I-70 west to the intersection of US 40 north. From Grand Junction, take I-70 east to the US 40 intersection. Follow US 40 to US 34 and the town of Grand Lake, the start of the byway.

This entire route is ideal for motorcycles; traffic is light, scenery is easily taken in without removing one's concentration from the road itself, and steep climbs and hairpin turns are minimal or nonexistent. The route is also ideal for those hauling a trailer or driving a large rig.

History: The byway itself is named in accordance with the famous North American river it follows, the Colorado. But there's more to this byway than just one of the most iconic rivers in the nation. The towns and communities that have sprung up along its banks are bathed in as much history as the river's gentle waters, which eventually become torrents of white-capped rapids. The byway begins just outside the western boundary of Rocky Mountain National Park, whose borders hold the true headwaters of the Colorado River. See the Trail Ridge Road chapter for more information on Rocky Mountain National Park.

Grand Lake. Home to the largest natural lake in Colorado, the aptly named Grand Lake has evolved slowly over the years. It's the first stop along the byway when

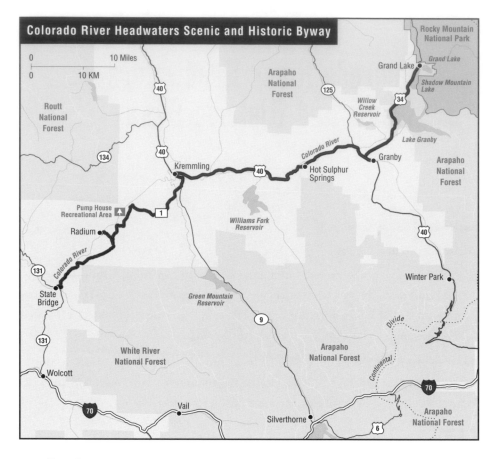

Colorado River Headwaters Scenic and Historic Byway

traveling from east to west, and according to legend, began life as a Ute settlement. The Ute passed a story down through generations about the lake regarding a villagewide massacre that took place there. It's believed that marauding Arapaho and Cheyenne descended upon the Ute settlement, killing the men and setting the women and children adrift on a raft that capsized in the middle of the lake, killing all on board. According to lore, the mist that rises from the lake in early mornings is the incarnation of these spirits, murdered hundreds of years ago. Because of this story, the area sat uninhabited for quite some time. But the discovery of gold in the nearby mountains rapidly changed this. Grand Lake became the final stop for prospectors and miners headed up into the surrounding wilderness in search of fortunes. Naturally, this drew savvy business owners, looking to cash in on precious metals without risking anything in the mines, by building supply stores along the banks of the lake.

When the hillsides were drained of their ore, the town became a retreat for well-off families who bought up land and began to develop the pine-ringed, high-mountain lake—a trend that continues today. As proof of fact, Grand Lake is now home to one of the highest-altitude sailing regattas in the world—a sport known for its upper-crust appeal. When its backyard was added to the western reaches of Rocky Mountain National Park in 1915, more Americans than ever saw the area's grandiose beauty. Since then, it has been growing as an outdoor enthusiasts' playground, especially for trout-hungry anglers.

Hot Sulphur Springs. It's long been told that an ailing Ute chief was once sent to live out the last of his days in this area. He spent his hours soaking in the natural hot springs, and drinking the mineral-rich waters. Within a short time, his health returned and he reentered the tribe as a poster child for good health. Since then, the magma-heated waters that bubble up from the ground have been revered as having curative properties.

Grand Lake boardwalk

Mile Marker 15 (US 34)—Grand Lake: At first blush, you'd think Grand Lake is a beach town in some coastal state. The stores are quaint, and small mom-and-pop shops dominate the main street with no chain establishment in sight. Its very purpose seems to be to please travelers, and its backyard of Rocky Mountain National Park has quite a bit to do with this fact. Even though the town is extremely popular with travelers, touring it isn't a rushed affair. People meander across the street, more intent on the sun-reflecting waters of Grand Lake and the snow-capped peaks of the Rocky Mountains that engulf this mining community turned tourist retreat. As you leave downtown, you should also be aware of people crossing on horseback, as it's the waypoint for **Sombrero Ranches,** home to über-popular cowboy-led trail rides.

The **Kauffman House Museum**—Grand Lake's only remaining log hotel—is wharfside, near the town's marina, and now spends its days edifying visitors on the history of the area. A boardwalk and marina with a clapboard pathway extend over the water, and sailboats and motorboats dock within its inlets. The lake is large enough to have created sand from the volcanic rock in the area. Because of this, picnic tables and volleyball nets can be found rooted in the soft, tan sand. Every building on every block appears to be a restaurant, inn, or rental facility; it's a wonder that an actual populace has a home in town that isn't already a place of business for the tourism industry. In this outdoors-centered town, you can rent anything that gets you around, including sailboats, motorboats, Jet Skis, sailboards, ATVs, Jeeps, horses, and, in the winter, snowmobiles, snowshoes, and cross-country skis.

The town's surrounding landscape has a gluttonous overabundance of grandeur. The deep greens of pine, dark blues of the lake, and the sky-scraping solidity of the granite peaks all combine to provide a spectacular scene. Unfortunately, the area, along with others in Colorado, has been afflicted with blight. The once endless sea of evergreen has begun to change to a tricolor patchwork. Greens, browns, and smoky grays are the dominant colors as trees slowly die. The pine beetle, a tiny insect, is killing hundred-year-old forests in a matter of a few years. As you look to the mountainsides, you'll see its mark.

The town is best seen on foot. Most people take advantage of this fact, making driving through town a slow affair. Shorts, T-shirts, and sandals are the uniform of choice during the summer, when temperatures easily hang in the mid-70s. People travel from doorstep to doorstep as they walk the length and breadth of

Grand Lake's special culture

the three-block downtown in search of souvenirs. Pace doesn't matter much, as the quaintness of the town is contagious. You'll find your normally tight grip on the steering wheel in response to children darting across the road soon replaced with a soft braking and a slight wave as you wish them a fun day in this high-altitude lakefront town.

At Mile Marker 15, on the eastern edge of town, is the entrance to an RV park and campground. Grand Lake's eastern portal welcomes you with a colorful sign. Roughly 200 yards after the sign greets you to Grand Lake, you can turn left to **Old Town Grand Lake and Village.**

Every block, connected by sun-worn walkways, houses a tourist-ready business. From ATV, bicycle, boat, and fishing gear rentals to shops selling ice cream, knickknacks, and necessities, the town is perpetually open for the tourist season. And on top of it all is ample free parking wedged in along its main and side

Grand Lake's recreational gateway

streets. Though spaces are plentiful, they often fill up completely come midday, when the critical mass of visitors arrives.

Most buildings have the façades of those seen in Western movies, with brightly painted false fronts and log cabin–style structures. Though they take on the timeless feel of the 1800s, it's obvious that these buildings have either been built relatively recently or their owners take pride in the façades. Speaking with store owners, it's evident that both are true—in spades. The shopkeepers and residents of this town take pride in their community, and it shows on their happy, sun-kissed faces.

Continue west to Shadow Mountain via Granby on US 34. To your left is **Grand Lake,** composed of dark blue water like that of the deepest sections of the Pacific Ocean. To your right are the stoic evergreens, protecting the hillsides that surround the giant basin of water. Dotting the lake, making wake, are motorboats pushing water aside in frothy waves through the otherwise calm surface of the lake. The lake is protected from wind by the surrounding mountains. But, as wind often does, it still finds ways to send wisps of air over the lake, providing just enough push for the many sailboats that also dash along its surface. Hard-packed dirt areas, serving as pullouts for **Shadow Mountain Lake,** begin along the left side of the road, just before County Road 469 (CR 469).

Once you remove yourself from the Old Town area of Grand Lake, it still feels like a California beach town, but with the trappings of a quintessential Colorado mountain town thrown into the mix. Being surrounded by wildlife and plant life gives the town a laid-back feel, but you don't have to put up with typical beach-town problems, like traffic jams and smog. Just outside of town is **Trail Ridge Marina and Rentals** on the left; look for a blue sign advertising a full-service marina. Just past that is **Lake View B&B.** Both are roughly 2 miles after Grand Lake's downtown. **Isolation Peak Lodge** and **Black Bear Lodge** are small accommodations, designed to cater to those who want to stay as close to the water as nature—or perhaps zoning laws—will allow; they're both found on the right. And, at Mile Marker 12, just after the cabins, is access to **Green Ridge,** with tent camping, picnicking, and a boat launch. The river doesn't appear as much as you'd think through this part of the byway. **Shadow Mountain Lake Picnic Area** is also found here, immediately after Green Ridge. The area is lightly used but small, so it can fill unexpectedly. The scenery is almost too perfect; with the road nearly abutting the waters of the lake, you feel the urge to skip stones right from your car window. To your right are glens and thickets that you'd think were the impetus for the movie *Bambi.*

You can get fried chicken to go at **Betty's ol' Café and Bakery** on the left-hand side of the road; on the right is **T Lazy W RV Park.** Both are on the outskirts of Stillwater, a town with an obvious sense of humor. Etched into their welcome sign is the message: A QUAINT LITTLE DRINKING VILLAGE WITH A FISHING, HUNTING, AND SNOWMOBILING PROBLEM. At this lakeside town, they don't beat around the bush about what they offer: pure, unadulterated recreation. Stillwater itself is built upon the banks and nearby hillside, stretching along the highway. If you find it difficult to get lodging in Grand Lake, consider Stillwater as a smaller, yet slightly more under-the-radar piece of real estate. Near Mile Marker 10 is **Cutthroat Bay Campground;** the road to the campsites leads to the lake. If you hit the Grand Lake Fire Protection building, you've just passed the turnoff. And if you decide to take this road to access the lake, look straight ahead of you, off into the distance through gaps in the pine trees, and you'll see the snow-veined granite peaks of the Rockies disappearing into the haze of the horizon. The road ends at **Cutthroat Bay Arapaho Recreation Area and Campground.** You need to buy a pass to make use of this outdoor recreation area.

The entrance to Stillwater Pass is on your right down CR 4 just after Mile Marker 10. It's about 0.5 mile after Mile Marker 10 that you get your first official sign marking this as a scenic and historic byway; but fear not, you've been traveling it since the town of Grand Lake. You are no longer surrounded by beetle-eaten pine; instead, to your left, you get a complete view of the lake. The bleached-white canvasses of mainsails can be seen, catching handfuls of wind to propel them along the lake in a slow, unhurried fashion. The banks of the lake are covered in picnic-ready grass that melts into the water. There is a sign at Mile Marker 9 identifying this body of water as Lake Granby and it marks a pullout ideal for photos of the scene, somewhat akin to the painting by Pieter Brueghel, *The Fall of Icarus;* look for it just before CR 42. The scene is set with the lake in the foreground, expansive and indigo blue, with boats and whitecaps gently riding the surface; behind that are evergreen-covered mountaintops, home to a great many creatures. And behind the rolling evergreen mountaintops are snow-covered peaks, which shrink the otherwise grand scene laid out before you. The entrance to **Stillwater National Recreation Area and Campground** is on your left, just before CR 41, which is equipped with a boat ramp, should you have the hardware to get out on the water. If you didn't bring a boat, travel a bit farther down the road to Mile Marker 8 to **Highland Marina Boat Rentals/RV Camp.** You don't even need a trailer; they'll set you up right on the dock.

Just before Mile Marker 8, the trees again engulf the road, with intermittent gaps that haphazardly provide windows into the scenery beyond.

Mile Marker 6 (US 34): On the left, just before Mile Marker 6, is a parking area with three informational signs. One of the signs provides information on some of the original workers who were transported en masse from the timberland of Michigan to tap the vast reserves of Rocky Mountain forest. Their outfit was considerable in size, and over the course of a short time, through necessity, they constructed a company town, complete with its own railroad. The area was quickly furrowed with canals and lakes, dug by imported Bulgarian and Japanese laborers. The waterways were used to transport timber to lower elevations, where the

Lake Granby

sawmill was located. When the main factory in the company town burned to the ground in 1908, the town went belly-up, and after a failed attempt to rebuild and regain prosperity, the railroad was cannibalized and used in other operations. US 34, on which the byway travels, was built atop the old railway tracks, and much of it still follows the railroad grade. What was left of the town now lies under Lake Granby. The same sign also provides information on Charles Lindbergh's connection to the area. In 1912 what was left of the currently submerged town was brought back from the brink of abandonment through its shrewd conversion into a resort town—an identity nearby Monarch still holds today. Then, however, it was called Ka Rose Resort, catering to the elite, among them Charles Lindbergh. Lindbergh would land his plane at the ranch of Harry Knight, of Mumm Champagne family, who also helped finance Lindbergh's historic flight to Paris. Ka Rose Resort eventually disappeared into the annals of history in 1946, when the government bought up the land to make way for the construction of the Granby Reservoir.

The second sign provides information on "The Nation's Backbone," or the Continental Divide. One of the more interesting facets of the divide is water flow. When it rains, water that falls on the eastern side flows toward the Atlantic, while water a few feet to the west makes its way toward the Pacific. The kiosk provides an image of the scene before you, identifying each of the peaks comprising the section of the divide in the background. Looking across the lake, the snow-veined granite peaks seen clearly on the horizon are, from left to right, Piute Peak (13,088 feet), Mount Tole (12,979 feet), Pawnee (12,943 feet), Shoshone (12,967 feet), Apache (13,441 feet), Navajo (13,409 feet), and Arickoree Peak (13,150 feet), among others.

The final sign provides information on water rights and issues of the arid eastern plains. In 1890 a study was drawn up to rate the feasibility of transporting water on the Western Slope across the Continental Divide to the east, in order to provide water to the heavily agricultural eastern plains of Colorado—this process was called trans-mountain diversion. At the time, the study found it to be both technologically and financially impossible. But the great drought in the 1930s, coined the Great Dustbowl and dramatized in Steinbeck's *Grapes of Wrath,* once again forced engineers to revisit the idea of transporting water across the divide. Technology and necessity had changed considerably over the 40 years separating the two studies, and this time they found the process plausible, though still difficult. The Colorado Big Thompson Project was undertaken between 1938 and 1957, at a cost of $160 million, and ensured a safety net for eastern-plains farmers, should a drought of that magnitude again threaten their livelihood. As of now, however, the plains are not making use of this system. There is another popular boat ramp at this parking area as well; while one of the smaller you'll encounter, it's also one of the most heavily used.

Roughly 0.25 mile past Mile Marker 6 is access to **Arapaho Bay,** a small sandy beach with a boat put-in, parking lot, tent camping, and hiking trails. To enter the area, head down CR 6. It's more of an isthmus than a full-blown beach, but it still makes for an interesting stop since you can dig your toes into sand nearly 1,500 miles away from the nearest coast. On the right-hand side of the road is Willow Creek access, again with a boat put-in, picnicking, and camping. You won't be

Rainbow Lake (behind Arapaho Bay at Lake Granby)

putting-in at Lake Granby; instead, the access takes you to Wilson Creek Reservoir, roughly 2.5 miles down the road, where the entrance is found.

You leave Arapaho National Recreation Area at Mile Marker 5. Once you leave the recreation area you enter ranching land as it transforms from forest to rolling green hills, mostly devoid of pine trees, and at any moment you expect Julie Andrews to burst forth, singing to nature. Next you enter the town of Granby. When the road forks, be sure to take US 40 west toward Steamboat Springs and Hot Sulphur Springs.

To the left are some of the unused railroad tracks running parallel to the road described in one of the earlier kiosk stops. Granby comes and goes quickly, as you only skirt the edge of it. You also cross the Colorado River here, and though it isn't very wide, it is flat and slow; you'd never expect it to have such powerful sections hundreds of miles downriver. Just after Mile Marker 210 on US 40 is the Windy Gap Reservoir, used to generate electricity for nearby communities. This constructed reservoir attracts wildlife in fairly good numbers. Make it a point to stop at the **Windy Gap Wildlife Viewing Area** on your left, which is at the turnoff for the town of Walden (CO 125) on your right. The reservoir is a small body of water held at bay by a rock-and-cement dam, which corrals the Colorado for a brief tenure, releases it to turn the station's turbines, and then allows it to continue its centuries-old course west.

White pelican at Windy Gap Reservoir

The landscape immediately changes after the Windy Gap Reservoir. The land has traded in the rolling hills of evergreen for dense groves of cottonwood that line the banks of the Colorado River. To your right is crumbling, exposed rock, akin to a child's drip castles made in soggy beach sand. On the left is a pullout beneath the first exposed rock face. It makes for an ideal spot to cast a fly. The river is still slowly rolling, but has turned color from blue-green to a distinctive brownish red, from where the river gets its name "colored red." Just before Mile Marker 208 are slight shoulders and pullouts, making it easy to find an eddy and have a go at the river's large trout population. If you wait until you pass this mile marker, however, you will run into quite a bit of private land, and owners are known to be loathe to let trespassing anglers throw in a line. If you absolutely have to fish on private land, be sure to garner the owner's permission first; it will save you a lot of hassle and let you concentrate on the river, instead of being on the lookout.

Mile Marker 204 (US 40) — Hot Sulphur Springs: At Mile Marker 204 hints of another scenery change can be discerned. Sagebrush begins to make an appearance, a telltale sign of an increasingly arid climate.

Enter the hilly town of Hot Sulphur Springs. It's a small, bucolic community with a few well-placed restaurants, hotels, and motels. The town is true to its name, sporting a hot springs resort and spa. Consider the **Riverside Hotel and Restaurant, Canyon Motel,** and **Stagecoach B&B** for food and lodging. The **Ute Trail Motel** is on the left as you enter town, with a circa 1950s neon sign to welcome you. There is also a historical museum, **Grand County Pioneer Village Museum,** on the left at Mile Marker 202, which also serves as home to the **Grand County Historical Association.**

After passing these businesses, you enter the small, quiet town of Hot Sulphur Springs in earnest. **Sportsmans' Café** on the left is a small white building, across from the **County Seat Grill.** And the **Hot Sulphur Springs Resort and Spa** is accessed by taking a right near the grill. It's a newer-looking structure, and is located across the river. As the springs are the town's main lifeline to prosperity — the town advertises the bejeezus out of them — you can't make a turn without finding directions leading you to its mineral-rich waters. When leaving town, you enter a small gorge, and you can see the environment's split personality. On one side of the road is a scrub-brush-covered hill, and on the other are thickets of evergreens. There are also

The namesake of Hot Sulphur Springs

patches of exposed rock, and while not impressive in their own right, they do serve to break up the scenery, both literally and figuratively.

The Colorado River picks up speed just after leaving town, with whitecaps beginning to paint its surface making it easier to see its actual flow. It's still no more than 15 to 20 feet wide, but you begin to believe in its potential to gain enough momentum to be known as the carver of the Grand Canyon. CR 50 is on your left, and is the forest access road to Beaver Creek stream. There is also a scenic pullout on your right, providing a closer look at the Colorado; look for it near the Colorado Division of Wildlife (DOW) Office just after the road crosses the river itself. Shortly after passing the DOW is a target range for pistol, shotgun, and rifle practice run by the wildlife office. It's an open range, whose backdrop is a sagebrush-covered hill. It's common to see soft plumes of white smoke wafting gently through the air, accompanied by the soft pop of rimfire or the louder bang of larger caliber firearms. Williams Fork National Forest access is on your left, down CR 3—the same turnoff to **Bar Lazy J Ranch** in the nearby town of Parshall.

At Mile Marker 197, the landscape changes dramatically, turning exclusively to dry and hilly terrain. This mile marker also indicates the entrance to the town of Parshall, which, admittedly, isn't much of a stopping point, and is less than 0.2 mile long along the highway. As you hit town, to the left is the business district, with a few whitewashed buildings. The Colorado River again makes an appearance and has once again changed. Once relatively narrow and fast paced, it has since calmed but has doubled in size, now measuring some 30 feet across. On the left-hand side is a viewing area, with a kiosk providing more information on this iconic river. The viewing area is a dirt pullout, about 0.5 mile past the town of Parshall. There is also fishing access here, so you can learn about the river, and then pull a fat brown trout out of its depths. The area is rich farmland, thanks mostly to the Colorado River itself, and a number of cattle and painted horses can be seen standing in the midday sun, motionless except for the occasional twitch of a tail.

At Mile Marker 194, you are provided with a sweeping view of the area. Previously, you were mostly hedged in by hills; now, like an art gallery wall, the view has been laid clearly in front of you, shimmering under the clear sky. You see more rolling hills, though this time you see them stand like a vast set of waves in the ocean, disappearing into the haze of the horizon. Cottonwoods, juniper, and

Colorado River near Hot Sulphur Springs

sagebrush are the only visible plants rooted in the tan soil. The land is taupe colored and arid, save for where the Colorado River has been rerouted to irrigate ranchland. If you look as far as your line of sight allows and off to the left, a granite peak breaks the hilly landscape: Sharp, jagged, and naked of flora, the mountain has signs of avalanche chutes and holds a permanent cover of snow. This land alludes to the fact that Colorado is built in an ever-changing format. For a few miles, you may see more shades of green than one thought possible, then, like a wing beat, it changes to an ochre-colored, dry landscape before quickly reversing itself. At Mile Marker 190, just before CR 39, you get an exceptional view of the distant peaks, which make a stunning juxtaposition—from this relatively dry area where even the waters of the Colorado dare not breach the banks to the cold, barren high-altitude climates of the Rockies.

Mile Marker 186 (US 40)—Kremmling: At Mile Marker 186, you enter the town of Kremmling, the self-proclaimed Sportsman's Paradise. **Red Mountain RV Park** is accessed via CR 22 on the right as you enter this small mountain community. Grand County/Kremmling Airport is on your left just before the official city limit; it's a very small airport, made more for crop dusters than passenger planes. It's also a very small town whose defining feature is a large sandstone butte that seems to be slowly disintegrating. However, this is your first chance to raft Colorado River waters. Look for the **Mad Adventures** office on the left; you'll find it by the silver school buses parked out front, which are used to ferry rafters from put-in to take-out. On the right, just after the rafting company, is the **Veterans' Memorial Park.** You can't miss it: There's a real Apache helicopter placed on a pedestal at the park's entrance. This town is also home to the Middle Park Fair and Rodeo, held in mid-September; look for the yellow sign on the left showing the rodeo grounds. The byway once again diverges, and you'll need to take a left down CO 9 to stay on the route—it's just before the **Cliffside Inn. Los Amigos,** allegedly home to the best Mexican food in Grand County, is also found at this intersection.

At Mile Marker 138, you are now driving toward the indigo-colored granite crags you saw earlier, and you get exquisite views of them as they frame arid, stunted hilltops. Mile Marker 137 is the end of Kremmling, and you again lose sight of the sky-touching peaks. It's the start of a popular cycling route, so take caution when checking out the scenery. While you lose the mountains for a mile or two, they will make their appearance at random intervals as the road turns and weaves its way in a haphazard western direction. Just after Mile Marker 137 you take a right on CR 1 to Radium, State Bridge, and **Pumphouse** recreational area. It's a hard-packed dirt road, not heavily trafficked. While the road is easy to drive in ideal conditions, should the weather turn wet or snowy be sure to drive with caution, as dirt roads, no matter how hard packed, can quickly become slick and muddy. At Mile Marker 2, you begin to gain altitude, giving you the sensation that you'll soon match the height of the granite peaks which are once again off in the distance to the southwest. Look to your left around Mile Marker 3 and you'll be able to look down onto the hill-studded valley in which CO 9 passes, where you were previously driving. The scene stretches out as far as you care to look, until it ends in more rock mountains—it's as if the higher you travel in altitude, the more you realize that, wherever you go, you're circled on the horizon by rocky peaks. **Kodi Rafting** is found out here, offering full- and half-day trips. There is a real dearth of mile markers along this section, but it's roughly around where Mile Marker 4 would be, if it were marked. Look for a log-cabin structure to your right; that's their main office. After Cody Rafting, pine trees begin to make a comeback to the left of the road, and a few aspens ring the lower edges of pine-covered hills, although to your right are exclusively sage and juniper. At Mile Marker 7 the valley walls hedge the road in and radiate up and out, creating a hollow wedge, where the road is the apex. The walls are just high enough to obscure your view. Just after Mile Marker 7, you'll encounter haunting rock formations that rock climbers would find intriguing. They appear as giant boulders, seemingly glued together to form a well-constructed wall. Around Mile Marker 8, you descend from the modest heights you have been traveling; the road is once again paved, and quaking aspens, shimmering in the breeze, surround both sides of the road.

Mile Marker 9 (CR 1)—Gore Canyon: At around Mile Marker 9, the valley in which you're driving drops off dramatically to your right and you'll silently thank the engineers who designed this road that they added a guardrail. It's unusual for a giant hole in the ground to sneak up on you; however, the gaping void of Gore Canyon does just that. There is a dirt pullout on the right, roughly 1 mile after the paved area begins, with an informational sign detailing the gorge's origin and impact on human history. While at the sign, look to the right for a view into the gorge. The cliffs are rugged and steep, filled with scree runs (fields of boulders left over after a rockslide), and a few tenacious pines grow precariously where they

Gore Canyon

can, defying gravity. If you've already driven, or plan on driving, the West Elk Loop, where the Black Canyon of the Gunnison is located, this gorge gives the appearance of its brother, and is still growing to match the Black Canyon's depth and severity.

Kiosks here again provide information about the Colorado River. It begins in Grand Lake, where your journey also began, and which also happens to be Colorado's largest natural lake—Blue Mesa Reservoir in the southwest region is the largest body of water in the state. It explains that the Hot Sulphur Springs were first used by the Ute for their curative properties. After Berthoud Pass was constructed, Hot Sulphur Springs was heavily marketed as a resort town, a distinction to which it still clings. The kiosk also speaks about the **Moffat Tunnel** near Winter Park. The completion of this railroad tunnel in 1928, through the Continental Divide, marks the point at which Colorado was placed on a direct coast-to-coast railroad route with Denver as a main depot. This directly aided in an economic boom, as well as a population swell. Denver's new place on the rail map can be greatly attributed to David Moffat, a poor New Yorker born in the 1860s. As an adolescent, he moved to Denver when it was still no more than a mining camp. Eventually, he made a tidy fortune in a trifecta of profitable banks, mines, and railroads. In 1903 he sought to build a trans-American railroad through Denver. The road on which you stand was originally part of his construction effort through this dangerous gorge. He never lived to see his dream to fruition, and his efforts greatly depleted his fortune. The path was finally completed in 1934, after the Denver and Rio Grande Narrow Gauge Railroad took over the project, and connected their tracks to Craig, the point at which the rails stopped shortly after Moffat's death, thus bridging the coasts through Denver and the Continental Divide.

The final kiosk details the Gore Canyon itself. The canyon is a 6-mile gauntlet of sheer walls and narrow sides, with the Colorado River running below. Moffat's men, who surveyed this canyon for laying tracks, must have had steel running through their veins: They dangled from ropes secured to the tops of cliffs by nothing more than a steel spike, and built walking paths of wood and steel pegs driven hard into the sheer granite walls. Miraculously, no man among them fell to his death. Because of their dexterity at precarious heights, they came to be known as "squirrels."

Another sign speaks to Sir St. George Gore's exploration, for which the gorge is named, though he himself never laid eyes on it. Gore arrived on a hunting expedition in 1854, guided by a local mountain man; Gore's group of 28 men reached the Colorado River in the fall, then named the Grand River. Though his namesake is the gorge, as well as a range of mountains in Colorado, he is perhaps best remembered as being a heartless and bloody hunter. In the three years he spent in this region, he and his party were said to have slaughtered two thousand buffalo, six hundred elk and deer, and around one hundred bears. His sheer disregard for the life of the land enraged both American Indians and whites.

The final sign, HEADWATERS GEOLOGY, provides a geological timeline of the area, dating back to 2 billion years. Among other facts, it explains that the Rockies that you see today are actually a second coming—the first mountains were washed away by the elements eons ago. In fact, the present-day Rocky Mountains lifted up from the earth's crust only 50 to 70 million years ago, a mere hiccup to a geologist. And 30 million years ago, more peaks were added to the range by numerous active volcanoes. At Mile Marker 9, the pavement again disappears, and you are once more driving along a dirt road.

The Bureau of Land Management–run **Pumphouse** recreation area can be found on the right along CR 106, just before Mile Marker 11. It's a day-use area, and a fee is required. As with the road you are currently on, CR 106 also cuts through sagebrush and juniper, signs of an overtly arid climate. After Mile Marker 13, the views once again open up and you see the route of Gore Canyon below you as it takes on the appearance of a lighting bolt cutting across the cracked land. At the intersection of CR 1 and CR 11 you can take a right to Radium or continue on to State Bridge.

Following CR 11 to Radium along the left is the Colorado River. There is a turnoff on the left to **Radium State Wildlife Area,** where anglers with the proper papers (wildlife stamp and fishing license) can drop in a line. You can purchase a stamp and fishing license in either Radium or State Bridge, if you don't already have one. **Mugrage Campground** is also located here, should you want to spend the rest of the day in the area and camp, then finish the few remaining miles of the byway in the morning. The campground is a small, sandy area on the river, under a grove of shade-providing cottonwoods, complete with fire pits and handicapped accessibility. After the wildlife area, the road narrows considerably, turning into a bending, one-and-a-half-car-width road. It's a good idea to sound your horn when rounding a blind corner, and as always, drive no faster than you feel comfortable. There are a number of rafters and kayakers floating down these sec-

Fly-fishing the Colorado

tions of water, and the largest concentration of rafters can actually be found here; during the high season, easily a half-dozen boaters can be seen within a few hundred yards of each other. Since the rapids around here are relatively mild, it's common to see a number of families in the boats, including children and older folks. The take-out/put-in is the Radium Boat Ramp in the **Radium Recreation Area,** a day-use park with a required fee, found to your left just before you cross the river into town. Pit toilets and a few picnic tables round out this one-purpose park. The town itself is quite small, with railroad tracks that run through it. There isn't much here, with the main element being its location near an ideal place to put in your own raft or kayak.

Continuing once again on CR 1, toward State Bridge, you cross the Eagle County line, and the road turns into CR 11. This can be a bit confusing, as the road you can take toward Radium is also numbered 11, though of a different county.

Before reaching State Bridge, you come across **Rancho del Rio** in the tiny hamlet of Bond; this waystation provides everything a traveler will need. It's a grocery and liquor store, and has showers, camping, and laundry facilities. It's in the location of the Colorado River Center, and has an excellent boat put-it or take-out. Even if you don't raft, snap a few shots of soaking-wet paddlers as they labor to get their boats into or out of the water. This is an extremely busy area, so don't expect a calm mountain scene; in fact, it can be a little hectic, and beware of drivers not concentrating on the road.

The river is so calm in these areas that the current barely moves the boats. It's common to see boaters dipping in their paddles and sweating a bit to get moving downstream, especially if there's a headwind. If you'd like to put in your boat in this area, but are loathe to jockey for position, there is a smaller and much less commercial site about 0.5 mile down the road. These sections of river are extremely popular with the less-than-hard-core rafter. You'll most likely see a number of people taking float trips through here, lounging in giant inflatables or inner tubes, drinking beer, and chatting among themselves as they let the current push them lazily along the wide surface of the Colorado River. The floaters eventually end up at the small town of State Bridge, which used to be anchored by a music venue/restaurant-bar, but since it burned down in the spring of 2007, there isn't much reason to stay, except to collect your raft after a trip down the river and head elsewhere. It's also here that the byway ends, at the intersection of CR 11 and CO 131. The last notable feature of the byway can be seen as you leave town—a tent city of raft guides. It's not a professional place, where you'd expect to find a lobby or even flush toilets; it's more of a bazaar for raft guides, and a good place to hire a local to take you down the river. A phenomenal spot to photograph rafters can be found along the bridge that leads out of town.

IN THE AREA

GRAND LAKE

Accommodations
Black Bear Lodge, 12255 US 34. Call 970-627-3654.

Cutthroat Bay Campground, 8 miles north of Granby on US 34, then 0.25 mile east on CR 46. Call 970-887-4100.

Green Ridge, 12 miles north of Granby on US 34, then 1 mile east on CR 66. Call 970-887-4100.

Isolation Peak Lodge, 12365 US 34. Call 970-627-8261

Lake View B&B, 164 Lake View Dr. Call 970-627-1200.

Sombrero Ranches, 304 W. Portal Road. Call 970-627-3514.

T Lazy W RV Park, 10553 US 34. Call 970-627-3753.

Attractions and Recreation

Highland Marina Boat Rentals/RV Camp, 7878 US 34. Call 970-887-3541.

Kauffman House Museum, 407 Pitkin St. Call 970-627-9644.

Trail Ridge Marina and Rentals, 12634 US 34. Call 970-627-3586.

Dining/Drinks

Betty's ol' Café and Bakery, 10658 US 34. Call 970-627-1934.

HOT SULPHUR SPRINGS

Accommodations

Canyon Motel, 221 Byers Ave. Call 970-725-3395 or 1-888-489-3719.

Hot Sulphur Springs Resort and Spa, 5609 CR 20. Call 970-725-3306.

Riverside Hotel and Restaurant, 509 Grand Ave. Call 970-725-3589.

Stagecoach B&B, 412 Nevava St. Call 970-725-3324.

Ute Trail Motel, 120 Byers Ave. Call 970-725-0123.

Attractions and Recreation

Grand County Pioneer Village Museum/Grand County Historical Association, 110 E. Byers Ave. Call 970-725-3939.

Dining/Drinks

County Seat Grill, 517 Byers Ave. Call 970-725-3309.

Riverside Hotel & Restaurant, 509 Grand Ave. Call 970-725-3589.

Sportsmans' Café, 512 Byers Ave. Call 970-725-3654.

PARSHALL

Accommodations

Bar Lazy J Ranch, 447 CR 3. Call 970-725-3437.

KREMMLING

Accommodations

Cliffside Inn, 113 N. Sixth St. Call 970-724-8949.

Red Mountain RV Park, 2201 Central Ave. Call 970-724-9593.

Attractions and Recreation

Kodi Rafting, 4995 CR 1. Call 970-668-1548.

Mad Adventures, 1421 E. Park Ave. Call 970-726-5290.

Dining/Drinks

Los Amigos, 109 S. Sixth St. Call 970-724-9243.

BOND

Accommodations

Rancho del Rio, 4199 CR 1. Call 970-653-4431.

Rio Blanco Ranch

5 Flat Tops Wilderness Trail Scenic and Historic Byway

Estimated length: 82 miles

Estimated time: 2 hours

Highlights: Fish for trout at the pristine, mountain-flanked Trappers Lake; hike or ride your ATV on hundreds of miles of unpopulated trails; go on a day-long horseback ride deep into the Flat Tops Wilderness; relax, stop frequently, and reset your inner urban clock to country time.

Getting there: From Denver, take I-70 west to CO 131 north to the town of Yampa. From Grand Junction, take I-70 east to CO 131 north to the town of Yampa.

Set atop one of the highest flat-top mountains in North America, the Flat Tops Wilderness Trail Scenic and Historic Byway is a path that takes travelers through rugged scenery and dirt roads, while introducing them to the origins of the National Forest System. Today, the National Forest System spans a total of 193 million acres, or, as the Forest Service is apt to point out, roughly the size of Texas. But, as with any grand design, its origins were much more humble.

History: This byway runs through what was once the White River Plateau Timberland Reserve, a parcel of land identified in 1891 as having natural characteristics that needed to be protected. Eventually, it would become the nation's second national forest—White River National Forest. A few decades later, Trappers Lake, roughly found at the halfway mark of this byway, fell under the 1964 Wilderness Act. The act stated that the developing hand of man in the area must be stayed, and no trees could be cut, nor mines dug. Because of these early efforts to sustain the natural integrity of the area, drives through the byway offer unspoiled

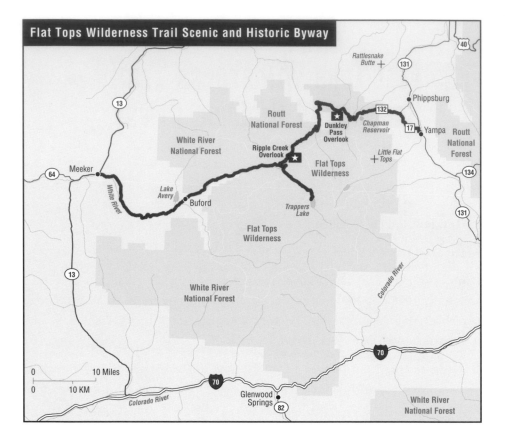

Flat Tops Wilderness Trail Scenic and Historic Byway

scenery and abundant wildlife. In fact, its identity as such has garnered presidential recognition: The White River National Forest was a favorite mountain lion hunting site for President Theodore Roosevelt in the early 1900s—an activity still available today.

At the western terminus of the byway sits the storied town of Meeker—the history of which reads like a Western dime novel. John Wesley Powell, for whom Lake Powell in Arizona is named, wintered here in 1868. You can still see the site of his party's respite at Powell Park. But even this historic figure is no more than a footnote in the town's history. In 1869, just a year after Powell and his party had added the site to their map, the area's first Indian Agency was constructed. In 1879, with a determination to set what he saw as Ute savages onto the path of the righteous, the post's first officer in charge of Indian affairs, Nathan Meeker, rode in. Meeker zealously began transforming the Ute into God-fearing Christians, but his last effort in turning their culture toward God ended in a bloody failure. Already unsettled by this foreigner's intrusion into their ways, the Utes became incensed when they found him plowing under their racetrack. This was the proverbial straw that broke the camel's back. The Ute attacked, killing Meeker and 10 other men under contract with the Indian Agency. They then razed the agency and held the area's other residents as prisoners for three weeks. This brought down the wrath of the already trigger-happy U.S. Army. In retaliation for the Utes' actions, a temporary fort was constructed near town and the Utes were exiled to eastern reservations. In 1883, with their charge completed, the army moved out, selling its fort to newly arriving settlers. Named after the slain agent, in 1885 Meeker became the first incorporated town in northwest Colorado. Today, Meeker is famous for its sheep ranching community, with an annual sheepdog championship held each fall.

Even with a backstory like that of Meeker, this is the kind of byway you travel not so much for the overt historical value, but for the scenery that shows itself at every turn. You won't see many other people along this route, except maybe the occasional rancher, herding his cattle along the road.

Intersection of CO 131 and Rural County Road 17 (RCR 17)—Yampa: The dirt roads of Yampa are at the eastern entrance to the Flat Tops Wilderness Trail Scenic and Historic Byway. This is a blip on the map of tourist stops, but the town can supply you with gasoline, basic food, and a few accommodations. In fact, many of the businesses may be a bit too authentic in terms of what a real frontier town once looked like. Take the **Royal Hotel,** for instance. Its whitewashed clapboards have dulled and chipped over the years, and its walls sit at less than a 90-degree angle from the dirt road leading into town. On its first floor is a dark-windowed bar resembling a prop from a midcentury cowboy movie.

The **Yampa Ranger Station,** a National Forest Service office, can also be found in town. Make it a point to stop here. It's open from 8 AM to 5 PM, Monday through Friday, but even when closed, a station outside is stocked with pamphlets about the byway and surrounding history. If you're really desperate to talk to someone face to face, and the ranger station is closed, the **Montgomery General Store** and **Weston's Country Store** in town have much of the same information you'd find at the ranger station. When the ranger station is open, rangers are on-hand to provide you with additional information about everything from weather and road conditions to how trout are hitting at Trappers Lake, the focal point of the Flat Tops Wilderness Trail.

At the entrance to town, look for a small grassy park on the left, surrounded by trees. Here is where you'll find the first official kiosk telling the tale of the byway, and about the town of Yampa. Ute were the first to traffic this area as they followed game and weather patterns throughout the region's fertile mountains. Later, settlers arrived and cultivated and farmed the land, a tradition and trade still evident in the region's many cattle and horse farms. For a while in the 1800s, the land was being ravaged of its natural resources. Trees by the thousands were being felled, water tainted, and game hunted to the point of endangerment. The residents of the area soon realized that if this course of action continued, the land they loved for its natural wealth would soon be laid barren. Because of this realization, and the actions of landscape architect Arthur Carhart, the area became the catalyst for the wilderness preservation movement. Trappers Lake, found nearly halfway through this byway, is often credited as being the birthplace of the first American environmental movement. Carhart was so inspired by the unadulterated raw beauty of this lake and its surrounding forests that he recommended that the president, for whom he was working, leave the land untouched so that future generations might enjoy the serenity there.

In Yampa's heyday (the town was originally named Egaria Park after a mythological water nymph that lived in the surrounding ethereal beauty), the town bustled with four hundred residents patronizing nine saloons, two real estate offices, two banks, and two churches. Cattle, spinach, and lettuce were, and still are, the town's main exports.

This is the last town to get gas for some time, so even if your tank is mostly full, topping it off is a good idea.

Mile Marker 1 (intersection of CO 131 and RCR 17)—outside of Yampa: To access the byway, return to CO 131 and head north. Look north for a glancing view of a strangely shaped butte, bulbous and bubbling from an otherwise flat land. As soon as you reenter the highway, you'll need to turn off it again. Take a left just past the blue byway sign marking the route on RCR 17. This can be tricky as there are three roads here—take the last of the three. Another byway sign on your left will confirm your turn.

The land along this route remains pastoral. Grazing cattle and horses swish their tails against both real and imagined flies in waist-high grass. Hogbacks and buttes dominate the undulating grazing land of this mountain basin. This is the stuff of John Wayne movies, where a gang is on the lam, running from the six-

Road to Yampa

guns of the Duke, and hiding out along the rocky sanctuary of dusty buttes. A few abandoned homesteader cabins, whose dilapidation puts them just beyond conservation, are slowly falling apart behind property fences. In the summer, adding a tone of softness to the rugged cowboy country are the budding yellow flowers of sagebrush, seemingly the only plant besides grass that grows here. This brush dots the land as far as the horizon can stretch.

Mile Marker 2 (turnoff for CR 132) — Rattlesnake Butte: At Mile Marker 2, the façade of **Rattlesnake Butte** demands a driver's attention as its towering plateau snakes across the land, high above the sagebrush and muted hills. The scene follows you for a bit, until you take a left onto CR 132 at Mile Marker 4.4. This turn will take you to Dunkley Pass, 14 miles away, and Vaughn Lake, 29 miles in the same direction. Kiss the asphalt goodbye as the road turns to dirt beneath your tires for the next few miles. Keep your eyes peeled for golden eagles, a common raptor in the area and the world's largest eagle. You'll know them from their bronze-colored plumage and high circling. These avian titans occasionally perch upon fence posts and telephone poles.

The landscape transforms after about 1 mile of bouncing along the decently graded dirt road. A shallow, narrowing valley replaces the high basin in which Yampa is located, and while sagebrush is loathe to disappear from view, aspens and evergreens are also seen.

Mile markers will be nearly absent from the road from this point forward, so start your odometer once the asphalt turns to dirt to follow along.

Mile 3 (CR 132) — Routt National Forest and National Forest Road 16 (FR 16): At roughly 3.5 miles along the dirt road, you enter Routt National Forest. A National Forest Service sign on the right will mark the official boundary. Once you cross the threshold into the forest, the road number changes to FR 16. As with the road change, you've crossed county lines, from Routt to Rio Blanco. The road then deteriorates quickly, though it still accommodates non-four-wheel-drive cars.

A plethora of aspens and evergreens covers every inch of real estate at 4.5 miles in. The hills in the area are rounded, yet so extreme that the road appears to be caught in the channel of a tumultuous ocean swell. **Chapman Reservoir** and **Little Flattops** are located on the left just after Mile 6.5 down FR 940. Chapman Reservoir is a short 1-mile detour off the byway. It provides camping and fishing opportunities. You may notice lonely roads traveling past the reservoir; these were built in the 1940s to salvage the timber ravaged by the spruce beetle. The log salvage trade still goes on today, with trees used in the construction of log homes.

Mile 13 (FR 16) — Dunkley Pass Overlook: At Mile 13 along the road, you reach the altitude of 9,763 feet at the **Dunkley Pass Overlook.** Take a left down the one-lane gravel road toward the overlook itself. After just a few yards, you'll end up in a small parking lot. Try the short hike to a scenic overlook that provides vistas across the **Bunker Basin Valley.** And in the distance, fighting the constant midday haze, is Pyramid Peak, at 11,532 feet.

Just past this turnoff are two informational kiosks overlooking the bubbling valley below, which are surrounded by a number of wildflowers dotting the landscape with yellow, purple, and white in summer. The informational signs give details on the Utes' connection to the land. They believed the birthplace of all life

was in these mountains. An easily ex-
trapolated belief, considering they
hunted and gathered much of their
food from these very hillsides. One of
the signs also identifies old Ute trails
used by the tribe during winter and
summer migrations, as recorded by
the Ferdinand/Hayden Expedition of
1874–78.

If you were unable to pull over at
Dunkley Pass and look down into the
view, the vista will still be strikingly
prevalent from the road. Views into the
hilly valley, ringed in mountains, are
omnipresent out your left window.
From time to time, groves of aspen will
obscure your view, but when they part,
you'll be rendered breathless as you
look into a valley filled with natural
beauty.

Scarlet gilia on the roadside

Mile 17 (FR 16): Mile 17 is the site of a
small trailhead, with parking available on either side of the road. Here, you'll see
one of the first of many signs welcoming hikers to the backcountry. The sign advises you to take certain precautions before venturing into the White River and
Routt National Forests, including what to bring and what restrictions to follow. It
gives you a basic history lesson of the area as well, again retelling the story of
the Ute and their five-thousand-year-old connection to the area. After they were
forced onto reservations, shortly following the Meeker Massacre, logging and
ranching cropped up where Utes once roamed, activities still visible and prac-
ticed in today's forest. Across from this trailhead, on the left, is yet another opportunity to take a gander into the tree-covered basin.

At Mile 20 you come to an intersection where you can take a right to **Pyramid Llama Ranch** or continue straight, toward Ripple Creek and the byway's
route. If you do decide to check out this left-of-center ranch, you'll have the opportunity to make use of their tent camping facilities.

This intersection also marks the point in the byway that, during the winter, is forsaken by plows. If it's snowing, venture at your own risk—though at times, the height of the snow makes even that proposition impractical.

Soon after this point you'll find yourself in the flat area of the basin you had been enjoying from above. Taking advantage of the lush surroundings and manageable terrain, ranchers graze cattle, horses, sheep, and llama here, adding to an already cookie-cutter scene of pastoral life.

Baldy Trail is located at Mile 22 and is open to both hikers and horseback riders, but closed to motorized vehicles. You can find this relatively popular byway trailhead just before the Pyramid Llama Ranch.

Immediately after the llama ranch, as if on cue, the road begins an enthusiastic incline. The evergreens have disappeared, and row upon row of perfectly spaced aspens appear, so thick that no other flora can be seen growing among them. Because of the saturation of aspens, this is the road to drive if you want to see their changing colors in fall. Mid- to late September is often the best time.

Vaughn Lake

A pullout with a pit toilet and trailhead for **East Fork Trail** is found at Mile 23. This stop is popular with horseback riders, and it's common to see a group of them gearing up for their trip into the backcountry.

Mile 27 (FR 16): At Mile 27, and after a number of hairpin turns and a gravel road with a dramatic incline, you come across another scenic vista on your left—an ideal mountain meadow scene, complete with the placid, mirrorlike **Vaughn Lake**. The meadow that surrounds the lake disappears into a hilly, pine-covered horizon. As the land rolls toward you, notice dried-up footprints of waterways, now slashes in the grass-covered land. A picnic area suitable for a respite is on the left, and there is a picnic area just after the turnoff. Shortly after this rest area is the turnoff to Vaughn Lake, with a few pullout camping spots and trails that lead to the water's edge. For those with a fishing license, consider casting a line, either lure or fly, and try your luck at the brown, cutthroat, and rainbow trout that populate this small body of water.

Routt National Forest, which you've been driving through, and **White River National Forest,** which you now enter, share a border at Mile 30. At this meeting of forests stands another informational sign, detailing the forest system of the area. It explains that, in the 1800s, when the Western land grab was at its height, the frontier was quickly transformed from wilderness to ranches, farms, sawmills, railroads, and cities. Because of the sudden influx of people, the once prolific forests were nearly stripped bare. Forest fires also scoured the wooded areas, killing off animals that human hands may have taken anyway without aid of flame. The forested areas of the West were in danger of disappearing even before most of the land became part of the United States. Luckily, residents became wise to the impact of their wiles, and a forward-thinking few rallied to protect and reestablish much of the greenery. Later, the U.S. Forest Service was established to protect public land and ensure the regulated use of this natural resource. The sign also welcomes you to White River National Forest, the second-ever national forest in the nation, which was created by President Benjamin Harrison. Behind the sign, a number of evergreens and aspens herald yet another view into a high-mountain basin.

At 0.5 mile down the road (now FR 8), you'll find two additional pullouts to the right and left. On the right is an entrance to a snowmobiling area that is used heavily after a good winter storm. In the summer months ATVs, horseback riders, and dirt bikers are often heard playing on the trails. The parking area is large, but graded with the hard and sharp edges of tire-popping rocks. The pullout to the left is another trailhead, which bars the use of motorized vehicles, allowing hikers to experience nature without the whine of a two-stroke engine. The faded red fencing of an abandoned sheep chute, once used to corral a flock, marks the trailhead.

Mile 31.5 (FR 8): At Mile 31.5, you'll find the **Ripple Creek Overlook.** Take a left down a one-lane gravel road through meadows filled with dense wildflowers in summer. The areas where wildflower petals don't dominate belong to sturdy evergreens. A short drive later, you'll come across the scenic overlook, outfitted with pit toilets and hand sanitizer. Be careful as you drive in: Daring ground squirrels make mad dashes in front of your tires, with cheeks filled to the limit with food. Park your car here and stretch your legs. This is the finest vista you'll encounter on the route. It again overlooks a valley basin, edged in mountains and saturated with rolling grassland, dotted with trees, and carpeted with even more flowers. A short nature trail loops around the area, through tiny groves of pine and thigh-high grasses and flowers. A number of signs informing readers about various plants and animals have been erected along this short walk. As you walk the trail, look for elk hoofprints, a common sight in the soft gravel/dirt mixture.

After leaving the overlook, you'll hit a turn that opens up an unencumbered view of the valley filled with the dark spikes of evergreens. The scene is so full of evergreens that the tops of the trees indicate where the mountains and hills are; it's impossible to see one speck of dirt. This area is also open grazing land, so be aware of wandering cattle.

Mile 35 (FR 8): At Mile 35, there·is another pullout on the right, housing a kiosk that explains the role of fire in the area. In 1898 an untamable fire swept across the landscape, burning nearly 80,000 acres of verdant forest. Today, a new forest has grown in its place. If you look to the hill in front of you, a pattern of light and dark green emerges. This is the fire line that separates the trees in the new forest from the older ones that survived the blaze.

On your left, at Mile 36, is the **Ripple Creek Lodge.** It's a small cabin community where you can rent lodging with a few modern amenities while still staying in the middle of the wilderness.

Just after the cabins is FR 205; take a left here to access the star of the byway,

Trappers Lake

Trappers Lake. A relatively quick 10-mile drive down this dead-ended forest road will lead you to the lake.

At Mile 37.5, look to your right, down the valley, and you'll see a strong-flowing river cutting its course with exploding whitecaps. On the right, at Mile 40, another kiosk appears, this time with information about **Rio Blanco Ranch**, originally named Himes Ranch, one of the first hunting lodges in the region. The lodge welcomed such dignitaries as President Theodore Roosevelt, who commonly visited this slice of forest. Across the river is a lake with half a dozen red log cabins sitting on its banks. This is the historic homestead. On the far hillside, you'll notice acre upon acre of burned trees from the Hayman Fire. This act of arson quickly spread beyond the control of professional firefighters, and caused Bill Owens, the governor at the time, to declare on national television that the entire state of Colorado was burning. While far from the truth, the Hayman Fire

Trappers Lake and its surroundings

turned out to be one of the worst fires in Colorado's recorded history. A few more miles down the road, you'll find the burnt-out toothpicks that were once proud evergreens, standing on either side of the road, and any vestige of live pines is gone. The underbrush, while stunted, is growing back well, an indication that the forest may yet renew itself.

At Mile 43.5, you'll find **Trappers Lake Lodge,** a rather large facility for being located in the middle of nowhere, near the end of the road. It sells fishing tackle and groceries, and offers a place to stay for the night, should you have the urge to extend your trip. Look for the tin-roofed, green log-cabin structure on your left. A few additional trailheads and campgrounds can be accessed near this lodge as well. There are two access points to the lake: the first is to the Trappers Lake Trailhead. The trailhead is popular with anglers and hikers. The parking area sits in a tiny bowl of hard-packed dirt, and the lake is obscured by its high walls. If you want nearly immediate gratification, take the road to the **Trappers Lake Campgrounds.**

Greenback cutthroat trout, the state fish, are prolific in these serene waters. You're allowed to keep any that you catch, as long as they're less than 10 inches long. The larger fish need to be released after hooking. This ensures the once-endangered fish will be able to reproduce. Brook trout also swim in these waters. There are limits on these as well, but not on the size, so if you hook a lunker, feel free to keep it.

Trappers Lake: When you first access the trailhead, don't be fooled by the small, algae-filled lake you see from the parking area. Hike past this pond to access the trip-defining Trappers Lake. A 10-minute walk along the trail will provide a stunning view of the lake, but if you decide to keep hiking, the trail will accommodate. It's an easy 0.5 mile hike to Trappers Lake from the parking area. When hiking the trail, you'll come across a fork. Be sure to take a left at the fork, as this is the quickest route to the lake.

This is probably one of the quietest places you'll find in Colorado. The only

Old animal pens

White River Valley

sound is the lapping of water on the shore. The lake is surrounded, for the most part, by the ash and white coloring of Hayman fire-torched trees. On the opposite shore looms a giant butte that looks like a natural rock amphitheater. The scene is serene, and as if in a library, you feel compelled to whisper. The forested area nearest you appears blissfully untouched by the fire, and still-verdant pines grow near the water's edge. A few rowboats skim the water with oars in fluid motion, like the legs of a water walker skating across the surface. A few other non-motorized boats lay on grassy or earthen banks, wherever there is room. No road leads in here, so the boats you see had to have been packed in. Backtrack down FR 205 to return to FR 8 and the rest of the byway.

Mile 54 (FR 8)—Snell Creek Corrals: Shortly after returning to the byway, you'll come across a kiosk in front of a still-functioning community corral. Watson

Ranches owns the corral, but when not in use by Watson, ranchers in the community are free to pen their animals here.

At Mile 60 you come across the **Lost Creek Ranger Station and Information Center.** Stop in during the work week to speak with rangers about the White River National Forest. This also marks the very edge of the tiny town of Buford—which is the first chance since Yampa to get gas and purchase food and drink. The most significant facet of this section is that the road becomes paved, so your jostled joints get a respite.

As you near the township of Buford, at Mile 63, the land again turns to meadow, and expansive ranchland appears, with a few more houses here and there. While Buford is by no means a booming metropolis, it is the first real piece of civilization you see since beginning the byway. The White River also gently flows in the valley basin. Cottonwoods again enter the scene, growing along the banks, with their greedy roots seeping up the river water. These are towering trees whose size is deceiving—be aware that their branches' connection to the trunk is fairly brittle, so having a picnic under one of them is not a good idea.

In this ranching community, it's common to see a tractor sitting fallow in a field, waiting to be started up to rumble through its daily chores. A number of bays and painted horses also populate much of the property here. Neatly squared off hay bales, stacked one on top of another, cover much of the farmland, ready to be stored for winter. Each of these elements lends itself to an exceedingly Old West feel.

At Mile 69, like a line in the sand, the trees change. The aspens and evergreens are replaced by grasses and sagebrush, covering the entire valley. Just after this change of scenery, you finally hit a gas station at the **Buford Store and Lodge.** This outpost sells gas and food, and has restrooms. It also provides cabins for weary drivers.

Seven Lakes Lodge is at Mile 72, and offers another locale where you can hang your hat. **Sleepy Cat Guest Ranch,** at Mile 74.5, offers hunting trips, fishing opportunities, and as with many of these backcountry affairs, hearty, rib-sticking food. Red cabins trimmed in white are scattered over the property. Scour the surrounding area for mule deer, often seen grazing on the cattle's grass, as fences don't mean much to these nimble animals. **K-T Ranch,** at Mile 86, is also a nearby option. Look for the large, octagonal, two-story building, painted yellow and topped with a reddish roof.

Meeker

Just after this ranch is a major viewing area, with a line of kiosks that give a timeline on the cultures that lived in the area and used the byway route, stretching from Ute to white settlers. You've almost completed the byway at this point, but if you'd like to stay just a bit longer, there's a covered picnic area here, set in a cedar-shingled gazebo.

Mile 89 (FR 8): At Mile 89, near the lodging of the **Green Cabins** (which are true to their name), and at the mortar-and-stone viewing area overlooking the basin, is the end of the Flat Tops Wilderness Trail. The nearest town is Meeker, a handful of miles south on the adjoining CO 789/13. While not officially on the byway, the town is a perfect place to stop, refuel both your belly and your gas tank, and maybe stay the night.

Meeker is a small town, where once a year championship sheepherders and their sheepdogs compete for top honors. And while it's now known statewide for this competition, it started its life as the site of a massacre in which Meeker, a naive and inexperienced Indian Agency officer, pushed the Utes into violent action.

CO 789/13 skirts the southern edge of town, and grabs a number of travelers since it provides easy access to small food joints and budget motels. While this is perhaps more convenient, a walk through the downtown area just two blocks to the north is a must, regardless of its small size.

Today, this sleepy small town has wide, well-laid-out streets. The most opulent hotel in town is the **Meeker Hotel and Café.** If you get squeamish around stuffed wildlife, you may want to find other accommodations as the lobby is outfitted with mounted heads, antler fixtures, and stuffed animals in action poses. Every element of the hotel, if not made of animal, is made of heavily lacquered and sturdy wood, the kind you'd expect to find in a frontier town of the 1800s, the century from which this hotel dates. Even if the décor isn't to your liking, the soft beds and friendly service will most likely seal the deal. Other lodging options are available, and since the town is so small, each is relatively centrally located to Meeker's stores.

With this town, the byway is complete. Travelers who end up in Meeker are a bit removed from any bustling burg. So if the hour is late, consider staying the night and continuing on to Denver, Grand Junction, or other points in the morning.

View of Meeker from Cemetery Hill

IN THE AREA

YAMPA

Accommodations
Royal Hotel, 201 Moffat Ave. Call 970-638-4538.

Attractions and Recreation
Yampa Ranger Station, 300 Roselawn Ave. Call 970-638-4516.

HAYDEN

Attractions and Recreation
Pyramid Llama Ranch, 1258 RCR 19. Call 970-276-3348.

MEEKER

Accommodations
Buford Store and Lodge, 20474 CR 8. Call 970-878-4745.

Green Cabins, 1240 CR 8. Call 970-878-4810.

K-T Ranch, 4160 CR 8. Call 970-878-4881.

Meeker Hotel and Café, 560 Main St. Call 970-878-5255.

Rio Blanco Ranch, 3050 Trappers Lake Rd. Call 970-878-4865.

Ripple Creek Lodge, 39020 CR 8. Call 970-878-4725.

Seven Lakes Lodge, 36843 CR 17. Call 970-878-3249.

Sleepy Cat Guest Ranch, 16064 CR 8. Call 970-878-4413.

Trappers Lake Lodge, 7700 Trappers Lake Rd. Call 970-878-3336.

WHITE RIVER NATIONAL FOREST

Accommodations

Trappers Lake Campgrounds. Call 970-945-2521. Details on all five campgrounds (Bucks, Cutthroat, Horsethief, Shepards Rim, and Trapline) found under "NW Flat Tops Area" at www.fs.usda.gov/detailfull /whiteriver/recreation/?cid=stelprdb 5361718&width=full.

Stations of the Cross Shrine, San Luis

6 Los Caminos Antiguos

Estimated length: 129 miles

Estimated time: 4 hours or more, allowing time to make plenty of stops on the way

Highlights: Hike the Great Sand Dunes and take pictures at sunset; ride to New Mexico aboard the Cumbres and Toltec Narrow Gauge Railroad; hike up the Stations of the Cross; enjoy New Mexico–inspired cuisine at one of many roadside cafés; pet an alligator at the Colorado Gator Farm in Mosca.

Getting there: From Santa Fe, New Mexico, take US 84/285 north for slightly more than 31 miles. Follow US 285 north as it diverges from US 84. Continue along US 285 for 75 miles to the New Mexico–Colorado border. Continue to Antonito, and proceed west on CO 17 over La Manga Pass and Cumbres Pass to the New Mexico border. From Denver, Colorado, take I-25 south for 161 miles to Walsenburg. Take exit 50 west onto US 160 toward La Veta. Continue along US 160 for 11 miles, then drive past the turnoff for CO 12 to La Veta, continuing toward Fort Garland. Stay on US 160 to the town of Alamosa, 26 miles. From Alamosa, travel south on US 285 to Antonito for 28 miles. Then proceed west on CO 17 over La Manga Pass and Cumbres Pass to the New Mexico border. Note: This route takes you over various parts of the Los Caminos Antiguos Scenic and Historic Byway.

At 120 miles long and 50 miles wide, the San Luis Valley is a sprawling swath of high-altitude desert roughly the size of Connecticut. The valley sits atop the Rio Grande Rift, an underground split in the crust of the earth caused by ancient volcanic activity. If uncovered by digging, the rift would be about 30,000 feet

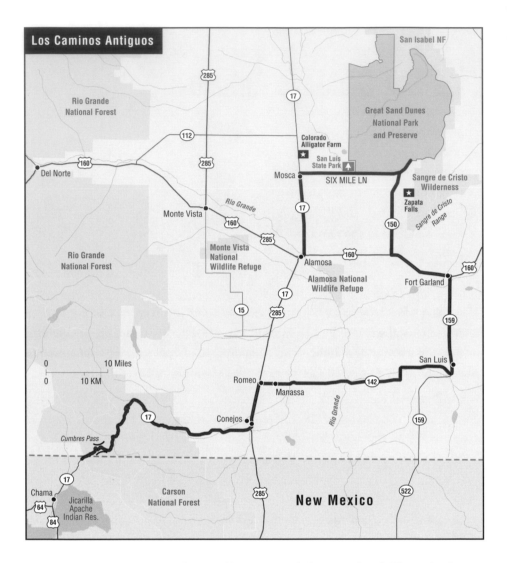

deep, making the bottom of the valley 4 miles below sea level. There is also an aquifer under the valley, making it ideal for agriculture. The Rio Grande, with its headwaters nearby, flows southeast through the valley to New Mexico.

The Sangre de Cristo ("Blood of Christ") mountain range rises up behind the valley, spanning from Salida, Colorado, to Santa Fe, New Mexico. The Sangres boast a number of incredibly high mountains, notably the 14,345-foot Blanca Peak, Colorado's fourth-highest mountain. The mountain range as a whole is a designated national wilderness area. When you glimpse the pristine creeks, small lakes, and waterfalls created by the snowmelt here, and, if you're lucky, some bighorn sheep, black bears, elk, and mountain lion, you'll see why this land should be preserved. Moreover, hundreds of thousands of sandhill cranes migrate through the valley every spring, and the Great Sand Dunes provide a unique mountain-meets-dune experience that you can only find in a handful of other places around the world.

In addition to its stunning natural landscape, the San Luis Valley boasts a fascinating confluence of cultures. Its Spanish, Mexican, and American Indian heritage show up in the flavorful chilis offered at local eateries, the adobe architecture interspersed with more modern buildings, art in the New Mexican tradition, and other facets of culture. In that sense, the San Luis Valley feels more like New Mexico than what you traditionally associate with Colorado.

There's also a bit of an eccentric bent to the area. The valley has been a known UFO-sighting hotspot for generations. In Mosca, you'll find a geothermally heated alligator farm, where you can sign up to wrestle one of the reptiles. Hot springs, sand dunes, and, a little off the byway, New Age capital Crestone offer further evidence of the unique character of the valley. Wherever you drive in the San Luis Valley, keep your eyes peeled for the strange and unusual.

History: Los Caminos Antiguos translates to "the ancient roads." This Colorado scenic and historic byway is drenched in history, from pre-Columbian to Anglo and Mexican heritage. As you drive along the byway, Spanish adobes, Mexican-style arts and crafts, old Catholic churches, and 16th-century Castilian dialects might make you feel like you're traveling not only through southern Colorado, but through history itself.

The San Luis Valley used to be the territory of the Ute, who are thought to have lived in the region as early as A.D. 1300. Apache, Pueblo, Navajo, and other tribes later joined them in the region. In 1694, Don Diego de Vargas, the first Spanish conquistador to explore the region, climbed to the apex of Cumbres Pass and identified the San Luis Valley. More conquistadors followed and eventually Spanish colonial migrants settled in the valley with the American Indians, leading to around 250 years of a rather strained coexistence.

It was during this time that the surrounding Sangre de Cristo Mountains got their name. One story claims that a priest was shot at sunset. As he lay dying, he saw the setting sun painting the mountains a deep red and shouted "Sangre de

Cristo!" before he expired. The other story claims that the range was simply named for the red reflection on the mountains at sunset.

During the early to mid-1800s, the Spanish and later Mexican governments, eager to move people into Mexico's uninhabited northern frontier, started offering land grants to settlers in order to develop the area. Mexican settlers established the town of San Luis; after the United States annexed Nuevo Mexico in 1851, San Luis earned its claim to fame as the oldest town in what would eventually become Colorado.

Not long afterward, settlers began striking silver and other ore in and around the San Juan mining district. This good fortune lured a railroad connection through La Veta Pass and into the Front Range in 1871. Around this time, Alamosa, now the valley's biggest town, was established by the Denver and Rio Grande Narrow Gauge Railroad, which dropped off settlers at the cottonwood-shaded location and eventually built the town into a major railway intersection.

Rich in ore, timber, and agriculture, the San Luis Valley was soon settled by a variety of groups, from Amish and Mormon to Japanese American. As more and more ranches and railroads popped up throughout the region, the valley grew deforested and grizzly bears permanently disappeared from Colorado's mountains. Despite that early natural fallout, however, the San Luis Valley remains the home of some stunning natural features.

Mile Marker 1 (CO 17)—Conejos Canyon: The 129-mile drive starts on CO 17, where it meets the New Mexico border. As you drive the route, you may notice an old steam-powered train snaking its way down a narrow-gauge railroad built into mountain rock. This is the **Cumbres and Toltec Narrow Gauge Railroad,** which CO 17 roughly traces through the Toltec Gorge of Los Pinos River and over the 10,022-foot summit of Cumbres Pass. The pass is the crack in the mountains through which the Spanish used to enter the San Luis Valley. Today, in winter, people find a web of snowshoe trails here.

Conejos Canyon has a history as rich as the abundant landscape surrounding it. Early homesteaders raised sheep here, then dyed and wove the wool. Weaving traditions here still mix Native American and Spanish designs. Weavers use native plants such as chamisa (for a gold color) and chokecherry (a rose-red color) to dye the wool. Various campgrounds and bed & breakfasts make the Conejos Valley an ideal retreat for fly fishermen and anyone who just wants to take it slow in a beautiful setting.

Cumbres Pass

Cumbres and Toltec Narrow Gauge Railroad

Mile Marker 39 (CO 17)—Antonito: A short while later, you'll leave the valley and find yourself in Antonito, where the scenic railroad starts. The old steam engine winds its way through 64 miles of sometimes precarious precipices, some of which you may have seen on the drive through the valley, to end up in Chama, New Mexico. The scenery from a cozy window seat unfolds into an incomparable panorama of wildlife-filled hills and breathtaking rock formations. The route, which crosses the border between Colorado and New Mexico seven times, has been deemed a National Historic Site. If you have time to spare, you absolutely must take a rail trip on this scenic railroad.

Because the train ride is roughly 60 miles long and takes several hours, riders might consider staying overnight in Antonito, which offers some lodging. Find a filling dinner at the popular **Dos Hermanas Steakhouse** on 435 Main Street, which specializes in carnivorous Mexican fare like fajitas and *carne asada*.

Mile Marker 41 (US 285)—Conejos: Keep driving north of Antonito on US 285 and you'll pass Conejos, an old, established Hispanic town where Colorado's oldest church, Our Lady of Guadalupe, is located. The church was built as a jacal, or Spanish adobe structure, then reconstructed to its current form in 1858. Its age is a careful claim, though—residents of nearby San Acacio claim that their town has the state's oldest church. Pull off and take a closer look at the Conejos church, which in summer and autumn is a refreshing respite from oppressive heat.

The byway swings right at Romeo onto CO 142. Be safety conscious when you drive this stretch of road. People like to pass, and sometimes nobody seems to be looking straight ahead. Boxing fans might enjoy the sometimes-open **Jack Dempsey Museum** in Manassa. There's a big statue of this Manassa native out front, donated by townsfolk and dedicated to the "Manassa Mauler." After Man-

Colorado's oldest church, Conejos

Jack Dempsey Museum, Manassa

assa, look for Mile Marker 4, where you can take a right turn to the historic **Los Cerritos Cemetery.** This well-kept cemetery contains tombstones from the turn of the 20th century.

Several miles out of Manassa, you'll cross a bridge over the historic Rio Grande. This now-sedate river used to create a death-defying experience for anyone who crossed it. Modern agriculture has made the river narrower, shallower, and markedly calm. Crossing it on foot these days is more of a high-water wade than a wrestling match with fate. Birdwatchers might enjoy the abundance of small water birds here.

Mile Marker 75 (CO 142)—Stations of the Cross: Just before you enter San Luis, you'll see a sign for the **Stations of the Cross Shrine.** If it's hot, grab a smoothie at the nearby **Café Rosa Mystica,** then follow the meandering dirt hiking path up to the shrine. Bronze statues accompanied by quotes depict the Passion of Christ. The church at the top boasts not only modern Southwestern architecture that begs to be photographed, but is also a cool, artful sanctuary inside. Walking farther up the western flank of this hilltop, which has almost 360-degree views of the valley, reveals a shrine to Jesus overlooking the valley, the terra-cotta busts of various martyrs, and plenty of cactus life. At the right times of day, it's a peaceful photographer's paradise.

Mile Marker 77 (CO 142)—San Luis: You'll soon arrive in San Luis, undisputedly the oldest established town in Colorado. Nestled near the base of the 14,047-foot

Stations of the Cross Shrine, San Luis

Culebra Peak, this town, with its adobe buildings and 860-acre *vega*, or communal tract of land, might make you think you've crossed into New Mexico. Early settlers, including men, women, and children, dug the communal irrigation ditch here, which is the oldest water right in the state. Today, farmers often use this traditional ditch irrigation over modern systems.

Keep your eyes open for tidbits of Hispanic history and culture in downtown San Luis, which is recognized as a National Historic District. A good place to start is the **San Luis Museum and Cultural Center** at 401 Church Place. In a surprising convergence of old and new, the museum is housed in a solar-powered, 17th-century building. Find the award-winning La Cultura Constante de San Luis exhibit downstairs for a short immersion in southern Colorado's Hispanic culture. Wander upstairs to see a marvelous collection of santos (Hispanic religious items) as well as other crafts. If you're looking to buy traditional blankets or woven items, which still come from local sheep and are dyed by colors made from local plants, ask the curator to connect you with San Luis's weavers and embroiderers.

More interesting sites abound in this town. The **Costilla County Courthouse** at 352 Main Street is a Colorado historic site that's currently being redone. The **Sangre de Cristo Catholic Church** at 511 Church Place, with its serene garden area, is still the hub of worship in this small town.

El Convento Bed & Breakfast at 512 Church Place, a restored 1905 building with former lives as a schoolhouse and a convent, is a good place to overnight in San Luis. Two of the four upstairs bedrooms have kiva fireplaces, traditional round fireplaces used by American Indians. Adobe walls, handmade furniture, and the calm quiet make it a good place to overnight. Homemade breakfast is served daily.

For a bite to eat, hit up the **Covered Wagon,** a family restaurant with wholesome eggs-and-pancake breakfasts and hearty lunches. Make a coffee pit stop at **Ventero Open Press Fine Art,** where proprietor Randy Pijoan runs a nonprofit where young people can make and display fine art. He also happens to be a fountain of local knowledge. Grab snacks for the next leg of the trip at the **R&R Market,** an 1857 general store that is Colorado's oldest continually operated business. Both establishments are located on Main Street.

Between Fort Garland and San Luis lies the massive **Sangre de Cristo Wilderness Area.** This pristine nature preserve spans an impressive 226,455

Fort Garland

acres in the Sangre de Cristo Mountains. The area has more than 400 miles of streams and trails and 60 alpine lakes. Four of Colorado's Fourteeners stretch up out of the wilderness, and you'll see them as you head to Fort Garland: Little Bear Peak at 14,037 feet; Mount Lindsey at 14,042 feet; Blanca Peak, the fourth-largest mountain in the state at 14,345 feet; and Ellingwood Point at 14,042 feet. If it's summertime and you're feeling adventurous, strap on a pair of hiking boots and summit the moderately challenging Blanca Peak. Be aware that the trailhead is located at the end of a treacherous four-wheel-drive road.

Mile Marker 93 (CO 159)—Fort Garland: **From San Luis, turn north on CO 159 to Fort Garland, a historically important outpost that evokes frontier life. Formerly a station for Union soldiers during the Civil War, then a base for Kit Carson in 1866, Fort Garland used to be known as a rather harsh, desolate frontier outpost. Today, the fort isn't quite as isolated, and its reconstruction has made it an ideal place to explore Colorado history. The **Fort Garland Museum** displays**

Barracks at Fort Garland

Hispanic, pioneer, and American Indian artifacts. A recently added exhibit about buffalo soldiers rounds out the experience. The folks from the American Historical Society who run the place will also give you directions to **Pike's Stockade,** a replica of the fort where Zebulon Pike and his men spent a winter as they attempted to explore the area in 1806–07.

Mile Marker 119 (CO 150)—Zapata Falls: Head west for 12 miles on US 160, then turn north on CO 150 toward the **Great Sand Dunes National Park and Preserve.** Take a small detour a couple of miles before the park, where a road takes a right toward **Zapata Falls.** With its panoramic valley views and short hike leading to 60-foot falls, this area makes a perfect photo stop.

Mile Marker 121 (CO 150)—Great Sand Dunes National Park and Preserve: Great Sand Dunes National Park and Preserve lies just a few miles north on CO

150. You'll see the dunes long before you enter the park, which is a 25-mile detour from the main road. They're unusually dark, as though they've sucked the
brownish violet hue right off the mountains towering above them, and they cast
wavelike shadows in the sunlight. They're also unusually tall: The tallest is 750
feet high, the highest in North America.

How did 30 square miles of sand dunes make it into the middle of a mountain range? As the visitors center will explain, a westerly wind picks up sediment
from the floodplains of the Rio Grande and its tributaries. The sand gets blown
to the northeast until it reaches the Sangre de Cristo Mountains, which create a
natural wind block. The wind, out of breath, dumps the sand, which then forms
the dunes.

The dunes, high as they are, sometimes get hit by lightning, creating an electrical charge so strong that it melts sand. Wormlike minerals called fulgurites result from a lightning strike. They have the white, calcified look of the tubeworms
you sometimes find on a beach, but they're actually melted, then solidified, sand.

In the summer, the dunes are popular among hikers, four-wheelers, barefoot
explorers, and sandcastle/kite festival celebrants. They're also handicapped ac-

Great Sand Dunes and their surroundings *Seth K. Hughes*

Great Sand Dunes *Seth K. Hughes*

cessible: Ask at the visitors center for special big-wheeled sand wheelchairs. In the winter, the dunes stand in snowy solitude and are breathtaking in the moonlight. Head to the visitors center for the lowdown on walks and natural history here. You can camp at either the park campgrounds, which have toilets and picnic tables, on the dunes, or in the backcountry (with a permit obtainable at the visitors center). You can also pick up free hiking permits, as well as browse the well-stocked bookstore.

Off-roading opportunities exist on Medano Road, a primitive road that follows Medano Creek along the edges of the dunes. During warmer seasons, hikers and backpackers will find trekking opportunities both in the dunes and in the mountains behind them. While it's always important to bring water on a trek, it's absolutely essential here in the dunes. In the summer, be very cautious about lightning, which often accompanies refreshing afternoon thunderstorms.

If you're car or tent camping, camp at the 88-site **Pinyon Flats Campground.** If you have an RV, the **Oasis Campground** offers electric hook-ups and other amenities. If you're not camping at all, try the basic but comfortable **Great Sand Dunes Lodge,** with patios overlooking the sand dunes and Sangre de Cristos connected to every room. The lodge also has a restaurant, gift store, and convenience store.

After the Great Sand Dunes, the byway turns and heads back toward CO 17 via Six Mile Lane. Along the way, take out the binoculars and point them at birds in **San Luis Lakes State Park.** The state park, which is also a lovely spot to get views of the dunes and the Sangre de Cristo Mountains, is a natural display case for wildlife, despite the many boaters that are often on the water. Raptors and shorebirds are here year-round; migratory birds, such as sandhill cranes, make this place their seasonal home. You may also see rabbits, kangaroo rats, coyotes, elk, and reptiles. Head Lake, and its surrounding smaller lakes, is home to even more birds. Ask the rangers where you can join a guided nature hike. Ducks nest here from February through August—vehicles are not allowed in the north areas during this time. There's a fully equipped 51-site campground nearby where you can camp for a nominal fee.

Continue south on CO 17 and you'll see signs for the **Colorado Alligator Farm** at 9162 CR 9 North in Mosca. You heard right—this is the place where ge-

---

The first Ute who emigrated along Los Caminos Antiguos had their dogs pull their belongings. Generations later, when the Ute first encountered the Spaniards, they told stories of men riding giant dogs, referring to the Spaniards' horses.

The San Luis Valley was once a vision-quest destination for more than 12 American Indian tribes. The Navajo claimed that people who traveled in seedpods landed on Blanca Peak to communicate with our dimension. UFO sightings continue to this day.

Crestone, located at the foot of the western slopes of the Sangre de Cristos, is known by the spiritual crowd as a hub of powerful energetic vibrations. Once considered sacred by American Indians, the town now attracts seekers and followers from the New Age, Buddhist, Hindu, and other traditions. Look for the UFO viewing platform on the way north.

othermal groundwater keeps an outdoor lagoon at a steady 87 degrees Fahrenheit, supporting more than one hundred alligators and other warm-water reptiles at a lofty 7,500 feet. You might get an adrenaline rush during feeding time, when the reptiles thrash in excitement with just a chain-link fence between them and you. The staff will even take a picture of you and an alligator for a few extra bucks. Anglers can ride a boat and fish for tilapia, catfish, and largemouth bass. Keep an eye out for their latest exotic reptiles and a lone ostrich.

Mile Marker 150 (CO 17) — Alamosa: Nearly 30 miles north of the beginning of the byway lies Alamosa, the largest town in the San Luis Valley. Alamosa, or "cottonwood grove," was historically a major railroad stop along the Rio Grande. In the old days, one remarkably large tree located near both the Rio Grande and the railroad served as the town's gallows. Early train riders were often welcomed to town by a swinging corpse.

Surrounding Alamosa are the spongy canals and wetlands around the Rio Grande. You'll find the **Alamosa and Monte Vista National Wildlife Refuges** here. Throngs of migratory birds take respite here, from cranes and teals in the summer to majestic bald and golden eagles in the winter. For more information, as well as self-guided driving tours, head to the U.S. Fish and Wildlife Service at the Alamosa National Wildlife Refuge on El Rancho Lane. If you're here in mid-March, don't miss the Crane Festival, where flocks of migrating sandhill cranes fly overhead and people celebrate their passage with wildlife art exhibits, a photo contest, wetlands education, and food.

Today, the town serves as a major intersection for valley travelers. You'll find antique shops, a variety of restaurants, a theater, galleries, and other shopping — and quite a few motels. It's a good place to get a meal and rest for the night. Chain hotels, such as the **Holiday Inn Express Hotel Alamosa** on 3418 Mariposa Avenue, are easy to find in town.

You can indulge in an all-you-can-eat Mexican buffet at **Calvillo's Mexican Restaurant** on 400 Main Street, which serves everything from sopapillas to ceviche. **Milagros Coffeehouse** at 529 Main Street offers quality coffee, reasonably priced café fare for breakfast and lunch, as well as a gallery, used bookstore, and community information center. A light breakfast here is the perfect way to end your journey. Fortunately, there's plenty of beautiful road to see on the way home, no matter which direction you travel.

IN THE AREA

ANTONITO

Attractions and Recreation

Cumbres and Toltec Narrow Gauge Railroad, 5250 US 285. Call 719-376-5483.

Dining/Drinks

Dos Hermanas Steakhouse, 435 Main St. Call 719-376-5589.

Jack Dempsey Museum, 412 Main St., Manassa 81141. Call 719-843-5207.

Los Cerritos Cemetery, at Mile Marker 4 on CO 142, Manassa 81141. www.themanassaproject.org/los_cerritos_cemetery.html.

SAN LUIS

Accommodations

El Convento Bed & Breakfast, 512 Church Pl. Call 719-672-4223.

Attractions and Recreation

Costilla County Courthouse, 401 Church St. Call 719-672-3681.

San Luis Museum and Cultural Center, 401 Church Pl. Call 719-672-3611.

Sangre de Cristo Catholic Church, 511 Church Pl. Call 719-992-0122.

Stations of the Cross Shrine, junction of CO 159 and CO 142. Call 719-672-3685.

Dining/Drinks

Café Rosa Mystica, 405 Main St. Call 719-672-3550.

Covered Wagon, 213 Main St. Call 719-672-3156.

R&R Market, 367 Main St. Call 719-672-3346.

Ventero Open Press Fine Art, 316 Main St. Call 719-672-0557.

FORT GARLAND

Attractions and Recreation

Fort Garland Museum, 29477 CO 159. Call 719-379-3512.

Pike's Stockade, 29477 CO 159. Call 719-379-3512.

GREAT SAND DUNES NATIONAL PARK AND PRESERVE

Accommodations

Pinyon Flats Campground. Call 719-378-6399. www.nps.gov/grsa/planyourvisit/campgrounds.htm.

Oasis Campground. Call 719-378-2222. www.greatdunes.com/camping.html.

Great Sand Dunes Lodge. Call 719-378-2900. www.gsdlodge.com.

MOSCA

Attractions and Recreation

Colorado Alligator Farm, 9162 CR 9 North (off of CO 17). Call 791-378-2612.

ALAMOSA

Accommodations

Holiday Inn Express Hotel Alamosa, 3418 Mariposa Ave. Call 719-589-4026.

Dining/Drinks

Calvillo's Mexican Restaurant, 400 Main St. Call 719-587-5500.

Milagros Coffeehouse, 529 Main St. Call 719-589-9299.

Independence Pass

7 Top of the Rockies

Estimated length: 122 miles

Estimated time: 5 hours

Highlights: Immerse yourself in the Wild West in Leadville; enjoy the haute cuisine and coutoure of Aspen; explore Camp Hale, a lesser-known piece of modern U.S. history; drive the spectacular Independence Pass, taking photos along the way; stop at ghost towns and imagine what life was like in the 1800s.

Getting there: From I-70 east from Grand Junction or west from Denver, turn off on exit 171 at Minturn for CO 24. Take a right on CO 24. Follow this road into the town of Minturn, where the Top of the Rockies, otherwise known as the 10th Mountain Division Memorial Highway, begins.

The 122-mile Top of the Rockies Byway, with average altitudes over 10,000 feet, seems to touch the sky at every bend. The two tallest peaks in Colorado, Mount Massive and Mount Elbert, both higher than 14,400 feet, are visible from this byway. Indeed, flatlanders may want to bring supplemental oxygen, extra water, and take it slowly—the altitude here rarely falls below 9,000 feet.

Even at such breathtaking heights, there's a lot of life on this 122-mile route. As the byway winds its way through the San Isabel, Pike, and White River National Forests, you may see bighorn sheep and rare mountain goats standing at precarious angles on rocky mountainsides. Up above, hawks and turkey vultures scour the skies, while robins and woodpeckers make homes in pine and aspen trees. In the spring, wildflowers like Indian paintbrush, columbine, and a variety of others form an almost psychedelic splash of color on deep green fields.

The sky-high mountains comprising the Sawatch and Mosquito Mountains

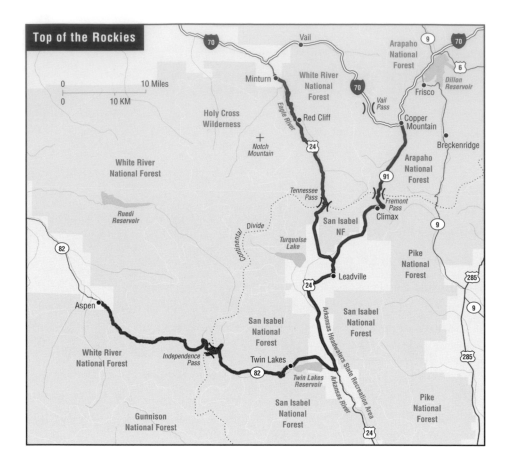

are punctuated by hidden lakes left by ancient glacial melt. The largest and most visible of these are the Twin Lakes, located at the foot of Mount Elbert. A beautiful and remote area for fishing, these lakes also provide enough pristine scenery to keep hikers and photographers gawking for hours.

History: The Ute were the original inhabitants of the these mountains. Small families would cover large areas of land in the summer, hunting elk, deer, and buffalo; gathering seeds and berries; and occasionally planting squash and corn for autumn harvest. After they'd exhausted their food-finding circuit, they would travel to a major meeting point near a river and winter with other tribes. It was during the winter that they had their celebrations and ceremonies, including weddings.

After Europeans arrived in the area, the Utes' territory grew smaller and smaller until they were eventually squeezed out from the region entirely. Meanwhile, the more intrepid of the Pikes Peak gold-rush crowd crept their way up to the high country, stumbling upon a find that would define the legacy of the area.

You'll find the thumbprints of mining and Wild West history all over the Top of the Rockies. Leadville, formerly the second-largest town in Colorado, teemed with famous figures, from Horace Tabor to Doc Holliday to Oscar Wilde. Aspen, another silver boomtown, is now a world-famous upscale ski resort and city. Camp Hale, where the military trained World War II fighters for mountain warfare, is on this byway, as are a smattering of ghost towns that whisper of boom-times past. Take your time to absorb all of the historical sites on this byway. You'll come home with a deeper knowing of Colorado's history and have had a real taste of the Wild West.

Mile Marker 144 (US 24)—Minturn: Minturn is in the 2.3-million acre **White River National Forest,** one of Colorado's biggest recreational playgrounds. It contains Colorado's two highest peaks, Mount Elbert and Mount Massive, both of which tower above 14,400 feet. Perhaps best-known for its ski resorts, which include world-famous Vail, the forest is also full of trails that can be accessed by four wheels or by foot. Award-winning fishing, some of the state's best rafting and boating lakes complete this adventure-filled national forest.

The Top of the Rockies Scenic and Historic Byway begins at the border of the White River National Forest. You'll see the Top of the Rockies sign at Mile Marker 144, around 1 mile after the Minturn boundary sign. In summer, grassy hills of lupine and wildflowers flank this section of the byway and in winter, you'll get slope-hungry just looking at the smooth hills on either side of you.

More of a railroad town in the past, Minturn is now an eclectic mixture of old Victorian houses, expensive condos, industrial workshops (such as granite-carving studios), and quaint, tourist-friendly shops and cafés. Not as upscale or impersonal as Vail, this little town is a study in modernization. You can witness the contrast between old and new Minturn firsthand if you compare the traditional old mining houses in the south to the new developments at the north end of town.

Minturn's proximity to the **Holy Cross Wilderness Area** makes it a good starting point for hikers and cyclists in the summer, and Nordic skiers and snow-mobilers in wintertime. Try the Grouse Creek Trail 0.5 mile past Mile Marker 144, a popular local spot. Kayakers and rafters will enjoy the rapids on the Eagle River, which runs through the center of town. For those interested in enjoying a river-

The city of Minturn has been working for years on restoring the Eagle River, which was corrupted by heavy metals and silt from mining and highway-building activity. It wasn't a pretty sight: Fish had their gills glued shut by heavy metals like cadmium and zinc, while trees, affected by erosion and bad water quality, were also dying off. These days, things are looking a lot better. The city has successfully restored brown trout populations and replanted native grasses and shrubs to reduce bank erosion. From the looks of it today, the Eagle River is becoming a thriving, living body of water once again.

Oscar Wilde, on a lecture tour of the West, ended up at the Tabor Opera House in 1882. David H. Dougan, the mayor at the time, named a new lode at the Matchless Mine "the Oscar" in Wilde's honor. One thing, however, really stuck with Wilde. Upon visiting a local saloon (as he wrote in his 1882 essay "Impressions of America"), he "saw the only rational method of art criticism [he] had ever come across. Over the piano was printed a notice—'Please do not shoot the pianist. He is doing his best.'"

side picnic, Little Beach, accessible from Cemetery Road shortly after Mile Marker 145, is a pleasant summer retreat with a playground, picnic area, basketball court, and river access for wading or splashing around.

There's just enough to do in this scenic little town to make it a popular off-the-beaten-track tourist destination. If you're in the mood for a filet mignon and all-you-can-eat salad bar, the **Minturn Country Club** on Main Street is your place. If you want to stay the night, try the **Minturn Inn,** a 1915 log-home mountain retreat that's one of the oldest buildings in town. As accommodations go, its stylish log-home furniture and down comforters make it a higher-end option, though you can get rooms for as little as $99 during the off-season.

After leaving Minturn, the road begins a noticeable climb. Note the Eagle River to your left—this river eventually joins up with the Colorado and, after some traveling, drains into the Gulf of California. Flat-topped rocks line the mountain to your right. Look for large aspen groves, which in the fall are awash in golden leaves. As you gain elevation, pine stands replace the aspen groves, adding a deep, somewhat mysterious green tinge to the mountains.

There are plenty of good lookout spots as you continue to drive, especially around Mile Markers 146 and 150. The latter has a viewpoint where you can look down into the Holy Cross Wilderness Area and see railroad tracks snaking through the bottom.

Mile Marker 151 (US 24) — Gillman: You'll soon come across a small ghost town. This is the old mining town of Gillman, an abandoned mining works that the city of Minturn is turning over to developers, who are looking to raze the area and put in a high-end resort. At the time of writing, the town was fenced off and off-limits to visitors, though it did make for a few intriguing photographs.

Notice the big mountain parallel to the highway 0.5 mile after Gillman. This is **Notch Mountain,** which stretches up to 13,237 feet. Pullouts and viewpoints along the way give you plenty of places to take in your surroundings.

A few hairpin turns later — watch for cyclists in the summer — you'll see a picturesque steel arch bridge spanning more than 200 feet above the Eagle River. This is the Red Cliff Bridge at Dowd Junction, a beautiful piece of civil engineering built in 1941 and rehabilitated in 2004. The bridge was built to provide an important commerce link between I-70 and Leadville. It's now on the National Register of Historic Places.

Around Mile Marker 154, the Eagle River becomes a slow, meandering stream. You reenter the White River National Forest. There's a picnic area here, as well as the **Horn Silver Campground.**

Notice that some of the pine trees around here look brown and bent, if not completely wasted. This is due largely to the mountain pine beetle, an ongoing scourge to lodgepole, ponderosa, limber, and Scotch pine trees in the Rocky Mountains. Beetles burrow inside the trees, then consume them from the inside out, leaving characteristic reddish brown foliage on the dead trees. Recent outbreaks are leading to dramatic effects on the scenery here.

Mile Marker 158 (US 24) — Camp Hale: Notice the old cement foundations and dirt roads in the Pando Valley to your left. This is all that remains of **Camp Hale,** the only site ever developed by the U.S. Army for winter and mountain warfare training.

Before the 10th Mountain Division, the Pando Valley had on several different guises. A glacier formed the valley several million years ago — notice the moraine, or piles of rocks, at the north end of the valley, as well as the jagged 14,000-foot peaks that surround it. These are evidence of glacial activity. Later, in the 1800s, miners tapped the valley. When they couldn't find much, people settled in and used the valley to grow potatoes and lettuce.

This quiet farming valley changed drastically after Pearl Harbor led the United States to become heavily involved in World War II. The U.S. government, with an eye toward defeating Axis powers in the Alps, built Camp Hale in 1942 to train troops for mountain warfare.

Soon after Camp Hale was finished in November 1942, more than fourteen thousand men moved in for intensive mountain combat and survival training. They were accompanied by horses, mules, and a canine corps. They trained in everything from skiing—either at Slope B at the south end of the valley or at nearby Ski Cooper—to climbing, wilderness survival, and snowshoeing. They also tested winter gear while they trained. At its height, Camp Hale accommodated more than one thousand buildings, as well as training grounds, weapon ranges, and barracks that housed German prisoners of war. They also built a hut-to-hut system in the nearby Rockies that's still in use today by recreational skiers and snowshoers.

In January 1945, the 10th Mountain Division landed in Naples, Italy, the last U.S. division to enter the war. On April 20, 1945, they led the Allies through the Po Valley—the first Allied crossing of the Po River—and through the Alps, where they pushed out the Germans. On May 2, 1945, the war ended with the Germans surrendering.

A few months later, in October 1945, the 10th Mountain Division was inactivated. The government dismantled Camp Hale in various stages over the next 20 years, using it on occasion to train covert guerilla forces for the Cold War, including a group of Tibetan fighters. In 1956 the facility was turned over to the U.S. Forest Service, which still manages it as public land. It's now on the National Register of Historic Places.

Today all that remains are the crumbled foundations of the barracks and the **Camp Hale Memorial Campground.** There's good ATV off-roading here, as well as access to the 10th Mountain Division hut system, where you can hike, mountain bike, ski, or snowshoe between huts.

At Mile Marker 159, **Pando,** an old refrigerated train depot turned adventure outfitter, has rafting, fishing, ATVs, and a restaurant. Near Pando was an icehouse that enabled railcars to carry refrigerated produce from the Western Slope to Denver.

Stop at the five interpretive signs just before Mile Marker 160 to learn more about Camp Hale. After this viewpoint, the road keeps climbing. Soon, you're not weaving into the mountains so much as you're rolling on top of them. The road at this point lives up to its name.

Mile Marker 160 (US 24) — Tennessee Pass and Camp Hale Memorial: You're truly at the top of the Rockies when you hit the 10,424-foot **Tennessee Pass,** located atop the Continental Divide. Stop here to read the story of the 10th Mountain Division, which is similar to the one at the viewpoint below, and admire the polished memorial plaque dedicated to the 990 men in the division who were killed in action.

Just south of the Camp Hale Memorial is **Ski Cooper,** the original training ground for the 10th Mountain Division. Today, it's a small, family-friendly resort known for its affordable lift tickets. Across from the memorial is the **Tennessee Pass Trailhead,** where you can access the 10th Mountain Division Hut Trail System and the Colorado Trail in both summer and winter. In summer, mountain bikers enjoy the trail for single-track fun.

As you descend Tennessee Pass, you'll notice that the scenery changes. Barren, high-alpine tundra replaces pine stands, lending astonishing views of the big, bald peaks gazing at the road from miles away, including the 14,421-foot Mount Massive. You'll also start seeing ghost towns, such as **Rancho Escondido,** the first boarded-up old town to your right as you descend the pass.

Mile Marker 80 (CO 82) — Twin Lakes: Travelers on their way to and from Leadville used to use Twin Lakes as a rest stop. The area was first known as Dayton, when prospectors settled there in the mid-1860s. In 1879 silver was discovered in Leadville and Aspen. At the time, there was no direct route between the two towns, so workers went about building one. The Twin Lakes area became a major hub through which not only the Leadville-Aspen road, but the Denver and Rio Grande Narrow Gauge Railroad tracked. As increasing numbers of visitors noticed the vast beauty of the Twin Lakes area, tourism became a main draw. Mining magnate James V. Dexter opened the Interlaken resort on the south shore of the lower lake. The rich and famous flocked to the area to fish, hunt, and boat.

Today, the state's largest glacier-formed lake, a stunning deep blue in the solemn shadow of the twin peaks of Mount Elbert and Mount Massive, still draws thousands of hikers, photographers, climbers, fisherman, and nature lovers. Hik-

Twin Lakes

ers can visit the Interlaken by hiking along the Colorado Trail from the dam at the south side of the lake. Kayaking and canoeing are other popular ways to explore the lake; rentals are available in town.

Visitors can also visualize life in the old tourist town, now a National Historic District, by exploring paths around the shed, log cabin, assay office (which tested the purity of precious metals to protect consumers), and Red Rooster Tavern, all abandoned now, but in decent shape. You'll find plenty of lodges and cabins at which to overnight, as well as a café, antique stores, and a small visitors center.

Anglers will find fishing access, a campground, and boat ramp between Mile Markers 79 and 80. Several lookouts provide scenic photo opportunities; hiking and camping abound around the lake as well. If you're a birdwatcher, try the easy hike to Lily Ponds around sunset; you'll see plenty of avian life here, including large wading birds like herons.

After Twin Lakes, the Top of the Rockies continues through the dramatic and wild Independence Pass to Aspen. This 40-mile stretch summits at a 12,095-foot pass that steals your breath away, both due to altitude and astounding scenery. Note that this pass is only open from June to September. From the lakes, the byway starts winding its way into an increasingly dramatic canyon. Notice the mammoth mountains surrounding the pass. These are part of the Collegiate

Peaks Range, which includes 13,000-footers named Champion, Geissler, Twining, and Grizzly.

The road winds through a canyon, following the meandering of the Roaring Fork River to a T intersection, where you'll turn left. Look to your left and you'll find the river a constant companion. Just out of Twin Lakes are a couple of campgrounds. Both are to the left, and the second abuts **Snyder Falls,** which you can also see if you pull off the road roughly 5 miles from Twin Lakes. You continue a sweeping curve through the Roaring Fork Valley. The road is cut out of the mountains, and you may notice some erosion at the edges. If steep drops without guardrails aren't enough to slow you down, the single lanes around blind turns will. Be cautious: You may run into a situation where you and someone going the other way end up stopped in a head-on dilemma where someone has to back up and pull over.

As the road turns north, you'll hit the first of four hairpin switchbacks. After this switchback, you hit Mountain Boy Gulch, carved out of steep tundra and cliffs. Nary 1 mile later comes the next 180-degree switchback, shortly followed by another. Then, the views at the summit of Independence Pass open up like a pair of unfolding giant hands. The parking lot here offers postcard-perfect mountain views as well as the chance to do some high-alpine hiking. You may see parasailers floating around the sides of mountains. If it's hot, cool off your feet in the frigid tundra lakes on the north side of the summit. It's a prime place to stretch your legs and have a snack.

Next, the road starts its descent into Aspen. To your left, you'll see a series of 12,000-plus-foot peaks. Cliffs, forests, and waterfalls define the right hand, or north, side of the road. There are a couple of trails to your right that lead into the White River National Forest; those on your left lead into the Collegiate Peaks Wilderness Area. Trails are generally quite long and somewhat time consuming.

One exception is the town of **Independence,** located on the south (left) side of the road roughly 2 miles from the summit, after the first postsummit switchback. It's a ghost town that was abandoned in the early 19th century, and is worth a peek. A walking trail leads you to several buildings and informational signs telling you more about the town's history.

Enjoy the dramatic scenery before your next stop, roughly 9 miles from Aspen. Between Weller Campground and Lincoln Creek Road are the **Grottos.** Here, a series of pools ripe for summer swimming make for a good cool-off point.

Top of Independence Pass

A nearby ice cave, which usually stays frozen through summer, makes for another good place to manage the heat. If you go back to the Grottos' parking lot and walk down the highway, you'll find the **Devil's Punchbowl,** yet another swimming hole with a high rock outcropping you can dive off. Nobody knows exactly how high it is, but estimates range as high as 25 feet.

As you continue down to Aspen, the trees get denser and the scenery more colorful. Thick pine groves contrast with towering red cliffs and waterfalls to make for an outdoor roadside paradise. Look for rock climbers dangling from nearby cliffs. In no time, you'll snake your way past Aspen Mountain and into the famous town of Aspen.

Mile Marker 42 (CO 82)—Aspen: Aspen was Ute country until miners settled there in 1879, finding so much silver ore that Aspen soon surpassed Leadville in silver production. The rest of its history aligns closely with many other Colorado mining towns. Aspen made loads of money on silver until the Sherman Silver

Purchase Act, which doubled the U.S. government's purchase of silver, artificially raising the price of the metal, was repealed in 1893. The resultant panic caused many inhabitants to go bust. The town shrunk steadily to a population low of 750 in the 1930s.

Fortunately for its residents, Aspen was surrounded by some seriously smooth snow. Investors started eyeing the area for ski development shortly before World War II interrupted their plans. In 1946, just after the war, 10th Mountain Division veteran Friedl Pfeifer and Chicago container magnate Walter Paepcke joined forces to create the Aspen Skiing Corporation, assigning Olympic ski champion Dick Durrance to head the design and production of Aspen's new ski resorts. Thus, Aspen Resort, and later, in the late 1950s, Snowmass, Buttermilk, and Aspen Highlands were born.

From those auspicious beginnings came some of the best skiing—and one of the most high-end resort towns—on the planet. Aspen's reputation as a culturally rich and prohibitively expensive resort town is well earned. Amid the fine European-style cafés, spas, hotels, and multimillion-dollar homes, you might spot some of the world's wealthiest mountain lovers. Goldie Hawn, Jack Nicholson, Michael Douglas, and a slew of other actors call this place a part-time home. If you're a star-seeker, consider Aspen an outpost of Beverly Hills.

Hunter S. Thompson at the Aspen Farmers Market

That said, the town is historically progressive, almost utopian, in its management. Elizabeth and Walter Paepcke founded the cultural component of the town on the "Aspen Idea," a "model of civilization where…activity, art, music, and the humanities…would enrich the spirit and elevate society, [culminating] in [a] complete person living in a community that [nourishes] the mind, body, and spirit of its citizens." That quote is

Downtown Aspen

directly from the City of Aspen, and it aptly describes the cultural atmosphere that you might experience as you walk past the beautiful people on Aspen's Main Street, filled with metropolitan-caliber galleries, restaurants, boutiques, and yes, mink-clad shoppers and million-dollar real estate dealers.

Speaking of mink, you might just find the fur you've been looking for at one of Aspen's high-end boutiques. The downtown shopping district offers boutiques, Italian shoe stores, organic cosmetics stores, outdoor gear from golf to backcountry skiing, fine art galleries, furniture, and more. Think classy and European, with prices to match.

If drooling at expensive items is not your pace, Aspen abounds with outdoor activities. In summer, catch a free bus to Aspen Highlands at **Rubey Park** in downtown Aspen, then board the Maroon Bells bus, which for $6 ($2 for children) takes you up to some beautiful hiking at Maroon Bells and Crater Lake, three times per hour during daytime. The hiking here ranges from flat, wide lakeside paths to challenging, multihour hikes. Fit folks might try Crater Lake for a mountaintop reward. Note that you can't drive up here from 9 AM through 4:30 PM, making the bus a necessity.

Hiking up Aspen Mountain is another option, though it's masochistically steep. For a $22–$24 fee (the latter being on weekends), you can take the Silver Queen gondola to the 11,212-foot summit. The gondola only takes about 14 minutes, and runs daily from June 15 to September 3.

Those staying a while might want to check out the summer music festivals that happen here almost daily. These include the **Aspen Music Festival,** offering performances seven days a week between June 21 and August 19. The **Aspen Chamber Symphony** plays most Friday evenings year-round, while the **Aspen Festival Orchestra** rehearses Sunday mornings. That's not to mention the many concerts and themed festivals that come through town every year, such as the **U.S. Comedy Arts Festival** in early November of each year.

Staying overnight comes at a price, most often in the $300 range. The **Sky Hotel,** Aspen's boutique hotel, offers trendy indulgence in the premium price range. The town of Glenwood Springs offers more budget options, and you can find campgrounds on Independence Pass.

Finding delectable dining in a town like this isn't hard. Aspen's dining options are comparable to those of a major city in both variety and quality. Try **Mezzaluna** at 624 East Cooper for midrange Italian, or **Matsuhisa**, a part of renowned chef

Hummingbird in Aspen

Nobu Matsuhisa's upscale sushi chains, on 303 East Main Street.

To continue on the byway, backtrack Independence Pass to Twin Lakes. As you drive out of Twin Lakes, notice the Mount Elbert power plant on your right. It's not much of a tourist attraction, but it does provide power to surrounding areas by pumping water from the Twin Lakes through its 170,000-horsepower turbines.

Shortly after the power plant is the sign for the **Arkansas Headwaters State Recreation Area.** This 148-mile kayaking and rafting favorite stretches along the Arkansas from just below Leadville to the Pueblo Reservoir in southeastern Colorado. The Leadville section in particular is renowned for its difficult, scenery-intensive kayaking.

Spiky granite rock outcroppings appear as you backtrack to Leadville in a lunar, high-mountain landscape. At Mile Marker 183, you'll see another ghost town, as well as the **Arkansas River Ranch** and the **Hayden Meadows Ranch. Crystal Lake,** another scenic alpine area, can be seen at Mile Marker 181. Past the lakes, you'll see the Leadville Fish Hatchery, then a small red ghost church just after Mile Marker 179.

1 Mile South of the Intersection of US 24 and CO 91 (US 24)—Leadville: Leadville, with its rich history of mining, outlaws, and boom-and-bust fortune, is one of the nation's only fully preserved mining towns. This National Historic Landmark town still boasts more than 50 original 19th-century structures, including the famous **Tabor Opera House.** Indeed, this 2-mile-high city's entire story remains largely intact today, from the abandoned mines that provided famous figures like Tabor and Guggenheim with piles of money to the **National Mining Hall of Fame** that celebrates them posthumously.

A SUMMARY OF LEADVILLE'S WILD WEST HISTORY

Leadville, the byway's de facto capital, has enough colorful characters and outlaw stories in its history to fill library shelves with Old West tales. In 1859, the Slater

Party, a group of gold diggers, discovered a whopping $8 million worth of gold while prospecting in the California Gulch. Word of their discovery spread like wildfire, and soon prospectors had built their cabins and hoist houses—above-ground structures associated with mine shafts—not only in the town of Leadville, but throughout a series of towns in an area now known as Lake County.

So many prospectors settled in the area that all the gold ran out one year later. The process of separating the gold from its pesky black carbonate encasing caused communal groans until 1877, when two veteran miners discovered that the outer stuff wasn't useless solidified black gunk, but lead, containing large amounts of silver. A resurgence of people flooded to the area, and by 1880 there were more than forty thousand residents, making Leadville the second most populated city in the state.

People made millions, almost overnight. The "Unsinkable" Molly Brown of *Titanic* fame married J. J. Brown in Leadville, where he owned a lucrative mine. Other well-to-do mine owners included the Guggenheims and Horace Tabor, a New England merchant, who hit pay dirt when he casually acquired a stake in what turned out to be a ferociously deep mine called Little Pittsburgh. Tabor went on to acquire stakes in several such mines, and by 1878 he'd not only become mayor of Leadville but had founded two newspapers, a bank, and an opera house. Estranged from his former wife and intoxicated by opulence, he and his new wife, known as Baby Doe Tabor—she was many years younger than him—were the subjects of one of Colorado's most legendary rags-to-riches-to-rags stories. Legend has it that he whispered the words "hang onto the Matchless," his mine in the outskirts of town, to Baby Doe just before he passed away. She took his word as gospel and immediately moved to a cabin next to the mine, where she died years later in poverty, frozen stiff from the cold.

Law was an afterthought throughout Leadville's gold rush years, as men broke into fistfights and fatal gun battles over the precious metal in the area. Local lore has it that the sheriffs became so frustrated with the area's many outlaws that they began staging sting operations in an attempt to regain control. One such sting involved a stagecoach on the old road between Buena Vista and Leadville, where stages filled with gold occasionally rumbled between the two towns. Gold-hungry outlaws regularly held up and hijacked these coaches. In 1879 one ambitious sheriff decided to take action by crouching in wait for the next outlaw. It worked: Just as the stage was rambling by the outlaw jumped out of hiding to take it over. The police officer, sensing his opportunity, shot the out-law dead. However, he was completely floored when he tore off the outlaw's hood—it was his wife he'd killed. Unable to muster up what it took to bring the body back to town, he buried her right next to the road where he'd shot her. Passersby can still see her tombstone off US 24.

Until the U.S. economy crashed in the panic of 1893—causing the government to repeal the Sherman Silver Purchase Act, and the price of silver to hit rock-bottom as a result—Leadville and its environs were the Wild West at its most prodigal. More than 30 mines produced more than $15 million worth of silver, gold, and lead per year. Leadville's wealth attracted handfuls of visiting notables, including Oscar Wilde, Doc Holliday (who had his final shoot-out here), Susan B. Anthony, Jesse James, and Buffalo Bill.

In 1881 the Denver and Rio Grande Narrow Gauge Railroad built a narrow-gauge route over the Tennessee Pass. At 10,240 feet, it was the highest mountain pass railroad in the U.S. The railroad was later upgraded to a standard gauge, and it remains one of the highest in the country.

In 1896, after the economic crash, the town of Leadville attempted to recapture its flagging economy by building the biggest ice structure in the U.S. The Crystal Palace, finished in 1896, didn't attract as many visitors as locals had hoped, and the economy kept waning until around 1918, when a huge deposit of

Downtown Leadville

molybdenum was discovered 14 miles northeast of the town. Molybdenum, which is used to produce high-strength steel alloys, was in huge demand during World War II.

Molybdenum mining kept Leadville afloat until the 1980s, when the government closed the city's mines. Around that time, the Environmental Protection Agency poured funding into fixing the sizeable contamination problem that years of mining had wrought on the community. Leadville took this as an initiative to spur tourism and outdoor recreation opportunities in the area. Nowadays, activities like skiing in the winter, rock climbing in the summer, and the Leadville 100—a famous marathon and mountain bike race—draw people from around the world into Leadville.

> Perched at 10,152 feet, Leadville is the highest incorporated city in the nation. Pilots won't be surprised to find the highest airport in the U.S. here, too: Lake County Airport, at 9,927 feet, lies at a single-engine cruising altitude. Finally, golfers will find the second-highest golf course in the U.S., Mount Massive Golf Course, at 9,680 feet.

LEADVILLE TODAY

Driving in, you'll see the freshly painted Victorians and Old West nostalgia that defines the town. History lives on in displays and little placards on street corners, buildings, and in display windows. Above, a cold mountain sky is often streaked with artistic, high-altitude cloud formations. In spring, summer, and fall, flower gardens and weeping willows add an additional dash of old-time charm to the town. There's plenty of parking either downtown or on one of the residential streets stretching away from it.

The best way to see Leadville is on foot. Start at the **Leadville Chamber of Commerce** on 809 Harrison Avenue and load up on maps. They offer maps for a walking tour of the downtown's historic district (a national landmark of more than 70 square blocks), as well as a driving route of the mines surrounding the area.

The **Leadville Heritage Museum,** located on the northeast corner of Harrison Avenue and Ninth Street, was originally opened in 1904 as the Carnegie Library. In 1971 the town transformed the library into a museum. Highlights include a scale model of the doomed Leadville Ice Palace, an art gallery, an exhibit of 10th Mountain Division artifacts, dioramas of mining history, and a variety of other exhibits.

The **National Mining Hall of Fame** on 120 West Ninth Street commemorates the people working in the mining industry. Exhibits include a walk-through replica of an underground mine; a quartz wall from a mine in Telluride; gold, silver, and other ore specimens; hands-on educational exhibits on industrial minerals; and other educational displays.

Leadville City Hall was the town's post office from 1905 to 1973. Its current incarnation as the seat of the city's government includes local history displays in the lobby. Look up as you enter—those little attic windows were where the old postmaster used to spy on his employees, or so the lore goes. It's on the northeast corner of West Eighth Street and Harrison Avenue.

The 1879 **Tabor Opera House** used to be packed with wealthy miners entertaining their ladies with Broadway shows. These days, the likes of Houdini and the Metropolitan Opera have been replaced by modern top-notch shows. A self-guided tour reveals a well-preserved, ornate interior. It's located on East Third Street in downtown Leadville.

Want to see the cabin that Baby Doe Tabor perished in, 36 years after her husband? The **Baby Doe Tabor Museum and Matchless Mine Cabin and Hoist House** is filled with Baby Doe memorabilia, including the cabin she was found frozen in. It's located on East Seventh Street in Leadville.

Donkeys on the street during Boom Days, an annual Leadville summer festival

Downtown Leadville

On the southwest corner of Poplar and East Seventh stands Leadville's landmark **Annunciation Church.** Its finely crafted wooden steeple has overlooked
the town since 1879. Inside the steeple, a 3,026-pound bell named the St. Mary
marks services and ceremonies. "Unsinkable" Molly Brown, who survived the
sinking of the *Titanic,* was married here in 1886, and Baby Doe Tabor was buried
here in 1935. Note that the church is still active, so be respectful when entering
if there are services in session.

Back in the 1800s, some of Leadville's residents truly lived like Western kings.
This plush lifestyle remains preserved at the **Healy House & Dexter Cabin Museum.** Mining investor James V. Dexter equipped his rather small log cabin with
an astounding collection of art, precious stones, coins, and hunting paraphernalia. He even started a private poker club here at the turn of the 20th century. The
Healy House, a stunningly preserved Greek Revival clapboard, is something of a
contrast to Dexter's log cabin, but lavish nonetheless. August R. Meyer built the
house in 1878 for his bride. Some time later, it became a boarding house for local
railroad men and townsfolk. One of the boarders was Dan Healy, the house's
namesake. The Healy House now boasts Victorian furniture collected from around
Leadville, including from the Tabor estate. Guided tours are available.

For an authentic scenic tour of Colorado mining country, catch the **Leadville,
Colorado, and Southern Railroad's** two-and-a-half-hour guided railroad trip
from Leadville to Climax, the highest unincorporated town in Colorado.

Antique bottles at the Western Hardware Company, Leadville

Once you've had your fill of historical museums, a stroll down Harrison reveals a wealth of gift shops, art galleries, restaurants, and outdoor stores. In the summer, motorcyclists love to come up here and clink beers at local saloons. You might also notice Colorado Mountain College, which offers outdoor education.

Accommodation-wise, the town has its share of roadside and chain motels. Among the handful of historical places to stay in town is the **Governor's Inn,** where Colorado governor Jesse McDonald used to live. The quaint bed & breakfast is located near downtown, on 129 West Eighth Street.

The historic **Silver Dollar Saloon** on 315 Harrison Avenue is a full-service Irish pub where you can drink brew and reminisce about the Old West. **Quincy's Steak and Spirits** on 416 Harrison Avenue has a Sunday filet mignon special, popular with the locals.

The **Delaware Hotel** has a fully stocked gift shop selling everything from elk racks to Old West costume wear. It's packed to the gills with Western kitsch. Despite the cheesiness, don't miss this place, even if you're not a fan of the Old West. It has a traditional restaurant and is a full-service hotel. Self-guided tours showcase period furniture, outfits, dolls, and the like; much of it is for sale. As in the gift shop, the number of pieces inside is overwhelming.

As you continue down Harrison Avenue, you'll see a plaque commemorating the May Company. The May Company stores were started in Leadville in 1877. David May opened his first department store in a tent on 318 Harrison Avenue. It occupied the site of the tablet that commemorates its start in 1877. In 1888 the store moved to Denver. After that, it became a nationwide chain before being bought up by Macy's in the 1990s.

On the way out of Leadville to the north, old abandoned buildings speckle the outskirts of town, a sharp contrast to the downtown area's freshly painted appearance. At the intersection of US 24 and CO 91, take CO 91 north. As you climb out of Leadville, notice the huge Climax molybdenum mine sitting atop Fremont Pass.

Mile Marker 14 (CO 91)—Robertson, Kokomo, and Recen: Stop off at the lookout point here. It looks like little more than a couple of lakes and carefully arranged dirt piles. However, almost a century of history literally lies buried underneath what's now a flat, mud-covered valley.

Three bustling towns—Robertson, Kokomo, and Recen—used to take up the space now flooded by mine tailings. When the first people moved here in the late 1800s, the valley was green, the lakes had trout, and wildlife such as elk still visited from adjacent mountains. Kokomo alone had 12 hotels, a newspaper, and enough saloons and brothels to keep the men of the Wild West in a hedonistic haze for weeks. It was also the site of the highest Masonic lodge in the nation, Corinthian Lodge Number 42. In 1881 fire consumed all but a few buildings in town. Kokomo never recovered. The three Recen brothers that founded the neighboring town of Recen donated the land to Kokomo residents whose houses had burned down. The town was later christened Kokomo-Recen, then changed to simply Kokomo. This version of Kokomo survived until 1965, when the town's nine registered voters agreed to abandon the town. Climax Molybdenum Company assumed ownership of the town, which was soon covered in mine tailings from the Climax Mine.

The third town, Robertson, also had a relatively short life span. It was ravaged by fire both in 1907 and 1916; the town never recovered from the second fire. There were just a few abandoned buildings left when the town, like its neighbors, was covered in tailings from the Climax Mine.

These days, the county is working to rehabilitate the valley. Trout, which were absent from the lakes for decades, live here again, and elk have been spotted in parts of the valley. The fruits of this long-term project are still hard to decipher, but interpretive signs reassure visitors that the valley will once again be filled with wildlife and plants in the near future.

At Mile Marker 15, past a small lake, the road circles around the San Isabel National Forest, then enters the White River National Forest again. You'll see the sprawling Climax Molybdenum Company in front of you. This is where Leadville derived the lead that is its namesake. The mine at one time employed more than sixty thousand people. Molybdenum, a mineral used to harden steel, took off during World War I, when it was used chiefly to make radio tubes, chemical compounds, dyes, and plane parts. The nearby township of Climax used to house one thousand employees until a 1959 strike, when it became a ghost town. The reason you don't see houses here now is that they were all trucked to the West Park subdivision in Leadville later in the 20th century.

The mine is on **Fremont Pass,** at Mile Marker 11, at an elevation of 11,320 feet. After Fremont Pass, the road winds back down through the White River National Forest and ends up at **Copper Mountain,** a popular ski resort right off I-70. There's lodging, tourist information, and places to eat here. Copper Mountain makes the perfect modern rest stop after your expedition into the past, and is a place to let the high-mountain magic of the Top of the Rockies really sink in before you continue with your journey.

IN THE AREA

MINTURN

Accommodations

Minturn Inn, 442 Main St. Call 970-827-9647.

Attractions and Recreation

Minturn Country Club, 131 Main St. Call 970-827-4114.

ASPEN

Accommodations

Sky Hotel, 709 E. Durant Ave. Call 970-925-6760.

Attractions and Recreation

Aspen Chamber Symphony and Aspen Festival Orchestra, 2 Music School Rd. Call 970-925-3254.

Dining/Drinks

Matsuhisa, 303 E. Main St. Call 970-544-6628.

Mezzaluna, 624 E. Cooper Ave. Call 970-925-5882.

LEADVILLE

Accommodations

The Delaware Hotel, 700 Harrison Ave. Call 719-486-1410.

Governor's Inn, 129 W. Eighth St. Call 719-486-1865.

Attractions and Recreation

Annunciation Church, southwest corner of Poplar and E. Seventh Streets. Call 719-486-1382.

Baby Doe Tabor Museum and Matchless Mine Cabin and Holst House, 3940 CO 91. Call 719-486-4918.

Healy House & Dexter Cabin Museum, 912 Harrison Ave. Call 719-486-0487.

Leadville Chamber of Commerce, 809 Harrison Ave. Call 719-486-3900.

Leadville City Hall, 800 Harrison Ave. Call 719-486-2092.

Leadville, Colorado, and Southern Railroad, 326 E. Seventh St. Call 719-486-3936.

Leadville Heritage Museum, 102 E. Ninth Street. Call 719-486-1878.

National Mining Hall of Fame, 120 W. Ninth St. Call 719-486-1229.

Lake County Civic Center Association/Heritage Museum, 102 E. Ninth St. Call 719-486-1878.

Tabor Opera House, 308 Harrison Ave. Call 719-486-8409.

Dining/Drinks

Quincy's Steak and Spirits, 416 Harrison Ave. Call 719-486-9765.

Silver Dollar Saloon, 315 Harrison Ave. Call 719-486-9914.

Royal Gorge *Seth K. Hughes*

8 Gold Belt Tour

Estimated length: 131 miles

Estimated time: 6 hours

Highlights: Drive over the red-walled Royal Gorge; indulge your inner rock-lover at Florrissant Fossil Beds and pan for gold in Cripple Creek; test out Lady Luck at one of Cripple Creek's many casinos; use one of many opportunities to raft, rock climb, hike, and bike; tour the darkly fascinating Museum of Colorado Prisons in Canon City.

Getting there: From Denver, take I-25 south to US 24. Travel west on US 24 to the town of Florissant. From Grand Junction, take I-70 east to exit 171, and then take US 24 south and then east to Florissant.

History: This byway is where water carved gorges to a depth and width so extreme, sunlight touches the bottom of their valleys only a few hours each day. The fossilized bones of thunder lizards, partially encased in rock and earth, have been extracted for science and human curiosity. And, of course, there is gold, once so plentiful it took five hundred mines and an immeasurable amount of will to extract it. The history of the Gold Belt Tour Scenic and Historic Byway covers eons of time and encapsulates a variety of interests for those who travel it.

Royal Gorge. The seemingly omnipresent Arkansas River is the sculpting force of the 1,200-foot deep Royal Gorge located at the southern edge of this byway. The first visitors to this area were prehistoric people and American Indians, most notably the Ute, who used the rocky outcroppings as cover for their winter camps, and found its bountiful wildlife a nearly inexhaustible source of food. It's thought

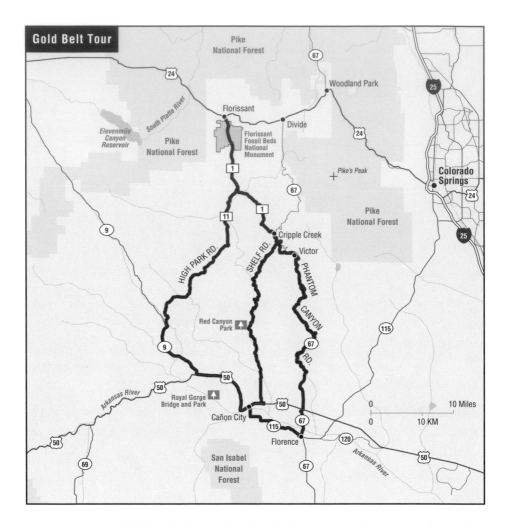

that a number of Plains Indians also found their way to the gorge as they followed game trails east.

In the mid-1600s, Spanish missionaries documented the area during their evangelical sojourns through the region. Later, European trappers and traders stumbled upon this game-rich area and brought stories of its landscape back to the burgeoning nation's populace. In 1806, the fabled Zebulon Pike, for whom a nearby mountain is named, was sent on a scouting mission by the U.S. government soon after the Louisiana Purchase. His party set up camp along the Royal Gorge's eastern entrance and sent an exploratory group into its depths to achieve a cursory look at this intriguing geological gem.

Roughly 70 years later, in 1877, the gorge found itself as the centerpiece for a small-scale private war. Two railroads, the Santa Fe and the Rio Grande, both wanted to lay track through the valley to aid in the transport of silver ore, found upstream in the Arkansas River. The company that laid its tracks first would be capable of achieving a large financial incentive. Taking advantage of the fact that law enforcement still had some catching up to do in the region, both railroad companies engaged in a type of industrial sabotage that would have made the Environmental Liberation Front proud. From dynamiting tracks to threatening their opponent's workers, the two railroads openly engaged in a hyper-regional war. It escalated when both companies hired what essentially amounted to paramilitary groups—though they called them posses—to protect their work and property.

Eventually, the matter was settled in court, with the Rio Grande Railroad gaining exclusive rights to lay their tracks. However, when the silver boom went bust with the repeal of the Sherman Silver Purchase Act in 1893, everything related to silver felt the financial shockwaves, including the Rio Grande's route through the gorge.

While the tracks no longer carry railcars filled with precious metal, a rail company still runs a scenic train through the gorge to this day, the **Royal Gorge Route Railroad.** Even without precious metal, it was obvious the area could be a gold mine; developers just had to change their focus to the area's tourist potential. In 1929 the construction of a suspension bridge to connect both rims of the gorge was completed. When finished, it stood 1,053 feet above the Arkansas River, becoming the highest suspension bridge in the United States.

Visitors are still invited to drive or walk over its gravity-defying heights. An incline railway, traversing a 100-percent grade, was built in 1931, and an aerial tram crossing 2,200 feet from rim to rim of the gorge was constructed in 1968—both of which are still operating. In the spring of 2012, the **Royal Gorge Bridge and Park**—the operation that manages the suspension bridge and runs the incline railway and aerial tram—opened what they claim to be the world's highest zip line, called "The Soaring Eagle." This thrill-seekers' dream ride suspends visitors over the gorge's 1,000-foot drop as they careen from rim to rim at 35 miles an hour. There are several campgrounds nearby; the **Royal Gorge KOA,** a large campground that supports RVs and tents as well as featuring climate-controlled cabins and a playground, is a good place to stay if you're seeking proximity to the gorge itself.

Petrified tree stump, Florissant Fossil Beds

Florissant Fossil Beds National Monument. Long before railroads, gold rushes, and even before the American Indians first set foot in the region, prehistoric creatures roamed the land of Colorado. Envision the Oligocene epoch, the time when South America separated from Antarctica, or roughly 23 to 34 million years ago. The area where the Florissant Fossil Beds are now located was once the site of a large inland lake, which probably served as a watering hole for a multitude of animals and a source of hydration for the area's once-copious plant life. When the region eventually became volcanically active, much of the life in the area was snuffed out and engulfed in the petrifying coat of lava. Today, the well-preserved remains of an ancient redwood forest and innumerable insects are found buried in the earth. The area has since been designated a national monument, dedicated not only to fossils but also to some of the homesteaders who settled there millions of years later.

Gold. Deep within the bowels of Rocky Mountain granite were woven innumerable veins of gold and silver ore, which made fortunes, and at times broke the spirits of those trying to extract it. One of the most bountiful areas for extracting gold was in Colorado, near the modern-day towns of Victor and Cripple Creek. It's been said that from 1896 to 1910 more than 22 million ounces of gold were extracted by five hundred mines from the area, amounting to a fortune of gold larger than both the California and Alaska gold rushes combined. Much of the discovery can be credited to Bob Womack, the first man to tap the bonanzas criss-crossing through the area. He did this in 1890, just 14 years after Colorado was inducted into the Union. Word of his find quickly spread, and like stockbrokers on a hot stock tip, fellow prospectors flocked to the area, hoping to duplicate Womack's luck—and many did.

Mile Marker 270 (US 24)—Florissant: Scenic driving is the most popular activity on the Gold Belt Tour, though there are plenty of activities if you want to stretch your legs, including the most common: camping, biking, hiking, fishing, walking, rock climbing, and river rafting, which are all easily accessible along the byway. Because of its many claims to fame, the Gold Belt Tour has not only been designated as a Colorado State Byway, but also a National Scenic Byway in 2000. A kiosk seen as soon as you enter town marks the entrance to the route and breaks the byway down into geographic and historical sections, showing us three legs.

The first leg is the Cripple Creek mining district, founded in the 1890s. The kiosk explains the route wagons took between Florissant and Cripple Creek during the largest gold boom in American history—as of 2005, the area has produced more than 731 tons of gold. The eastern leg of the byway follows Teller County Road 1 (CR 1), also known as Phantom Canyon Road, the route of the Florence/Cripple Creek Railroad—once the busiest narrow-gauge railroad in the West. Shelf Road, the middle leg on the byway, retraces a toll road used by stagecoaches bound for Cripple Creek and the valley of the Arkansas River. The road itself was blasted out of the side of Four Mile Canyon. The final leg is High Park Road, a route once used by prospectors bound for the Cripple Creek mining district and points south.

If you look to your left, toward a slight mound a few hundred yards away, you'll see the meadows where Chief Ouray—leader of the Tabeguache band of Ute—camped whenever he was in the area. Near this meadow is the stunted and slightly domed Fortification Hill. It was used by the Ute as a stronghold, and includes small reinforced walls, riffle pits, and hollowed-out boulders used to store grain. The site now rests on private property, so you can't access it without permission. And while the items on the hill are hard to discern, it's still possible to imagine braves hunkered down, weathering an attack.

On the right-hand side of the road, a small roofed-in area with cedar shingles covering three signs is embedded in masonry rock. The signs welcome you to Florissant, the northern gateway to the Gold Belt Tour Scenic and Historic Byway. They expound on the rich cultural legacy of the many different people who influenced the area, provide information on world-class fossils of the area, and describe its diverse activities.

As soon as you enter town, just past the stone-and-mortar kiosk, you'll come across a brown government sign directing you to turn left onto CR 1 to **Florissant Fossil Beds National Monument,** also the beginning of the Gold Belt Tour; you'll see **Thunderbird Inn** at this intersection. After turning down the road, look for the **Pikes Peak Historical Society Museum** on your right.

The **Hornbek Homestead** is on your right at Mile Marker 16. This log-cabin-style 1878 homestead is now nearly overrun with prairie dogs. An informational plaque near the site provides information about what you're seeing. The homestead is in impeccable shape. You can look through the windows and walk through the doors of some cabins in the compound. An old wagon is also on-site, and the complex is completed by a storage shed, main home, and a root cellar built into the side of a small hill. The homestead sits in a grassland basin, surrounded by pines. There are no large mountains, but numerous hills make it a rolling land-scape. The part of the basin untouched by pine is, in the summer, covered in wild-flowers and knee-high grass.

Mile Marker 16 (CR 1)—Florissant Fossil Beds National Monument: The turnoff to the Florissant Fossil Beds visitors center is on your right about 0.75 mile after Mile Marker 16. This is a day-use area, with gates opening at 9 AM and closing at 5 PM from Labor Day to Memorial Day, and 8 AM–6 PM all other times. A $3 fee is required to enter and is good for seven days. A wooden booth outside the visitors center has a drop box for money, and tags for paying visitors to take as proof of payment. Since it sits only 1 mile down the road from the Hornbeck Homestead, the scenery is a mirror-image of the prairie-dog-tunneled and wild-flower filled landscape of the homesteader's land. Wheelchair accessibility is easy to come by in and around the visitors center, with paved outdoor walkways con-necting various fossil finds, including the stumps of once-immense redwoods, and the fragile, fossilized exoskeletons of insects.

When leaving the park, turn right toward the mining-town-turned-gambling-hotspot of Cripple Creek. The surrounding area is extremely pastoral, with llama farms replacing the ubiquitous cattle ranches. The first llama farm you'll come

Llama farm off CR 9

across is on your right, at the intersection of CR 1 and Calle del Viento. When unsheared, the coats of these animals are shaggy and disheveled, and look as if an overzealous barber took what he needed in patches from their fur. The entire area has a certain down-home feel, a tight-knit ranching community where everyone knows their neighbor, and is all the happier for it. White picket fences outline property lines, providing a Norman Rockwell charm. Just after the ranch, look to your left for rock formations. These smooth-faced rocks are tan colored and tower hundreds of feet as they bulge out of the hillsides. They're akin to the rocks in Garden of the Gods near Colorado Springs, though they lack the signature red, and are easily double the size.

The scene here unfolds from meadow to pine- and rock-studded hilltop; then, in the distance, like indigo on a canvas, stands the outline of the backbone of America, the Rocky Mountains and the Continental Divide. At Deer Mountain Road, just before CR 12 and at nearby Mile Marker 10, look to your left for another view of these improbable boulders. It's a wonder they haven't rolled off the side of the mountain. The whole area seems to be built from these boulders, precariously placed one upon another, and it looks as if the roots of the hearty pines that have dared to grow between the crevasses are all that tether them to the mountain. Also at Mile Marker 10, the meadows dead-end into larger, more robust mountain peaks covered in evergreens and ochre rocks. There is yet another llama farm, **Stage Stop Llamas,** at Deer Field Circle on your left. This is an ideal photo shot to fool your friends into thinking you're in the Andes, as the llamas graze in a small meadow with Incan-wall-like rock formations behind them.

Continue straight on CR 1. The intersection with CR 1 and CR 11 is still part of the byway, but you won't see CR 11 again until the last leg. Just after the intersection, you leave the vast meadows and enter environs on the exposed rock and evergreen hills.

At Mile Marker 6, aspen begin to crop up, indicating that the road is rising in altitude. RV camping can be found just after Mile Marker 4 at **Lost Burro Camping and Lodging.** Access to this area is through a grove of pines down a lonely dirt road.

Mile Marker 3 (CR 1)—Cripple Creek: The scenery dissolves from pine-covered hills to rolling meadows as you enter the outskirts of town. A gas station is the first real business you see as you cross the town's threshold. Downtown Cripple Creek is a National Historic District, thanks to its gold-laden history. As you delve deeper

Cripple Creek

into town, you'll see what looks like an earth-toned flat-top mountain. Don't be fooled: What at first looks like a natural occurrence is really the effect of strip mining.

You will quickly come to a four-way stop at B Street and Carr Avenue. Take a right toward the business district. You'll pass an old stucco home on your left, doing its best impression of an art gallery as it advertises a stop to view its pieces. Your next turn is a left on Bennet, the next block over. The **Westward Ho Motel** will be on your right, and on your left is the **Jackass Café,** selling coffee and various food items. **Cripple Creek Inn** stands at the threshold of Cripple Creek's business district. This, the epicenter of town, consists of old brick buildings stretching no more than eight blocks. The most distinguished of these historic buildings is the **Teller County Courthouse,** a building still used for its original purpose. On the right, as you enter town and directly across from the courthouse, is a park dedicated to prisoners of war and those missing in action. It's composed of a tiny grassy area, gazebo, and large artillery gun.

Cripple Creek is one of five towns in Colorado graced with gambling licenses, though this one is by far the quaintest and least Vegaslike of the bunch. The town has worked hard to dilute the impersonal feel that plagues many casinos by exuding a heavy dose of personality and an Old West attitude. Even today, Cripple Creek provides visitors with the feeling that they've stumbled upon a romanticized frontier town, with a dash of civilization and old-timey gambling thrown in. In addition to the town itself, the streets are notorious venues for chrome-laden Harleys, both classic and contemporary, all very well kept.

Cripple Creek's downtown is tourist-centric, with every square inch filled to capacity with Western-façade storefronts. One of the most historic and opulent hotels in town is the **Palace Hotel & Casino** between First and Second Streets. Public parking is available in a lot directly across the street from the hotel, which makes for an ideal starting point if you decide to meander through town. Restaurants, knickknack stores, and several tastefully done casinos fill out the town. If you choose to stay at one of the town's many historical accommodations, consider the **Imperial Hotel,** an elegant and tastefully restored hotel that features quality Italian dining and the Gold Bar Room, a theatre hosting frequent shows. The **Carr Manor,** an old schoolhouse, is another good option.

At the end of the town's main street, which runs into a historic and still-functioning narrow-gauge rail line, take a left on Fifth Street. To your right, you'll immediately notice a forest-green railcar with markings identifying it as the one-time property of the Midland Railroad Company. The second life of this passenger car is as the **Cripple Creek Information Center.** Inside, helpful staffers provide pamphlets and word-of-mouth advice on the town, train, and other attractions. Ask for the walking tour of historic downtown, especially if you're into the gold lore of the area, including striking miners and bonanzas of ore. And if not, ask about current discounts or deals at area businesses. The itineraries of lucky travelers will coincide with summer melodramas, music, and movies at the historic **Butte Theatre** in town.

Behind the parking lot–stationed railcar/welcome center is the **Cripple Creek and Victor Narrow Gauge Railroad.** This still-functioning rail system's defining features are its diminutive size—akin to that of a glorified toy—and the color scheme in which it was painted. The train is painted with more colors than a rodeo clown's makeup, an effect that again adds to its child's-toy look. Because of its look and easy accessibility, the train is popular with kids, who often outnumber adults four to one. Rides depart from the train depot, connected by the same parking lot as the welcome center.

To continue on the byway itself, backtrack on W. Carr Avenue to Second and take a left toward Victor. Two route options quickly present themselves: one is a small dirt road, nearly mistaken for a rugged, rural driveway that leads down the middle spur of the byway along Shelf Road; the other is a paved route, leading down Phantom Canyon. If you aren't ready for a four-wheel-drive trip, or aren't properly equipped, continue along the paved path which has now become CR 67.

Outlaws and Lawmen Jail Museum, Cripple Creek

Continuing along CR 67, the road rises and twists slightly, cutting through evergreens and quaking aspen that shoulder their way between the pines to compete for patches of dirt. After a few turns, you can get a better view of the peeled-away sides of the strip-mined mountain, tiered like a Mayan pyramid. It's obvious from this mountain-moving endeavor that this area was once the site of the richest gold boom in American history. Old mining structures, riddled with holes connected by rust, still cling stubbornly to the mountainside, surrounded in dull yellow mine tailings. The stripped-down mountain before you is beautiful, despite the fact that it's being dismantled. The tailings of this modern-day mining are the color of a pastel rainbow—bronze, gold, and rust-tinged.

At Mile Marker 49, the road passes along an old, log-constructed, 30-yard tall and 220-yard long retaining wall left over from the mining days of yore. The logs aren't hewn, and were felled from surrounding thickets; parts of the wall no longer hold back the flow of yellow earth, as sections allow a fair amount of seepage. You may notice long, uninterrupted black plastic hoses running the height of the mountain. These are used as a drip system, constantly depositing water on the

Victor

exposed dirt to keep the potentially lung-burning dust down. Just after Mile Marker 49, you'll cross a modern bridge, look right for a change of scenery. Views into the valley basin present themselves, rolling with undulating hills of high meadow.

Mile Marker 46 (CR 67) — Victor: This town's much smaller than Cripple Creek, perhaps one-sixth the size, and does not have gambling, though its history can be found in spades. Brick and clapboard houses and businesses line the road. The most distinguishing feature is the whitewashed and gold-domed belfry ordaining Victor's **City Hall** to your left as you enter town. An old, reconditioned fire engine sits in its garage. The historic **Victor Hotel** is on your right, across from City Hall. Take a left on Fourth Street to continue along the byway, then take a right at the next intersection onto Diamond Avenue. You will pass the Colorado Trading and Transfer Company, a shuttered redbrick building with canary-yellow trimmed windows. Look around you once again for abandoned mining structures, which have been left to rot. The route can get a bit confusing here as you wind through the back streets of town, following the signage for the byway.

The number of mining structures here is almost absurd. Every mile you encounter half a dozen. Sometimes they're in open land; at other times, they're in people's front yards and backyards.

If you want to schedule a retreat in the area, look up the **D & B Ranch** bed & breakfast, tucked away in its own private canyon near Divide. One of the proprietors, Gary, hand-designed the three tasteful Jeffersonian cottages (they're really large enough to be considered spacious homes) next to a bubbling creek. Each is equipped with hand-selected antique furniture and full amenities, including breakfasts that the other proprietor, Jerry, makes for you. It's a quiet, peaceful retreat that is perfect for couples, families, and events such as weddings or reunions.

Mile Marker 2 (CR 67) — Phantom Canyon: Just before Mile Marker 2, the pavement ends. You've traded in manicured asphalt for the rock and gravel of Phantom Canyon Road. The rock on this road is extremely loose, and even in perfect conditions traveling too fast can cause a vehicle to fishtail, so be sure to enjoy the scenery at slow speed. Mile markers are as sparse as gas stations along this section of road — that is to say there are none. What would be around Mile Marker 8 into the canyon, the road narrows to a one-and-a-half-car width. To the left is an extreme drop-off where parts of the road have sheared away, making a jagged edge to the canyon side of the road. It looks as if someone took a giant bite out of the edge, leaving teeth marks where guardrails should be. Though this section maintains for a just a few hundred yards, the timid may swear it lasts for miles. Roughly 0.5 mile after you've left the left-hand drop-off, it's the passenger's turn to look down hundreds of feet as the guardrail-devoid edge threatens to suck the car over.

A few miles later, evidenced by a wooden bridge, the road again narrows to a single lane. The turns here are blind, as rock walls obscure your view; it's a good idea to sound your horn as you enter a blind turn to warn any oncoming, and equally blind, traffic. **Phantom Canyon** is composed of rock walls made of smoothed boulders separated by perfectly sanded fissures, while aspen and pine daringly grow where they are able. The rock walls are so precarious and improbable, it's a wonder they don't topple. Notice that many are topped with a single boulder, like the watchtower of a citadel. About halfway through the canyon you hit the rest stop at **Dunville.** You can find information here on the canyon and the trains that once ran across the same road you are now driving. Restrooms are

Phantom Canyon Road

also available here. The canyon begins to open up at this rest stop, and the rock formations, though still a fixture, are farther from the road.

Look for small signs along the canyon's road indicating various towns. Don't be confused by the lack of structures; the tiny markers are indicating where towns once were, mostly gold-mining and rail stops that have since disappeared into obscurity and have been reclaimed by nature. After a few miles, and a few more of the less-than-ghost towns, the canyon walls again hedge in the road.

As you follow this dirt road, try to avoid skidding along the gravel and dirt, where kiddy-pool-sized potholes make for a perilous drive. A gritty scent reminiscent of a rodeo arena fills your nose with an earthy smell. Although particulate clogs your pores, the touch of raw nature in the backcountry is a welcome sight. Occasionally, another car or truck bounces toward you, and slight waves are exchanged in acknowledgment of a compatriot in this relatively unused area.

After the "town" of Dale, the rock walls are at their peak, both physically and aesthetically. The boulder-constructed valley walls are more compact, covered in streaks of lichen and moss. The walls threaten to crush the road between them. Sections of the walls here are so close to your window you can almost reach out and touch both walls at the same time, as the road is barely large enough for a full-size truck to pass through.

Shortly after the narrow section of valley, the bumps in the road disappear for a brief yet joyous few yards as you cross **Steel Bridge.** It's a steel-framed, wooden-planked bridge that seems to have been taken from a coastal town's boardwalk. At the far end of the bridge are placards providing information on the 1897-constructed bridge and the railroad that once traversed a bridge that spanned the same spot, built years before the current incarnation and long since gone. About 1 mile after Steel Bridge is a 30-yard dynamite-blasted tunnel blown through granite. Very little in the way of finishing has been done to the tunnel, as the walls are just slightly less ragged than the road you're driving. The one-lane **Upper Tunnel** makes for a quirky and popular photo stop—there is a pullout on the right just before you enter. Just after the tunnel is a rest stop named Twelve, a prayer answered for those in desperate need of a bathroom break.

For most of the byway, Eightmile Creek has been running along the road. Though incognito for the majority of the way, the creek shows itself in earnest right after the Twelve rest stop. During the spring melt, the creek runs full force, but by midsummer, it's much more sedate. The creek's refusal to take a straight line through the rock canyon led, over many years, to the winding nature of the canyon itself.

Also after the Twelve rest stop is the second, and final, dynamite-carved auto tunnel along the road, **Lower Tunnel.** This tunnel is perhaps a few yards shorter than Upper Tunnel, but is no less impressive. A few miles after the tunnel, look for a small bridge marked 215. A small dirt road leads down to Eightmile Creek on the right, and is the first real chance for visitors to get out and dip their toes in the cold, clear water.

Near the intersection of CO 123, when the land opens up a bit and the rock walls disappear, pavement once again graces the byway. The rocks that remain have turned a deep red, like that of a Southwestern sunset. In the distance are the outlines of the serrated Wet Mountains. Although the immensity of the rock walls lingers in your mind from the last section of byway, these deep gray-colored behemoths dwarf them, even at a distance.

A few miles after this scene first presents itself the byway intersects with US 50. Taking this route west leads to Canon City and the **Royal Gorge Bridge and Park,** while heading east takes travelers to the town of Pueblo, the largest settlement in the southeast region of Colorado. It's a valid option for those who want to cut the byway short and return to a town with adequate lodging. There are quite a few buttes, hogbacks, and mesas in the basin before you reach the tiny, pastoral town of Florence, your next stop. Again, llama farms spring up about 1 mile after CR 67 crosses US 50 at Mile Marker 13. As you enter the town of Florence at Mile Marker 12, you cross a strong-flowing and muddy Arkansas River, roughly 50 yards wide.

The hamlet of Florence sits in a grove of cottonwood trees that leech off the Arkansas's banks. Houses are tucked into the folds of the open areas between trees. Houses are the well-kept, unpretentious structures of a hard-working, blue-collar community.

You might notice a few with boats in their driveways, ready for an outing on Lake Pueblo to the southeast. When you hit the intersection of CO 115 and Pikes Peak Avenue, take a right on CO 115 toward Canon City to continue along the byway. Once you do, you enter the business district of Florence, with hardware stores, antique shops, knickknack stores, coffeehouses, gas stations, and **Florence Rose Bed & Breakfast,** a Victorian-style B&B located on CO 115, roughly 0.5 mile before Mile Marker 7. At Mile Marker 7, you leave the town of Florence behind. Consider a stop in town if you'd like to continue the route at a later time.

At the intersection of CO 115 and US 50 is the town of Canon City. Take a right onto US 50 to begin the four-wheel-drive-only section of the Gold Belt Tour. To skip this section, travel left on US 50 toward Salida. Once you turn right onto US 50, the road travels though an area filled with both locally owned and chain restaurants, as well as gas stations and motels. Though not the prettiest section of town, it is perhaps the most utilitarian. Continue straight along US 50 for a few miles to access the **Winery at Holy Cross Abbey.** Once an abbey, it now functions as an intricately carved, steeple-laden stop for wine aficionados. A few more miles along the highway sits a tiny log cabin amid a heavily used road and surrounded by strip malls; this seemingly out-of-place structure serves as a tourist information center. Look for the large stegosaurus out front. Stock up on any additional tourism information here, find out about road conditions, or chat up the friendly locals. It's a good excuse to stretch your legs and gather your wits before starting the off-highway section of the byway.

After the welcome center, backtrack to the intersection of US 50 and CO 115 to Reynolds Avenue and take a right. It gets a little tricky in here, so be sure to keep your wits about you. If done correctly, you should pass a car wash on your right, then you'll enter a residential area, misleading in its own right. Roughly 1

Colorado Territorial Correctional Facility in Canon City

mile after turning onto Reynolds, take a right at Field. You'll quickly come upon a yield sign; stay right to continue onto Field toward Red Canyon and Garden Park Fossil Area. After this mazelike route out of town, you leave the high-mountain basin and once again head toward sandstone-dominated landscape. To your right babbles Fourmile Creek, with never-ending cottonwoods lining its banks.

At Mile Marker 3 is **Cleveland Quarry Recreation Site,** a day-use area with pit toilets and informational signs that delve into information about the fossil-producing quarry once found here. Just after this small park, on the left, is an informational sign at a small U-shaped dirt pullout, providing information on the **Garden Park Fossil Area.** The sign relates that a number of museum-quality dinosaur fossils have been found in the area, including stegosaurus and long-necked herbivores, among others.

Mile Marker 6—Red Canyon Park: At Mile Marker 6 is **Red Canyon Park.** As soon as you hit this landmark, the land cracks and yawns with valleys. The 500-

acre public park is synonymous with red rock formations, including sandstone towers that reach upward of 100 feet high. At Dilley Ranch, on your left, and roughly 1.5 miles after Red Canyon Park, the pavement once again disappears and becomes roughly graded reddish dirt. As is the norm, when the pavement ends, mile markers become scarce.

Quickly after Dilley Ranch, near Mile Marker 10, the road halves itself and become a one-lane affair as you officially enter Shelf Road. The driving here is slow going. It's a good idea to engage your four-wheel drive before continuing on. Shelf Road was originally constructed in 1892, and was considered cumbersome and precarious even by 19th-century standards. It was carved out of limestone cliff faces to connect Canon City to the Arkansas valley. The only route between the two cities, it was administered by tollbooth operators who lived in tiny cabins at the beginning and end of the road. The road was a venture bankrolled by entrepreneurs in Canon City, intent on squeezing money not only from the mountainsides, but from the pockets of travelers as well. Blind turns and loose dirt are still the norm, as are the sheer and guardrail-devoid edges of the road.

The striations of limestone on the left, if you can tear your eyes away from the drop-off, are impressive displays of pinks, reds, whites, and mauves.

Mile Markers 11 and 12 (Shelf Road): Just before Mile Marker 11, be daring and look straight down the gorge at the remains of one of the road-keeper's log cabins, sans roof. Looking straight ahead, large sandstone buttes present themselves, each sporting more striations, with segments perhaps 20 feet wide and colored with pastels.

At Mile Marker 12, the drop-off reaches an extreme, and the cliff sides are sheerer, composed of cracked boulder walls with rocks stacked upon one another. This section is one of the highest on Shelf Road. Immediately after reaching this pinnacle, you descend down toward Fourmile Creek and at Mile Marker 2 (the markers abruptly change) you cross a spillway bridging the sides of the valley. The tattered warning sign stationed before the river crossing advises against continuing on if water has crested the concrete spillway. As flash floods have been known to happen in this narrow valley, it's a warning with teeth. However, the water is usually at a respectable level and flows beneath the crossing. This stop makes for the best photo opportunity of the byway, with views up and down the valley, as well as to the heights of the red-rocked walls that envelop the road. The creek runs through it all—it's a "can't-miss" shot. Just after Mile Marker 3—the mile marker numbers are again counting forward—the waxy, dark-green gamble oaks grow in abundance, reaching into the road as if to scratch the paint off your car with talonlike leaves. Just after Mile Marker 3, the road begins a steep incline, and if you didn't already, engaging your four-wheel drive becomes a necessity.

After about 0.5 mile through the incline, look straight ahead and up toward the top of the far canyon's wall. You'll readily notice **Window Rock,** a nearly perfect square hole that looks like an intentionally carved window to the azure sky behind the red rocks. Bighorn sheep are common visitors to this wind- and water-carved landmark area. This is the last true landmark of this section of the byway. Around 1 or 2 miles after Window Rock, the byway descends and the strip mining on the near horizon lets you know that Cripple Creek is a short drive away.

Mile Marker 9 (Shelf Road)—Cripple Creek: With the ever-thickening of abandoned mining structures along the roadside, you once again enter Cripple Creek at Mile Marker 9. It's an interesting experience, traveling though wilderness to be

Downtown Cripple Creek

Window Rock on Shelf Road

greeted so abruptly by civilization, but Cripple Creek may just be the best town to welcome you back to your fellow humans. It looks unchanged since the 1800s gold boom, allowing you a taste of what a miner returning from a sojourn in the backcountry must have felt. The resurgence of smooth, black asphalt quickly steals that romanticized vision away, but lends comfort to your road-shaken bones.

To access the westernmost and final leg of the byway, travel north through town to the intersection of CR 11 and CR 1. To do so, turn left into town (Second Street), then left again onto Bennet, and, at the four-way stop and Westward Ho Motel, take a right, which is B Street. The final turn is left onto Carr Avenue (CR 1) toward the post office. Follow this road to the intersection with CR 11. Take a left onto CR 11 to finish the Gold Belt Tour Scenic and Historic Byway.

Intersection of CR 1 and CR 11: At the intersection of these county roads, there is a scenic and informational pullout providing more information about the byway, and probably most importantly, pit toilets. As you look to your left 1 mile after the intersection, take in the view of **Wright's Reservoir,** the largest single body of water on the byway. You can access the reservoir at Mile Marker 9. Picnic areas and pathways leading directly to its banks are available.

The rest of the byway is more of a connector road to Royal Gorge Bridge and Park than a scenic or historic section in its own right. Along the way, however, sights of 14,110-foot Pikes Peak to the north can be made out on clear days. And to the southwest horizon are the fairly faint silhouettes of the Sangre de Cristo Mountains.

Mile Marker 271 (CR 3A)—Royal Gorge Bridge and Park: The Royal Gorge Bridge and Park is home to the highest suspension bridge in the U.S., an aerial tram that traverses the gorge, and an incline railroad that scales a 100-percent grade—not to mention the **Royal Gorge Route Railroad** a classic railroad that runs along the gorge floor, alongside the Arkansas River. When you first see the bridge from the byway, it looks like any other suspension bridge. But as you near its entrance, you see the ground give way and form the dramatic, granite-walled, and aptly named Royal Gorge. While there is no official town, the Royal Gorge anchors a number of businesses that have hoped to ride the coattails of this popular natural attraction. An RV campground, restaurants, motels, gas stations, helicopter tours, and even river-rafting companies that shoot the intimidating class IV rapids along the Arkansas River through the gorge are in abundance.

IN THE AREA

FLORISSANT

Accommodations

Thunderbird Inn, 17801 CR 1. Call 719-748-3968.

Attractions and Recreation

Hornbek Homestead, 719-748-3253. www.reporterherald.com/columnists /ghost-towns/ci_20249241/adeline -hornbek-homesteaded-near -florissant.

Pikes Peak Historical Society Museum, 18033 CR 1. Call 719-748-8259.

Stage Stop Llamas, 8918 CR 1. Call 719-689-9010.

CRIPPLE CREEK

Accommodations

Carr Manor, 350 E. Carr Ave. Call 719-689-3709.

Cripple Creek Inn, 123 May Ave. Call 719-689-2288.

Imperial Hotel, 123 N. Third St. Call 719-689-2516.

Lost Burro Camping and Lodging, 4023 CR 1. Call 719-689-2345.

Palace Hotel & Casino, 172 E. Bennett Ave. Call 719-689-2992.

Westward Ho Motel, 236 W. Bennett Ave. Call 719-689-0622.

Attractions and Recreation

Butte Theater, 139 E. Bennett Ave. Call 719-689-6402.

Cripple Creek Information Center, corner of Fifth St. and Bennett Ave. www.visitcripplecreek.com /businesses/cripple-creek -information-center-train-car.

Cripple Creek and Victor Narrow Gauge Railroad, 520 E. Carr St. Call 719-689-2640.

Teller County Courthouse, 101 W. Bennett Ave. Call 719-689-2543.

Dining/Drinks

Jackass Café, 227 W. Bennett Ave. Call 719-689-3900.

VICTOR

Accommodations

Victor Hotel, 321 Victor Ave. Call 719-689-3553.

Attractions and Recreation

City Hall, 500 Victor Ave. Call 719-689-2284.

DIVIDE

Accommodations

D & B Ranch, 6250 CR 61. Call 719-686-9004.

FLORENCE

Accommodations

Florence Rose Bed & Breakfast, 1305 W. Third St. Call 719-784-4734.

CANON CITY

Accommodations

Royal Gorge KOA, 559 CR 3A. Call 719-275-6116.

Attractions and Recreation

Royal Gorge Bridge and Park, 4218 CR 3-A. Call 719-275-7507 or 1-888-333-5597.

Royal Gorge Route Railroad, 401 Water St. Call 719-276-4000 or 1-888-724-5748.

Winery at Holy Cross Abbey, 3011 E. US 50. Call 719-276-5191 or 1-877-422-9463.

FRONT RANGE

A view from Summit Lake Park *Seth K. Hughes*

Trail at Summit Lake Park *Seth K. Hughes*

9 Mount Evans Scenic and Historic Byway

Estimated length: 49 miles

Estimated time: 2 hours

Highlights: Enjoy the views from above 14,000 feet at the Crest House; put your bare feet in the crystal blue waters of Summit Lake; explore the ancient Ponderosa pine forest near Mount Goliath Trailhead; cheer on the road cyclists climbing this hill; tour Idaho Springs's Argo Gold Mine and relax in the hot springs.

Getting there: From Denver, travel down I-70 west toward the town of Idaho Springs. From Grand Junction, take I-70 east toward Idaho Springs. Take the Mount Evans Road exit on CO 103, just after the town of Idaho Springs.

History: The history of this, the highest paved road in the United States, is filled with feuding, burgeoning mining towns, and ravaging fires that gave the Front Range one of its most intriguing 20th-century ruins at an incredible altitude; its historical origins can accurately be traced to the time of World War I, Prohibition, and even the Spanish-American War.

In the late 1800s and early 1900s, when Colorado was a hotbed of growth, industry, and burgeoning state power, the mayors of Denver and Colorado Springs found themselves pitted against one another in a contest to prove which city was the brighter beacon for progress in a state that had been inducted into the Union merely two decades prior. They both realized that the way to bolster their cities was through economic dominance. And with the expansion of the railroads, and increased army presence throughout the region, tourism was coming of age in America. All throughout the new West, the prospect of money from the East flowing into the region buoyed the importance of tourism as a means to an

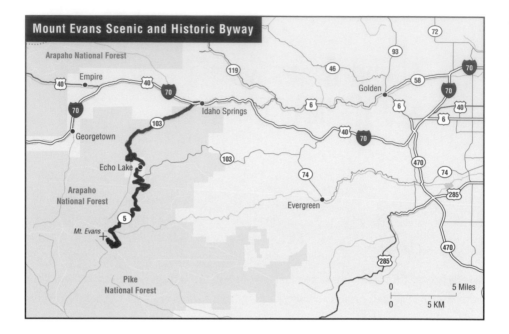

economic end. In fact, whether the gentry of these rising cities thought about it or not, the precious ore in the mines would one day be tapped, but money from tourism could prove to be a perpetual source of funds, long after the last bonanza had been discovered.

The American West was a source of fantasy and wonder to those who lived in the East. They were inundated with stories of hardship, perseverance, and heroism. Influential painters like Albert Bierstadt were capturing the landscape, painting the sweeping panoramas of geographical features never before imagined by Americans. After all, in comparison to the highest peaks in the East, like the Appalachian Mountains, the Rocky Mountains, especially in Colorado, smashed previous notions of scale in nature. Coupled with the romantic desire to see and travel the West, the idea of manifest destiny still lingered in the American psyche, drawing many to explore and visit the "unknown" areas west of the Mississippi River. At the time, the prevailing mentality of Americans was that it was their spiritual and social duty to expand and explore—summed up in the phrase "manifest destiny."

As leaders of Western towns and cities began to exploit and woo this cash source, ever-more-creative ideas of how to accomplish this goal emerged. And along the way, rivalries were sparked. Since their inceptions in the mid-1800s, the cities of Denver and Colorado Springs had been battling, first for recognition as the state's capital city, then for economic influence—a battle, some would argue, that still goes on today. It was Colorado Springs that first took advantage of the city's nearby mountains, which top out at more than 14,000 feet. When the city constructed a tollway on the road up the north side of Pikes Peak in the late 1800s, tourism began to gravitate toward Colorado Springs and away from the Denver area. This road was one of the first of its kind, as it made it easy for nonmountaineering types to interact with the behemoth mountains of the West.

But Denver has never been the type of town to roll over and shun the limelight. In 1917, Mayor Speer used his influence to procure state funds for the construction of Mount Evans Road, which would terminate at the summit, some 14,264 feet above sea level, while climbing more than 7,000 feet in 28 miles, making it the highest paved road in the U.S.—a record that still stands today. While this road didn't obliterate the tourism at Pikes Peak (it is still Colorado's most visited mountain), Mount Evans Road did give the Denver area an equal shake in enticing visitors.

Continual improvements, such as guardrails added on the switchback-laden route, were made, and in 1942 the construction of a stone-and-mortar restaurant at the summit was completed. This structure, known as Crest House, gave visitors another reason to visit the top. Now, they could grab a warm meal, browse the souvenir racks, and still take in the majestic views of the Rocky Mountains. Unfortunately for today's visitor, it burned down in 1979, leaving skeletal remains behind. Due to the cost associated with reconstruction and upkeep, it has never been rebuilt. This 20th-century ruin now affords only observation decks and windbreaks for visitors.

Not much has changed since the late 1970s. Road improvements are constantly made to battle the deteriorating effects of high-mountain winters on the asphalt. A few pullouts and a new section of road have been built, connecting Echo Lake to Bergen Park, allowing visitors more access to the mountain's tundra terrain.

Idaho Springs. As you travel along the busy and valley-walled I-70 heading west, the town of Idaho Springs stretches to your right. It's a small mining community turned tourist town. The town has three main visitor draws: whitewater rafting, tours of the once-prolific **Argo Gold Mine and Mill Museum,** and the natural hot springs that feed the **Indian Hot Springs Healing Waters Spa.**

The mine is striking, as it is easily the largest structure in town, built into the northern cliff wall and looming over the town. Its wooden walls are painted caboose-red. Its color is just slightly faded, enough to let you know it wasn't always just part of a guided tour but was once a working mine, whose riches fed Colorado's booming economy—a fact bolstered by sulfur-colored mine tailings surrounding it like a lion's mane.

The hot springs sign, like a beacon from the highway, nearly matches the Argo mine's call for attention. The sign shimmers with thousands of tiny metal plates, sending sunlight and headlights dancing off its reflective surface. Amid the shimmer, passersby can decipher a message: hot mineral springs, American Indian springs resort, cave baths, hot tubs, pools. You can access this relaxing getaway on Soda Creek Road, in the middle of town.

Downtown Idaho Springs is very busy, quaint, and exceedingly walkable. This is a tourist town, and for good reason: It is not only the gateway to Mount Evans, but it also offers a slew of other outdoor and indoor activities. Every block and shop along Miner Street, the town's main thoroughfare, is tourist-centered, with restaurants, bed & breakfasts, guide services, and knickknack stores. The entire town exudes the essence of an old mining town, with ornate and frontier-style buildings. Consider parking near the Old Town Hall at the corner of Miner Street and 17th Avenue; parking is free and ample.

Exit 240 (I-70)—Start of CO 103: This road is open until snow hinders the drive—some sections aren't plowed—but even in the summertime it can be an intimidating route. So unless you have nerves of steel, are incredibly confident in your driving abilities, or just have an absolutely insatiable desire to get to the top during inclement weather, wait for the warmer months to try this drive. On the flip side, the omnipresent cyclists don't populate the road during winter, so you won't have them to contend with.

Even in midsummer, small patches of hard-packed snow can still appear on the side of the road. These stubborn clusters look like hard plastic or Styrofoam, as they've congealed to retain the cold and are still pristine white, and not soiled brown patches one would expect on a heavily trafficked byway. Needless to say, there is no stopping to take pictures wherever you like, as the narrow road just won't allow it. Roadside pullouts need to be used to take a shot, unless you've got a willing photographer in the passenger seat. While well placed, the pullouts are not plentiful, so take advantage of them when they come.

Soon after passing the entrance sign to Idaho Springs is exit 240 (CO 103), which leads toward the Mount Evans Scenic and Historic Byway. Also found at this exit is access to the **Clear Creek Ranger District.** Stop here for maps of the route, printed guides on wildlife viewing, a plant-identification chart, and other trip-related paraphernalia. At the stop sign at the end of the exit, take a left to continue onto the byway and access the ranger station. A right leads you into Idaho Springs past the **Buffalo Restaurant and Bar** and a Shell station. This is the last gas station you'll see before beginning your skyward route, so if you don't have a full, or nearly full, tank, refill here. Be wary, as this busy intersection has awkward street lines and no stoplights.

Across from the ranger station is a public parking area of compacted dirt. Bicyclists with stamina find this a popular place to park. You'll see quite a few of them as they pedal up to the more-than-14,000-foot summit—fittingly enough, the parking area is right next to the Clear Creek Ambulance Station. This is an exceptionally popular ride for cyclists, so in addition to paying attention to the road and high-mountain scenery, you'll have to work on sharing the road with struggling, yet determined two-wheelers. There is no shoulder on this road, so bikers make use of the road, making it difficult to pass. Be patient when attempting any sort of maneuver. In addition to pedal bikes, motorcycles are also found in abundance, rumbling up toward the high altitudes.

After you cross the overpass to reach the ranger station, you may notice a number of giant, brightly colored rafts putting in on Clear Creek to shoot the rapids. Various local companies, like **Adventures in Whitewater,** are the experts on this section of river, and reservations can be made in the town of Idaho Springs. If you don't want to raft, but would like to see brave souls fight their fears, take the small pedestrian bridge over the freeway for an unencumbered view of rafters beginning their half- and full-day trips.

As you continue the drive, evergreens surround the road and lead up the mountain walls that corral you in. Chicago Creek also runs alongside the road here, fed from two lakes, Upper Chicago and Lower Chicago, situated near the top of Mount Evans. The über-popular **Cottonwood RV and Mobile Home Park** is on your left, 0.5 mile after Mile Marker 1, tucked into the folds of the base of Mount Evans. Finding a spot is doable, though many RVs tend to stay for extended periods, taking up some of the real estate for a good chunk of time.

After the RV park, the road begins an incline just enough so as to cause notice, though nowhere near the steep climbs to come. Just before Mile Marker 2, look to your left for an unencumbered view of a large, abandoned mining structure, whose green paint still hangs stubbornly to its wooden walls. Just after Mile Marker 3, on your left, is a small turnoff for **Big Spruce Cabins,** log-cabin dwellings lining the banks of the tiny Clear Creek. A fair number of houses are built along the banks of this miniature run of water. The walls of the creek have been built up with rocks to further tame the river and stay the hand of erosion that would otherwise slowly eat away at their foundations.

Mile Marker 4 (CO 103): At Mile Marker 4, you pass **Mount Evans Trout Fishing,** where they claim you can catch wild trout. While advertised as "wild," these trout are confined to a relatively small pond. If you have a tiny angler in the bunch, or you just want to massage your own ego, consider stopping by and dropping in a line: you're almost guaranteed to reel one in. And if you didn't start your drive geared up to hook a trout, Mount Evans Trout Fishing will supply you with everything from rod and reel to bait and hook.

After Mile Marker 4, shining leaves of quaking aspen ruffle in the seemingly nonexistent breeze. They seem to wave at you as you drive by, shimmering in the sunshine, showing drivers both sides of their leaves, one lighter than the other, giving the impression of mirrors reflecting sunlight. These animated trees grow thicker as you pass Mile Marker 5. Just after Mile Marker 5 is a pullout on the left, another popular starting area for bikers, as it makes a convenient spot to drop your car off until you're ready to reclaim it after the ride.

After Mile Marker 6, the valley narrows and you begin to wind quite a bit more as you follow the road that follows the creek that cuts a path down the mountainside. National Forest Service–run **West Chicago Creek Campground** is accessed on the right, 3 miles down West Chicago Road (County Road 114 [CR 114]); you'll see it just slightly before you enter **Arapaho National Forest**—all roughly 0.5 mile after Mile Marker 6. After you cross the forest's threshold, you double back on a turn. Look to your left for a view of an exposed granite cliff face, where even the tenacious pine have trouble clinging. With this dramatic curve in the road, the byway begins a no-nonsense ascent, with hairpin turns, sheer dropoffs, and (thankfully) guardrails (though these barriers do disappear later in the trip, when you feel the most dire need for them).

Just before Mile Marker 8, on the right side of the road, is a dirt pullout to the **Chicago Forks Picnic Grounds** of Arapaho National Forest. The picnic area is near the quietly babbling Clear Creek, and is within a grove of aspen and pine. Across the road from this picnic area is a turnoff for a phenomenal photo opportunity of the brook cascading down rocks. It's an image you'd expect to be milked for all it's worth in selling a tourist destination.

Just after Mile Marker 9, look to your left. The trees clear, and you're struck by the realization of how high you are. Across the valley you see other mountain peaks rolling away into the horizon, covered in evergreen and aspen. There is a scenic pullout on the left near here, at a hairpin turn just before Mile Marker 10, where you can focus on the view, instead of the road. And on the right, directly after the pullout, is another picnic area, **Ponder Point,** perched on an overhang that looks over the valley. It's a fitting name for the place. A BBQ stand is also available for those wishing to stoke up the grill In the fall, the ample aspen nearby add a hue of gold to the immediate area.

At Mile Marker 12 is a modest shrine, constructed of a masonry arch, with a Forest Service medallion. At one point in its life, it had a fountain attached to it, but now it's run-down and certainly isn't worth the stop.

Just after Mile Marker 12, look straight ahead and you'll see the granite peaks of Mount Evans. Even in midsummer, the bald granite tips, the highest in the area,

Summit Lake Park *Seth K. Hughes*

Drive carefully! *Seth K. Hughes*

are snow-crusted. Now, on the right side, you come upon **Echo Lake**—this is a popular stopping point for those on their way to the top, on their way back down, or for those who never had any intention of continuing on to the summit. Echo Lake's placid surface is home to nearly as many bobbers and hopeful anglers on its shores as there are fish in the water. This multipurpose site has restrooms, pavilions (usually the scene of a child's birthday party), a number of picnic tables dispersed throughout a wooded area, and two hiking trails—one that circumnavigates the lake, and the other that leads well into the forest and wilderness area to Lower and Upper Chicago Lakes, and then on to the summit of Mount Evans.

Mile Marker 13 (CO 103): Back on the road, take a right to Mount Evans at Mile Marker 13. **Echo Lake Lodge,** a large, forest-green, log-cabin-style building, is at this intersection. It's a popular waypoint for motorcyclists and those who want to stock up on a few for-the-road snack items. Another parking area for bicyclists is found along the left side of the road here, directly across from the lodge.

A few yards after the turnoff are ranger tollbooths, set up to collect a $10 entrance fee for cars. Look for a whiteboard prominently displayed near the tollbooths for a schedule of daily events held at various points along the byway. Often, these events are ranger talks on the flora and fauna of the diverse ecosystems through which this byway cuts. Basic information regarding current temperature, wind speed, and the like is also displayed here. The pass you purchase at the booth is good for three consecutive days, so if you're staying in the area, don't feel like you have to hit every spot on your first trip up; you can spread the wealth a bit—though most visitors choose to drive it just once within that time period, as they are on a tight schedule and there is quite a bit to do in this section of the state besides driving the highest paved road in North America.

Mile Marker 1 (Mount Evans Road): Mile Marker 1 marks the very first switchback turn after entering the toll area, and begins a trend that only ends when the road runs out of pavement, at the summit. No off-highway vehicles are allowed in this area, and trailers are highly discouraged, as the road can get a bit hairy, and there's no place to camp here anyway. Sticking to the road, unless you want to hoof a section or two, is the only way to see the area. Grand vistas at the beginning of this section are nonexistent, and the forest that surrounds you gives you the feeling of security, like you're being tucked into a comforting blanket. Then, at Mile Marker 3, the entire scene opens up as the forest blanket is thrust off, and the whole world is spread out at your feet. Look out on the horizon, ringed in mountaintops and evergreens. Guardrails disappear as you enter the park, replaced instead by steep drop-offs.

Between Mile Markers 3 and 4, the air in midday smells of sap and warm pine, a very calming and nature-defining scent. A crispness to the otherwise warm summer air can be detected, as a slight breeze tickles your skin just enough to cool you off. The pines soon begin to look gnarled, cracked, and twisted, evidence of the harsh winters these plants must endure. At this point, look out your right window; the road you were sure your tires were touching is nowhere to be seen. The sight of solid ground has been replaced by the vista of a sheer and immense drop-off. It's the same sensation one gets when looking out over the wing of an airplane at altitude. Below you, on the right, a view of Echo Lake presents itself, now far below. Its deep blue looks like a small, dark inkwell of indigo. You can now also see beyond the formerly horizon-defining tree-covered mountaintops. Past them are yet more mountains, though their lack of trees and ample veins of snow evidence their great heights. Clouds shed shadows on the vast forest floor beneath you. Giant swaths of transparent grays slowly roll across the land. Even the shadows of these giant clouds are dwarfed by the amount of acreage covered by these forests. You're now past the pine, and high tundra takes their place, with delicate yellow flowers dotting the landscape among rocks and short grasses. When you hit Mile Marker 4, the tundra begins in earnest, though the vistas remain.

Past Mile Marker 4, you begin to encounter the exposed granite domes of the higher altitudes. They are so enormous that looking at them while driving may cause the slight feeling of vertigo. The rock is smooth in areas and craggy in others, shaped and sheared by the tireless efforts of nature.

At 0.5 mile past Mile Marker 4 is a paved pullout area, often packed with cars.

Viewpoint about halfway up Mount Evans *Seth K. Hughes*

A picnic table and informational signs directing you to **Mount Goliath Trailhead** are both found here. This is an ideal photo stop to see the vast expanses of the valley below. Parking is quite tough to come by, as this is little more than a horseshoe pullout with no official parking spots. Giant boulders are piled up along this area, and nimble visitors climb among them as others take their photos. The mountaintops that you look over are akin to a tumultuous ocean that fades into the horizon, never calm, but trapped in midwave break.

Mile Marker 6 (Mount Evans Road): Just after Mile Marker 6, look down and you can see **Upper Chicago Lake,** one of the two lakes that feeds the creek in the valley. It's a thin, oval lake with a small cascading stream that tumbles over boulders and through pine to feed the trout-stocked **Lower Chicago Lake.** You can access the lakes from the summit, though via an arduous hike—most are content to see both lakes from afar. A number of dead trees can be seen near the lake; some laying on their sides and others still standing stoically, like a soldier unwilling to leave his post.

If you've been worrying about the sheer drop-off, Mile Marker 7 brings some relief, as the drops become less extreme. Guardrails are still absent, but at least you can release the grip on the steering wheel just slightly. After Mile Marker 8 you are very near the tops of the granite peaks. Here, you come across a giant concave wall, nearly encircling the snowmelt-fed Summit Lake—even in mid-July this lake is mostly ice-covered. There is a major pullout on the right, **Summit Lake Park,** that offers access to the lake's nearest bank, as well as a stop for a ranger talk, hiking trail (that leads 2.7 miles to the top of Mount Evans), and informational kiosks. When you get out of your car to take advantage of any of these activities, the change in temperature becomes obvious; it can drop at least 20 degrees Fahrenheit from when you started, which prompts the use of a light jacket, or at least quick movements and the occasional breath into cupped hands.

The road here is atrocious. While still paved, it rolls more than the hills in the distance. Take it slow or you're likely to jostle a few fillings loose. At the far end of the parking lot is a natural window across a valley, overlooking a striated red-hued rock wall, sheer, immense, and beautiful in its rawness. Kiosks stand at the short trailheads that lead down to the lakefront. The signs provide information on the beauty and rarity of the area, and details on why preservation of these types of natural features is environmentally important. As you read the signs, you look into the bowl that holds Summit Lake, with a granite, snow-speckled cliff holding in the waters of the far bank. When walking around the area, take it slow, it's easy to become short of breath at this altitude, even if you're accustomed to the elevation.

Back on the byway, you notice that the lake trickles down the mountain, not in a uniform stream, but seeps out, creating marshlands as it travels to lower elevations. It spreads out across the tundra, creating pockets of small pools that are actually slowly flowing water, composing a dispersed river, much like a floodplain.

Mile Marker 10 (Mount Evans Road): At Mile Marker 10, the road narrows and the centerline disappears. Just after this decrease in road size, look left and below you for an invigorating view of a rocky plateau. Its sides are sheer ochre-colored granite, with a pale pink hue. There are a few intense switchbacks just after this view, which force cars to take it slow. In fact, you come to a near complete stop while making the turns. There are still no lines or guardrails, but cyclists do persist, so an extra dose of caution is advised.

After Mile Marker 10, and the stick-shift-stalling switchbacks, you cross over to the other side of the valley and are afforded the opportunity to look down into the opposite side of the mountain for a new perspective. Again, mountains covered in relatively sharp granite and touched with snow still disappear into the horizon, but there are fewer of them and they are more densely packed. At the third switchback, after crossing to the other side of the mountain, is a small trailhead leading off into the wilderness. It's accessed via a small parking area, so it's hit-or-miss on finding a spot to park here. All this time you're increasing altitude at an astonishing rate; you can actually feel the air getting thinner with every foot you travel, and the ambient temperature again drops.

Trailhead at Summit Lake Park
Seth K. Hughes

At Mile Marker 12, around a sharp turn, look to the peak in front of you for a view of a large observatory, used by local colleges for gazing into the heavens. Spotting this landmark identifies the last few turns of the byway as you near the top.

There is a large boulder mound on your left as you approach the peak's parking lot. A trail zigzags up this small, few-hundred-foot mound and leads to the highest point on the mountain. It's common to see families making the short 10-minute hike to stand atop one of the highest points in the

Mountain goats at Summit Lake Park
Seth K. Hughes

continental U.S. The parking area is a hub of activity, as it's the final destination. The parking area is disappointingly small for such a draw, so you may have to circle a few times before you can find a spot. At the summit, you'll notice the modern ruins of an old restaurant, the **Crest House,** which once served the masses who reached the summit. It was constructed from rocks in the area, as transporting material up the mountainscape would have been inconceivable. The design of the building wasn't a typical boxlike structure either. Instead, its frame was constructed to mimic the contours and spikes of the mountain peak itself, so as to blend into, as opposed to taking away from, the view. To a hungry visitor's misfortune, a fire laid waste to the restaurant/gift shop in 1979 and the building was never rebuilt. The cost of maintaining a restaurant at this improbable altitude was the major reason for not rebuilding. Everything—including all of its water— had to be ferried up by truck every day. Now, it serves as a shelter from the wind and a stage for regular ranger talks about the animals of the area, including the powerful bighorn sheep, Colorado's state mammal, and the nimble mountain goat. It's quite often overcast here, though on rare days the clouds part, opening up views along the spine of America. If you happen to be one of the lucky visitors who catch nature with the blinds open, take as many photos as possible, as this view is vacation-defining.

At the far side of the parking lot is a kiosk explaining what, on a clear day, is visible. It identifies a number of nearby peaks, including Mount Warren (13,307 feet), Longs Peak (14,255 feet), and Rogers Peak (13,391 feet), among others. You can also see the Denver metro region way off in the distance, conditions allowing. There's also a sundial to the left of this mountain-identifying kiosk. The dial directs you to the exact coordinates of each mountain in respect to the peak of Mount Evans. It's cast in weather-dulled brass and is set in immovable stone. Look to the left of the dial for a brass U.S. geological marker, again set in stone. It's a bit obscure, but it marks the peak of the mountain, identifying it as standing at 14,127 feet. Again, to reach the true summit, hike up the rocky hill just behind you—this point will place you at 14,264 feet above sea level. On the right-hand side of the parking area are viewing stations that take quarters and allow you a view of the immense surroundings. There is also more signage here, which points out other peaks and altitudes. Try spotting each as you look through a spyglass.

Interestingly enough, there is cell phone reception here. So if you feel the urge to give someone a ring and let them know you've just reached the summit of a 14,000-foot peak, you've got the rare opportunity to do so. Take as much time at the summit as you can, it's not often you find yourself this high without the aid of an airplane. On the way back down, be sure to use a low gear and save your brakes.

View from the summit of Mount Evans *Seth K. Hughes*

Coming down from the summit *Seth K. Hughes*

IN THE AREA

Accommodations

Big Spruce Cabins, 3 miles south of Idaho Springs on CO 103. Call 303-567-2841.

Cottonwood RV and Mobile Home Park, 1485 Chicago Creek Rd., Idaho Springs 80452. Call 303-567-2617.

Echo Lake Lodge, 13264 Chicago Creek Rd., Idaho Springs 80452. Call 303-567-2138.

Indian Hot Springs Healing Waters Spa, 302 Soda Creek Rd., Idaho Springs 80452. Call 303-567-1303.

West Chicago Creek Campground, 6.5 miles south of Idaho Springs on CO 103, 3 miles west on FR 188. Call 303-567-3000. www.fs.usda.gov/rec area/arp/recreation/camping-cabins /recarea/?recid=28478&actid=29.

Attractions and Recreation

Adventures in Whitewater, Winter Park 80482. Call 970-726-3279. www.adventureinwhitewater.com.

Argo Gold Mine and Mill Museum, 2350 Riverside Dr., Idaho Springs 80452. Call 303-825-6513.

Clear Creek Ranger District, 101 CO 103, Idaho Springs 80452. Call 303-567-3000.

Mount Evans Trout Fishing, 4125 CO 103, Idaho Springs 80453. Call 303-567-4017.

Dining/Drinks

Buffalo Restaurant and Bar, 1617 Miner St., Idaho Springs 80452. Call 303-567-2729.

Heading up to the summit *Seth K. Hughes*

10 Trail Ridge Road: Rocky Mountain National Park

Estimated length: 48 miles

Estimated time: 2 hours

Highlights: Drive the tenuous Fall River Road—and get rewarded at the end; photograph the sweeping vistas at Mile 15; hike to one of the waterfalls at Glacier Gorge; visit during the elk rutting season in fall to hear these majestic creatures bugling; bring your binoculars and see if you can spot bighorn sheep, black bears, mountain goats, red-tailed hawks, marmots, and some of the park's other inhabitants.

Getting there: From Denver, travel north on I-25 to the junction with US 36. From Fort Collins, take I-25 south to US 36. Take US 36 north/west to the town of Estes Park.

History: Trail Ridge Road was actually the second road constructed through Rocky Mountain National Park. In 1920, five years after it was officially declared a national park by congressional approval, Fall River Road, the first road through the park, was constructed. The year it opened, roughly 116,000 automobile tourists drove this narrow, steep, and winding road.

However, problems with the road were many, and immediately evident. The road was, for the most part, completely unpaved, forcing drivers to traverse loose gravel. The lack of pavement wreaked havoc on the road's condition, especially after the winter months when the expansion and contraction of ice and blustery conditions knocked top layers of gravel free. Furthermore, inclines along the road reached an absurdly steep 16 degrees, making it nearly impossible for early cars to make the trip unimpeded. In addition to these issues, the road's path took trav-

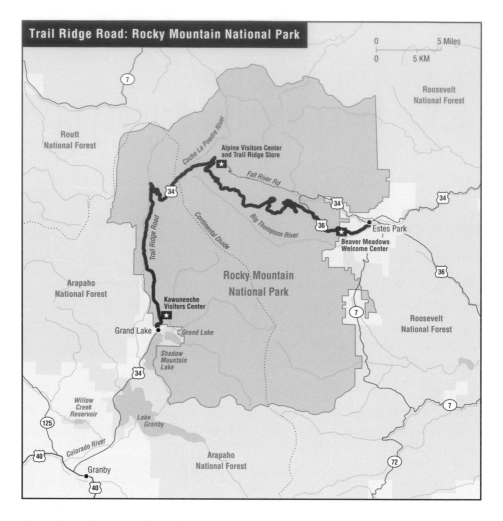

Trail Ridge Road: Rocky Mountain National Park

elers through areas where views down into the valley or even toward the horizon were completely obstructed. And due to the park's ever-increasing popularity, the amount of traffic on this narrow road exceeded its original design. In fact, while still open, Fall River Road is now nearly completely a one-way route, having been classified as too hazardous for two-way traffic some years ago.

With the safety, comfort, and enjoyment of the visiting public in mind, construction on the much-improved Trail Ridge Road began in September of 1929, just nine years after the completion of Fall River Road. Construction of Trail Ridge Road finished three years later, in July of 1932. Due to harsh winter conditions that often exist above timberline, laborers were forced to work solely during the summer, within a paltry four-month window. A small army of laborers (150 in all) used exceptional engineering know-how to build this road over a very short time period. When one season's work was completed, they had to hope that one summer's toils would not be swept off the mountain during the eight months of winter following each stint. After its completion, Trail Ridge Road crossed the Continental Divide in Rocky Mountain National Park at an elevation of 12,183 feet, had a length of 28 miles, and became the highest paved through-road in North America, a unique distinction it continues to hold.

Construction of the road required more than just laying asphalt. Since it was located within a national park dedicated to the pure, unadulterated beauty of the Rocky Mountains, construction had to be environmentally conscious as well. Two different construction companies were tasked with building sections of the road. Each was held accountable for the safety of flora, fauna, and high-mountain tundra. The goal of the park during construction was to maintain as much of the region's natural integrity as it could. Evidence of this is the park's decision to leave various vista-framing rock outcroppings along the road instead of blasting them off the mountain. Permafrost was another issue and a constant problem. If workers dug too deep into the terrain they could create fissures that would eventually lead to the road being washed away. But if they dug too shallow, the road wouldn't have the stability needed to remain on the mountainside. A careful balance between the two extremes had to be reached, and diligently watched, along every foot of construction. While the park tried to minimize the road's footprint, construction still required some blasting. To protect the landscape from being permanently scarred by blasts, natural dams and dikes, designed to funnel debris into a single location, were constructed before blasting occurred. When completed, tundra grasses and flowers were salvaged, then transplanted to road banks in an effort to cover "unnatural" exposure of soil, which ultimately helped curtail erosion in the delicate environment.

Columbine flower

Trail Ridge Road, the highest paved through-road in North America, cuts over the backbone of America, the Continental Divide. Not only do the lofty heights define this route, but so do the abundance of wildlife, including elk, deer, bighorn sheep, and mountain goats. The road itself provides a grand tour of Rocky Mountain National Park, one of Colorado's, and the nation's, most-visited national parks—a fact that becomes evident once you cross the boundary into its evergreen forests, upper montane, and high-mountain tundra.

Mile 1 (US 34)—Beaver Meadows Welcome Center: At the eastern entrance, this is 1 to 2 miles from Estes Park on US 34 west. Built of sandstone rock, it houses a half-dozen park rangers and volunteers, as well as behind-the-scenes staffers. A modest gift shop and educational center provide informational items on the park and its ecosystem. Parking is ample, with limited areas for RVs. While you are not yet in Rocky Mountain National Park, this is your first official source for park information. Park entrance will cost you $20, and credit cards are accepted. Unless you're buying from the gift shop or donating a few dollars, keep your wallet in your pocket—the entrance fee should be paid at the manned tollbooths at the park's boundary. A note to the cost-conscious: If you plan on visiting the park more than once over the course of a calendar year, consider buying the annual pass, which will set you back $40. *There are no mile markers in the park, so set your odometer from this welcome center, as mileage will be your gauge to sights along the byway.*

If you want to spend the day hiking around the park instead of driving the byway, you can leave your car in the parking lot (or even in the town of Estes Park) and catch the hikers' shuttle into the park, which deposits visitors at various trailheads within the park. While it's a free ride, you still need to cover the entrance fee.

It's important to pay attention to the calendar before even planning a trip along the length of the byway, as large stretches of its higher reaches are closed from Labor Day to Memorial Day, though the park is still open and offers sublime wildlife viewing and winter hiking, snowshoeing, and cross-country skiing in its open areas.

The tollbooths are just under 1 mile past the welcome center. There are three booths one-time visitors can access, making the entrance to this park relatively quick and easy. The fourth booth, on the far right, is designated for annual pass holders, and rarely sports a line.

Grazing elk *Seth K. Hughes*

After entering the park, you see the granite peaks of the Rocky Mountains ahead of you, tearing at the azure sky, and streaked with avalanche chutes. In your immediate surroundings are large hills choked with pine. After the toll-booths, continue straight at the Y to continue onto Trail Ridge Road. A left turn leads you to four different sites: Bear Lake, Sprague Lake, Glacier Basin, and Moraine Park. At these lower sections of the road, wildlife isn't the only thing you should be looking for—landscape artists are also a common sight, standing before their easels and rendering the Rocky Mountain bliss that envelopes both you and them into art. The start of the road here is flat and meandering, a laid-back affair. In the winter months, these lower altitudes are havens for elk that have descended to lower elevations in search of shallower snow and dormant grasses.

Upper Beaver Meadows, a trailhead that intersects an old Ute trail, is located 1.5 miles after the Beaver Meadows Welcome Center. After this landmark, the road begins its lofty trek skyward. There's an ideal photo opportunity 2 miles after the welcome center at a pullout on the right-hand side, large enough to accommodate two cars. The vista overlooks a small Rocky Mountain basin. In the not-so-distant horizon is a long row of peaks.

The invasive thistle grows heartily in this climate and is well represented at

At one time, Fall River Road was open year-round, but due to operating costs of clearing winter snow, it was decided that normal operations of the road would occur between Labor Day and Memorial Day, thus decreasing the number of man-hours it takes to maintain this all-American road.

the outlook, its hot-pink flowers standing starkly against the muted greens of the surrounding grasses. A number of black-eyed Susans intermingle with the thistles, and soften their extreme vibrancy.

On your left, roughly 100 yards after this first vista, is another pullout with much the same view, though this one also supports a trailhead. If both of these sites are full, don't worry. Every 100 yards or so another opportunity for stopping has been built into the shoulder of the road. If the day of your visit seems like the busiest of the season, a sentiment especially true during summer, remember that patience usually pays off.

In midsummer, no matter how patient you are, the campgrounds of the park are completely filled by midafternoon: Don't arrive at the park expecting to find a prime spot, or even any spot at all. It's a good idea to make reservations for a campsite before entering the park. Reservations can be made for two sites in the park: Moraine Park and Glacier Basin; the others are first-come, first-served. Make reservations online by visiting www.recreation.gov or by calling 1-877-444-6777. If you're unable to finagle a campsite within the park, consider camping at the privately owned sites near Estes Park—or Grand Lake, on the western entrance.

Roughly 3 miles after the Beaver Meadows Welcome Center, there is a large pullout with an informational kiosk and the same views. Just after the kiosk, visitors encounter another fork. You can either turn onto Fall River Road—the first, and now outdated, route through the park—or continue along Trail Ridge Road. To stay on the byway continue straight onto US 34 west.

The road dives down after you cross the intersection, and quaking aspen begin to make an appearance. The ubiquitous pines found in the park now start to grow closer to the road, hedging you in. The trees on the hillsides are so thick that it's hard to imagine any animal having enough space to travel through them.

Mile 5.5 (US 34)—Into the Park: At 5.5 miles into the route, there is a viewing area on your right with wheelchair access. The area is roughly 100 yards long, and looks like a dock without a bay, as it rises above supple grasses and through a grove of pine.

At the hairpin turn at Mile 6, there's a pullout to **Hidden Valley Parking Area and Trailhead.** It's easily accessible and is situated roughly 2 miles down the road. This area has been outfitted with restrooms and picnic areas.

A multitude of shimmering aspen leaves can now be seen shaking in the wind, and abut the edge of the road. At 7 miles in, aspen and evergreen fight for dominance along the roadside. Through the minimal spacing between their boughs, the smooth and partially tree-bare Rocky Mountain peaks can be seen.

Traffic along this road is heavy and slow, as everyone jockeys for a view, but you didn't come all this way for a quick drive. The best advice anyone can give is to expect to have a car ahead of you, a car behind you, and ethereal scenery filling every other gap.

Mile 7.5 (US 34)—Into the Park: At 7.5 miles in, you'll come across one of the most popular and heavily trafficked pullouts. You may come to a dead stop here as people try and get off the road. The hero of the scene is a lava-molded boulder sitting on the edge of the pullout and above a valley basin. A number of visitors choose to take a family shot sitting atop the jagged boulder. There's a nature trail along the left side of the road as well. It showcases a sheer drop-off into the valley, but for those with inquisitive children or a dislike of heights, fret not, a strong fence stands between visitors and the abyss. The trail is wheelchair accessible, and again, as is the norm with roadside trails here, no more than 100 yards in length. There are a few informational signs along this area that explain more about the road and environs.

Mile 8.5 (US 34)—Into the Park: After driving 8.5 miles, look to your right and straight down into the entirety of a high-mountain valley. At the bottommost area of the valley is a tiny river that snakes through the land. Be very careful as you look down, guardrails are absent from the side of the road. From time to time you will see a rock-

This is a popular motorcycle route. Harleys rumble loudly at high altitude, with a throatier gargle to their trademark sound. Road cyclists are also a popular bunch, fighting the effects of thin air as they huff it up the road and bomb down the steeps, conquering the highest continuously paved road in North America.

Alpine tundra *Seth K. Hughes*

and-mortar wall a few feet long, although these barriers don't inspire much confidence. Looking down the drop-off, you gain perspective on how high you've come in a short amount of time. At this point, pines and high meadow are all that remain; you've now crossed the threshold into the high montane region.

Mile 10.5 (US 34)—Into the Park: While most of the vistas showcase the grandiose, the pullout at Mile 10.5 focuses on the tiny natural intricacies of a mountainside. A cascading mountain stream tumbles down large rocks, frothy and clear. Rooted in the grassy edges of the cascade are wildflowers the colors of an oil painting. And beyond the banks are the true greens of pine, shielding this snatch of scenery from anyone but those looking on from the roadside. The well-used pullouts for this point-and-shoot scene are on the right. This is your last picturesque stop for views of high montane. Immediately after this pullout, the scenery morphs; there are fewer trees and those that do remain grow fewer needles than those in lower elevations. As the scene is unveiled, the tips of rocky behemoths emerge. The tops of these peaks seem to be composed solely of rockfalls and look unstable, as though removing a key stone would cause the entire mountain to topple down, covering the road.

If you look right, across a valley, the mountainsides are still covered in pine, thick as the fur on a dog's back. Near this juxtaposition is a popular photo pullout. Restrooms are also available here, making the stop one of the most popular along the first half of the route. At this vista, the trickle of a river with dramatic oxbows can again be seen running through flat, lush meadows far below. Looking down into the valley, you see pine trees covering the shorter mountaintops below you. A distinct tree line, above which trees refuse to grow, physically marks the boundary between life zones. As you were driving up Trail Ridge Road, the trees seemed immense and were the largest living creatures in view. Now, at this lofty altitude, they seem minute. From this distance they look more like moss covering a stone than a forest covering the Rockies. Be careful at this pullout, as turn signals are scarce and drivers abruptly dart in and out of the overlook.

Immediately after the pullout you'll round yet another turn. Look straight ahead, and pay no mind to the sheer drop-off that looms to the right. Taking center stage is a mountainside that is sliding off the face of the Rockies. It looks like a shelf of glacial size has crumbled away and sheared off, exposing a lichen-stained face of smooth granite. At this site, you enter the high-mountain tundra in earnest. Trees grow dwarfed and gnarled, like arthritic fingers, shaped by the unencumbered winds and cold snaps they constantly face. They are the last trees to grow on the mountainside before you reach the summit, the only ones hardy enough to challenge the elements and last for decades. Within this terrain are also patches of snow that rarely disappear, no matter how hot the summer. Their perpetual presence adds a contrast of white to the otherwise muted-green landscape. Yellow and white summer wildflowers, tenacious as they are beautiful, also grow from the fragile grasses at this altitude.

There are two opportunities at Mile 13 to pull over and gander at the scenery without fighting the slow ebb of traffic. Read the informational sign of the second pullout, which lets you know that you have entered the highest life zone in the park, as well as the most fragile. While the trees, grasses, flowers, and mosses are small compared with their low-altitude brethren, the time it takes them to grow to the height at which you see them is exponentially longer. The crack of one stem or the dislodging of a moss from a rock can take years to regrow. It's ironic, in a way, that while these species can handle subzero temperatures, extreme winds, and poor soil, they can't cope with a single footstep.

Mile 13.5 (US 34)—Into the Park: At Mile 13.5, look to the horizon and you'll see the silhouettes of Grand Teton–like mountains, armed with sharp pinnacles, veins of snow, and areas of crags and smooth caps. There is a pullout on the left-hand side of the road; it's popular, so you won't be alone.

At Mile 14, take a look out your left window, perpendicular to your car, and you'll see what looks like the highest peak in the park, which touches the clouds and nearly disappears into the cobalt blue haze of midday. A good stopping point is **Forest Canyon Overlook** on the left, at an elevation of 11,716 feet. The viewing area is accessed by a small, paved pathway, suitable for kids and the elderly.

At Mile 15, you've seen the last of any sort of tree. Iridescent purple and yellow wildflowers hug the area's short grasses. Views here are seamlessly spectacular. This section of road is what you'd expect of a national park dedicated to the grandeur of a continent's backbone. You're at the top of it all, looking over now humble peaks that breach the 11,000-foot mark. They cover the entire landscape around you, in every angle and every direction. Take the time to stop at an unmarked, and often less-crowded, pullout on the left just before Mile 16.

This is bighorn sheep country during the summer months. Herds of ewes can often be seen congregating on the high meadows, their brown coats superimposed over cotton-white clouds. Males are less commonly seen, though when they do make an appearance their large namesake horns demand attention. A telescopic lens or a pair of binoculars is the best way to catch every detail of these rare animals. If you look to your left at Mile 16, you'll find a view of two crisp and dark high-mountain lakes. Look for them as you pass near rock formations that look like a child's sand-drip castles on the seashore. Just after the rock formations is also a parking area with views of the lakes. Restrooms and a short hiking trail can also be found here.

Immediately after this scene, the road drops dramatically through a series of twists and turns until you come upon a meadowed saddleback. As with bighorn sheep, elk, who share their habitat, are also common visitors to this area. There is an open tundra area found shortly after the lakes, which is a popular grazing area for the sinewy creatures. It's common to see eager photographers and gawkers trampling over the tundra to get a better view of these animals, but again, this does irreparable damage to a fragile and ever-disappearing ecosystem. So fight the urge to follow the crowd and enjoy the elk from a respectful distance. There are pullouts on both sides of the road here, with ample room to navigate between other wildlife viewers. After a short descent, you again ascend toward thinner air.

Mile 18.5 (US 34)—Into the Park: At Mile 18.5, you come across a towering cliff. A kiosk here explains how this burnt sienna–colored high cliff came to be. It explains that a volcanic explosion caused the geological feature: The force of it blew

Elk bucks *Seth K. Hughes*

a hole in the mountaintop, shearing off one side of its crater. Debris from the explosion (scree) outlines the nearest lip of the volcanic basin.

Miles 19 to 30 (US 34)—Into the Park: At Mile 19, you begin your final descent down the Continental Divide to the other side. At 0.5 mile after this there is a parking area on your left, which has been built to provide views into the volcano-created basin. A few snow-fed cascades and the reemergence of trees can also be seen here. The dramatic peaks and valleys of the Rockies can still be seen ringing the entire scene.

At Mile 20, there is a popular parking area on your right that serves the **Alpine Visitors Center and Trail Ridge Store,** found at an elevation of 11,796 feet. The Trail Ridge Store is your stop for food, gifts, and Native American arts and crafts. The store accepts credit cards. The Alpine Visitors Center has informational displays and viewing areas, and also marks the official halfway point on Trail Ridge Road.

At Mile 21, you come across **Medicine Bow Curve** and an overlook that provides views of Medicine Bow Mountain on the right. At this point, Wyoming is a short 35 miles to the north, an area you can almost see on clear days. These mountains are much smaller than those immediately surrounding you. Their tops aren't devoid of roughage but are instead covered with pine trees, indicating their lower elevations. The rolling tops of these mountains disappear into the horizon, where the state of Wyoming sits.

At Mile 22, you are surrounded by slightly more dense evergreens, and wild-flowers grow in the niches spaced between them, indicating your entrance back into the montane.

At Mile 23.5, there is a scenic pullout that overlooks the return of pine forests. While hardly the most spectacular pullout, it is one of the least used and does welcome the trees back into the environment. At Mile 24, the road flattens out and you come across the **Poudre Lakes,** two more snow-fed bodies of water. There is a viewing area on your right. In addition, intriguing rock formations sit on the opposite bank of the nearest lake: They are square-peg structures, akin to guard towers, that stick straight up, roughly 75 feet, into the air.

At Mile 24.5, you come across **Milner Pass,** the pass that sits atop the Continental Divide, separating the continent. There is a major pullout at this pass, with parking, bathrooms, and hiking trails that lead to the banks of the Poudre Lakes. After these dual lakes, you come to the easily accessed **Lake Irene,** found on the right side of the road—look for the large paved parking area that serves the stop.

At Mile 25.5, you are exactly 2 miles above sea level, or 10,560 feet. Look for the national park sign indicating this altitude; it's nearly immediately after Lake Irene. At this point, the road becomes noticeably windy, and evergreens grow exceedingly close to the asphalt.

Far View Curve Overlook, with parking on your left, overlooks the valley floor, where evergreens spill over the sides but stop short of the grass-covered floor. On the other side of the valley, evergreens run up the walls until they are snuffed out by altitude. Rust-colored rock takes their place, reaching up to the mountain peak. The evergreens that you see as you look down aren't just the typical dark-green variety. Sadly, because of beetle infestation, a number of brown, dying trees can also be seen peppered throughout. It looks as if a painter's brush has randomly splattered red-brown drops onto a green canvas.

At Mile 29, aspens return, fighting a losing battle for space against the evergreens. At Mile 30, the evergreens are again dense, and a heady smell of pine strikes you abruptly. Sharp hills fill the roadsides, and trees grow up and down their faces, at times clinging precariously to exposed granite.

Mile 31 (US 34)—Into the Park: At Mile 31, the **Colorado River Trailhead** parking area is on your right. To your left is **Timber Lake Trailhead.** They are both paved areas, and relatively underused, with parking spaces available. The light use is most likely due to the camping restrictions here. Both hikers and horses are allowed on the Colorado River Trail, which is not for the unseasoned hiker. The entire area is thicketed, like a cloud forest in the Northwest would be. **Beaver Ponds Picnic Area,** a small one-table picnic area, can be found just before Mile 32. Since it has such a limited seating capacity, it's hardly ever vacant. On the right-hand side of the road, just after this semiprivate picnic area, is **Timber Creek,** a site offering drive-in camping among the pine trees.

Holzwarth Historic Site. The **Holzwarth Historic Site** is on your right and accesses old homestead cabins, one found near the parking area, and eight others at the end of a short 1-mile trail. There is often a ranger on hand who is there to answer questions about the site. Informational signs also detail its significance. The dwelling at the trailhead is a miner's cabin, one of the oldest structures still standing in the Kawuneeche Valley. It originally belonged to Joseph Fleshuts in 1902, who homesteaded 160 acres of the area with the intent to live on the land. U.S. law at the time made the land his. In 1911, however, he mysteriously vanished, and wasn't heard from again. The questions as to why he left and where he went have never been answered.

At 0.5 mile down the dirt trail lie the Holzwarth cabins. The Holzwarths lived at this site from the early 1900s until the mid-1970s, when they sold their land to the National Forest Service. The life of their homestead had always been that of a working cattle and dude ranch, right up until the 1970s. It originally went by the name of Never Summer Ranch.

The kiosks also talk about the Ute, who were among the first people from modern history to make use of the land. It's said that the Ute hunted game and gathered various plants in this area for more than six thousand years. Later, in the early 1800s, the Arapaho also made their way into this valley. Today, members of both tribes come to the area to embrace their culture, holding various ceremonies here.

Miles 34.5 to 40 (US 34)—Into the Park: Bowen Baker Trailhead and national forest access are on the right; there is a sign for the trailhead at Mile 34.5. A parking area, restrooms, and posted trail maps are available here. There is a small, unmarked picnic area 0.5 mile on the right after the Bowen Baker Trailhead. Near this picnic area is another trailhead, named Coyote Valley.

At Mile 37, the destructive work of the invasive pine beetle is sadly evident. All around you are the browns, reds, and yellows of dead and dying trees, which are being devoured by this tiny insect, a problem for which there is no feasible remedy.

From this point to the exit of the park, a few miles farther down the road, there are a handful of other trailheads, all leading hikers through pine forests and down trails designed for both the novice and expert hiker. Many of these trails cut through large swaths of afflicted trees, their hues adding a poignant touch to the pallet of colors. The road through this section of the park is flat and straight, as is the rest of the byway.

Mile 40.5 (US 34)—Into the Park, Leaving the Byway: At Mile 40.5, you arrive at the park's exit. Another row of ranger booths is there to collect the tolls from visitors entering from the west. Just after the booths is the last ranger station of the byway, Kawuneeche Visitors Center, at Mile 41. The Windy River Campground is across from the visitors center on the right-hand side of the road. The visitors center is set in a grove of pine trees. A stream babbles nearby. An easily accessed trailhead can also be found to the right of the visitors center, and makes for a fun little nature hike to shake out the atrophy of sitting for so long. This station is much smaller than the Beaver Meadows center at the eastern entrance, as this side of the park sees less traffic (unlike Beaver Meadows, whose popularity can be greatly credited to its proximity to Fort Collins, Denver, and the I-25 corridor, the state's major north-south artery). Rangers and volunteers are always on-hand during business hours, and can answer any questions that may have popped up during this 40-mile drive along the highest continuously paved road in the U.S. A small gift shop can also be found here.

IN THE AREA

For more extensive listings in Grand Lake, see chapter 4.

Attractions and Recreation
Alpine Visitors Center and Trail Ridge Store.
Beaver Meadows Welcome Center.
Holzwarth Historic Site.
Kawuneeche Visitors Center.
For all, call 970-586-1206. www.nps.gov/romo/planyourvisit/visitor_centers.htm.

SOUTHEASTERN MOUNTAINS

The Devil's Stair Steps

Near the town of Stonewall

11 Frontier Pathways and Highway of Legends

Estimated length: 185 miles

Estimated time: 6.5 hours

Highlights: Climb around the fascinating Bishop Castle; experience the singing waiters at Rino's in Trinidad; find one-of-a-kind antiques in the many shops in Westcliffe, Walsenburg, and Trinidad; catch trout at one of the many lakes and reservoirs on these byways; photograph geological wonders along the way, including the Sangre de Cristo Mountains, the Devil's Stair Steps, and Stonewall.

Getting there: From Denver, take I-25 south to the town of Pueblo. From Grand Junction, take US 50 east to Pueblo.

History: This byway is a crossroads of culture. Its well-worn path was first traversed by the Ute, then by Spanish and American explorers, including Zebulon Pike. Finally, fur trappers, prospectors, and homesteaders found their way into the area.

Pueblo. The first white settlement in the area was Fort Pueblo, built in 1842 for the protection of traders who sought to barter with the native Ute, mostly trading for buffalo hides. However, as with other forts during this period, strained relations between whites and American Indians boiled over. On Christmas Eve of 1854, a tribe of Ute was invited into the fort to join in the festivities. Taking advantage of the situation, the Ute attacked and razed Fort Pueblo, killing all but a few of the revelers. After the massacre, the site remained uninhabited by Westerners until 1860, when settlers began building over the timbers of the abandoned fort. Since the town was officially raised, it has found its foothold in industry, most notably with steel manufacturing. But fate dealt another blow to

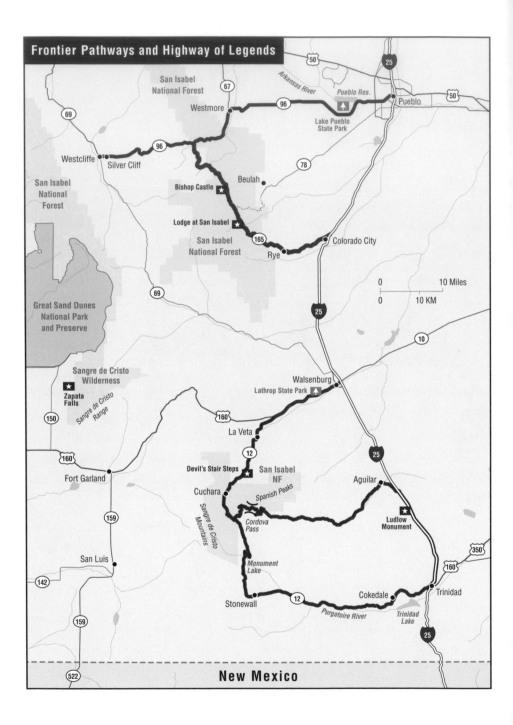

the town's livelihood in 1921, when the swollen waters of the Arkansas River, which runs through town, broke free of their banks and flooded much of the city. It washed away buildings, businesses, and family futures. Later, the river was rerouted and a series of levees and reinforced embankments held the Arkansas in check, and now a stretch of the Arkansas through town is a very popular tourist attraction, known as the riverwalk.

Westcliffe to Colorado City. Named for England's Westcliffe-on-the-Sea by town founder Dr. J. W. Bell, an English national, Westcliffe is Custer County's seat of government. It was originally one of Colorado's booming silver towns, but like other silver-based economies, the town, along with Silver Cliff, which touches its borders, lost much of its significance after the economy crashed in 1893, leading to the repeal of the Sherman Silver Purchase Act. Today, its sturdy pine trees and radiating hiking trails keep the town on Colorado's maps.

Highway of Legends Scenic and Historic Byway. Connected to the southern entrance of the Frontier Pathways by a short 25 freeway miles, the Highway of Legends Scenic and Historic Byway is an easy add-on to the route.

The Tarahumare tribe of American Indians believed the birthplace of creation was located in the Sangre de Cristo Mountains, the heart of which this byway crosses. It's easy to see from where this belief arose. The scenery is dominated by the serrated edges of these granite behemoths, which seem to nearly touch the sun.

One of the first documented Western expeditions into the area involved gold-hungry conquistadors. Having found traces of gold in the Sangre de Cristos, they enslaved a local American Indian tribe, forcing them to mine the metals. When they had obtained all they could carry, the Spaniards slaughtered the natives and collapsed the mine on top of the bodies. When returning south, a band of American Indians, intent on revenge, attacked them. The Spanish were slain, to a man, and their gold was never recovered. This cache of gold is believed by some to be still hidden away somewhere nearby.

The first true American exploration of the area occurred in 1860, when the Army of the West, a force sent to fight in the Mexican-American War, passed through. The initials of a few American soldiers can still be seen atop Fisher's Peak, carved into a large granite stone at its summit. A decade or so after the Union army marched through the area, homesteaders from New Mexico began to descend upon the region. They immediately began working toward incorporating the area into Colorado, creating the modern-day town of Walsenburg. Soon after, the discovery of coal in the surrounding mountains heralded a population boom around Walsenburg and Trinidad. On the coattails of coal miners came the fortune-seeking gold miners, intent on finding the next mother lode.

Although gold was to be had in these mountains, the veins did not sustain for very long. Coal, however, flourished. With this abrupt and exponential growth came the influx of crime in an already rough-and-tumble area. One of the most intriguing stories involves Bob Ford. After shooting his cousin, Jesse James, in the back for reward money, Ford moved to Trinidad—well, he tried to. Thanks to what was seen as cowardice for shooting an already-fabled outlaw in the back, Ford was run out of town by locals and forced to live with his sister in nearby Walsenburg. He was later shot dead in Creede, Colorado, by the sheriff—a relative of one of Ford's former robbery victims. Even the hero of the American West, Doc Holliday, and the Earp family passed through town; Holliday was eventually buried in the Western-Slope town of Glenwood Springs, located a few hundred miles away.

Mile Markers 49–44 (CO 96)—Pueblo: Frontier Pathways Scenic and Historic Byway begins in Pueblo, a familiar town to many Colorado visitors. The town is situated along I-25, Colorado's main north-south artery, and abuts the foothills of the Rocky Mountains. This one-time Spanish colony is now the most-visited city in Colorado's plains. Don't judge the town by how it looks from the highway; it is admittedly not the most breathtaking town in Colorado, but this is a gem of a town worth exploring.

In the post–World War II era, Pueblo's steel economy boomed, putting more than nine thousand laborers to work. In the 1980s, however, the steel boom went bust and half of its original labor force was laid off. Never a town to admit defeat, Pueblo began the arduous process of reinventing itself.

In 1921, the Union Avenue District, now Pueblo's arts district, was submerged beneath 11 feet of water as the Arkansas overflowed its banks. Truth be told, this nearly broke the spirit of the neighborhood and people were ready to pull up stakes and relocate. In fact, the area was mostly given up for lost until the 1980s, when a revival of sorts began to reclaim it, thanks in large part to the arts community.

With a revitalized riverfront area as its base, Pueblo now embraces tourism.

The Arkansas River has been tamed through town, and a riverwalk meanders along its banks. The city makes use of this area with regular summer festivals, concerts, and other events; lazy boat trips down this calm section of the river are also available to visitors.

The byway officially begins at the western edge of Pueblo at the junction of US 50 and CO 96. The town's largest green space, **Pueblo City Park,** is found at this intersection. It's more than just a swath of green grass, as one would expect from a park. Instead it is saturated with family-friendly activities, including a 18-hole golf course, an electric train ride for the kids, and an early 1900s carousel. Adjacent to the city park is the **Pueblo Zoo,** home to a literal jungle of animals and the largest lizard exhibit in Colorado. At the intersection, take CO 96 west toward Wetmore.

Before Pueblo was a steel town, it was a hub for the trading of buffalo hides and beaver pelts. Fort Pueblo, built in the 1840s, was the axis on which trade revolved. American trappers, Mexican traders, and American Indians all passed through the fort's adobe walls. Ultimately, the fort was razed in 1854 when tensions between traders, settlers, and American Indians boiled over. On Christmas Day, Ute attacked; the fort was abandoned soon after, a shell of its former self.

Although the fort was no more, the area was still an ideal crossroads for pioneers looking to traverse the Continental Divide. The area continued to be settled, with residents taking timber from the abandoned fort to build their new town. Years later, the city was built over the fort, burying it under streets and structures. In 1989 archaeologists began to unearth this nearly forgotten fort and began what would become the **El Pueblo History Museum.**

The museum opened in 1990 on the fort's original site, now located at 301 North Union Avenue. Visitors to the museum are treated with displays on early settler and American Indian life on the prairie as they walk among unearthed walls of the original fort. The museum is now an anchor for the town's **Union Avenue Historic District** and the **Pueblo Loop Tour,** both ideal for learning more about the history of the town. Consider walking or biking these loops. Maps are available at the El Pueblo History Museum.

Mile Marker 49 (CO 96)—Lake Pueblo State Park: A mere 5 miles down the road from the intersection of US 50 and CO 96 stands an architectural monolith: **Lake Pueblo Dam.** The steel and cement spines of the convex dam stand against the 4,500 surface acres of Lake Pueblo. You can find one of the better views of the dam at the **Division of Wildlife Office** at Mile Marker 50 on the right-hand side of the road. It's also home to the **Bighorn Archery Range.**

The state park itself is a boater's oasis. Fishing, sailing, Jet-Skiing, and swimming are popular on-water activities. The park also has terrestrial draws, including 18 miles of hiking and biking trails. The longest is **Dam Trail,** which travels 16.5 miles along a paved pathway and runs north to south between the lake's two marinas. More than four hundred campsites are also available here, the majority of which have full electrical hook-ups for RV users. While open year-round, the park is most heavily used from Memorial Day to Labor Day, when campsites are known to fill quickly. Luckily, reservations can be made by visiting the park online. When at the park, be sure to look around, past the vast flatlands and muted buttes to the north and west, where views of the lush Wet Mountains and Pikes Peak can be seen.

Mile Markers 49 to 27 (CO 96): Cresting the hill after Lake Pueblo State Park, the Wet Mountains take over the forefront of the horizon as you enter a wide basin. Roughly 30 miles of a valley basin separate you from mountains once documented by famed explorer Zebulon Pike. Lonely farmhouses are peppered over the land, perhaps a dozen in all, each with a long dirt driveway leading to its front door. Look to your right, and the sight of the city of Pueblo West sprawls in the distance.

Along this lonely section of byway, the soft soils have been eaten away by the elements, leaving brittle sandstone shelves cut into the walls of small, sporadically placed valleys, with cattle grazing along their rims. This scene continues for roughly 10 miles.

Look to the north after about 20 miles of driving along CO 96 to see more of the Wet Mountains. You begin to realize you're in a grand basin. The snowcapped Pikes Peak to the north is the highest pinnacle visible.

Notice how, like ripples in an ocean, the ground begins to rise up and turn a sun-faded green. The Custer County line is the division of this geological feature and is also home to soil conservation in this arid, drought-prone area. Look to the red-roofed barn on the right for the expansive soil conservation research center. It's along this county line division that you begin to transition into a life zone with juniper and pinyon heartily growing; then, nearing the town of Wetmore, the flora changes to lower montane, with evergreens and aspens.

Mile Marker 36 (CO 96)—Wetmore: The town of Wetmore is little more than a blip on today's map, but it was once full of buckskin-clad trappers headed deep into the Wet Mountains in search of pelts. Today's town is a small ranching and farming community set in the shadow of the Wet Mountains. As you enter town, the **Wetmore General Store** is to your left. Look for the faded Pepsi mural painted on its roadside wall. It's a town where you can expect to see children in their Sunday best, biking home from church. This community still embraces its small-town roots.

The air begins to have an alpine feel as you leave town and gain altitude. At the end of town is your last chance to stock up on goods in the area; the **Wet Mountain Goods General Store** is one of the last buildings on your way out of town.

Nearly immediately after you breach the boundaries of Wetmore, you'll enter into the evergreen-laden **San Isabel National Forest**. Originally called a forest reserve, and created to stay the hand of homesteaders in the area, the San Isabel National Forest of today is still an ecological gem. While originally classified solely for timber, cattle, and watershed use, in the early 1900s it became clear that recreational activities would also be popular in these areas. Today, the National Forest Service oversees this and more than 150 other national forests nationwide. Their mission is to maintain the environmental integrity of the area, as well as provide recreational and economic benefits to the community. The San Isabel National Forest is no exception, and it covers a good portion of the Wet Mountain Range.

The byway cuts through the forest along CO 96 for roughly 10 miles. Juniper and sagebrush give way almost immediately to pine that covers sharp, small, and exceptionably climbable hills. After driving nearly 30 miles, your first true hiking experience presents itself: the trailhead to **Lewis Creek Trail** in the **San Lewis National Forest**.

To the left is **Hardscrabble Canyon**, a small granite gorge carved by the babbling brook that's still running. For information on the area—including wildlife and the many life zones the road will follow—stop at the **Hardscrabble Wildlife Viewing Area** at Mile Marker 23. The informational kiosks here give you all kinds of gems about the surrounding area. One sign advises you to look for Colorado's state mammal, the bighorn sheep. Another printed sign gives visitors information on animal populations in Colorado, as well as identifying animal tracks. Yet another sign details the numerous life zones of the Wet Mountains and identifies its highest point, Greenhorn Peak, at 12,347 feet. While reading the signs, you are standing at 7,000 feet of elevation. There's also a sign that advises you to keep a sharp ear out for the Mexican spotted owl and Virginia warblers. Another sign explains that the byway goes through five zones: alpine, subalpine, montane, foothills, and grassland. The final sign gives an abbreviated history of the byway, beginning with Matthew Kinkead in 1844. Kinkead established the first American-owned cattle ranch in the Rocky Mountains. It was originally built near this spot at the junction of North and South Hardscrabble Creeks.

Look for rock features throughout this section of the byway like **Lover's Leap,** near Mile Marker 16, and **Big and Little Sinking Ocean Liners** near Mile Marker 18. At Mile Marker 18, there is a pullout on the right, providing access to snap a few shots of the granite pinnacles of the "ships," which do their name justice—though it does take a little imagination to make out their forms.

The road winds quite a bit more after this point, so if you want to take pictures, use the amply provided pullouts. The babbling brook from earlier now gains momentum from time to time, cascading over small boulders along the left side of the road. The drive seems to perpetually wind between two valley walls, just high enough so you can't see over them, and they're laden with evergreens.

Mile Marker 6 (CO 96)—Wet Mountain Valley: Wet Mountain Valley separates the relatively diminutive Wet Mountains from the skyscraping majesty of the Sangre de Cristo Mountains. The Sangre de Cristos stretch for nearly 100 miles, and

Near Westcliffe

lay claim to 6 of Colorado's 54 Fourteeners. Among these needlelike behemoths of granite are Crestone Peak (14,294 feet), Kit Carson Peak (14,165 feet), Challenger Point (14,080 feet), Humboldt Peak (14,064 feet), Mount Lindsey (14,042 feet), Little Bear Peak (14,037 feet), Blanca Peak (14,345 feet), and Ellingwood Point (14,042 feet). It's an irresistible string of mountains that expert climbers find hard to pass up.

Mile Marker 1 (CO 96) — Silver Cliff: The barely-on-the-map town of Silver Cliff was once a boomtown, riding the coattails of artificially high silver prices. Thanks to the Sherman Silver Purchase Act, which was passed to keep silver prices high, the town and its members found nearly unlimited wealth hidden beneath layers of dense rock. Within less than 10 years (1878–85), miners had extracted more than $3 million in silver and copper, a testament to the feverish pace at which they worked. By 1880 Silver Cliff was the third largest town in Colorado, proclaiming a population of 5,040 people, a drastic difference from today's populace of a dwindling 350 souls. The town's demise can be credited to two factors: the first was the repeal of the Sherman Silver Purchase Act, and the second was the tapping of the area's mines. Most of the precious ore is now gone, but the area is still honeycombed with mine shafts and strewn with abandoned mining structures. A stop by the **Silver Cliff Museum** at 606 Main Street in what was once the town hall and fire department, built in 1879, will edify you on more of the town's, and the area's, history. The museum is open Friday through Sunday, Memorial Day to Labor Day, but special tours can be arranged in the off-season by calling ahead.

Mile Marker 0 (Intersection of CO 96 and CO 69) — Westcliffe: The town boundary between Silver Cliff and Westcliffe is somewhat imaginary. The two towns blend together like the colors of a sunset, their borders all but indistinguishable from one another. Each town shared much the same history, which pertains mostly to mining. The reason these two towns were built nearly on top of each other was due to the Denver and Rio Grande Narrow Gauge Railroad. In 1880 the Denver and Rio Grande began buying up as much land as it could west of Silver Cliff in order to lay tracks to access miners hitting pay dirt in the silver mines. Instead of expanding the town boundaries, they created Westcliffe as a rail stop. Wherever tracks were laid, profits followed, and businessmen began setting up shop near the railroad's terminus, in Westcliffe.

The old firehouse in Westcliffe

At 302 South Fourth Street stands the 1891-constructed **Westcliff School-house.** In what we hope isn't a testament to late 19th-century spelling, the "e" in the town's name was omitted from the school's sign. This National Historic Landmark a fully reconstructed two-room schoolhouse, and one of only six original schoolhouses still standing in Custer County. Arch Scherar was the stonemason who built the schoolhouse, as well as a few of the other stone buildings in town, among them the town's jail. Local lore has it that when Scherar constructed the jail, he purposely left a few stones loose, perhaps foreseeing his own future in the town. For disputed reasons, he was at one time locked up in his own creation. He then used his purposely shoddy work to escape. Tours of the schoolhouse are arranged by calling the Custer County Historian at 719-783-2699.

After your visit in Westcliffe, you'll need to turn the car around and head back along CO 96 to the junction of CO 165, which you take south toward Rye.

Beulah. While not explicitly on the byway, this backwoods town is known for the precious rock it mined, and it isn't gold or silver. Beulah red marble, used in the construction of Colorado's state capitol, is so rare that every known reserve of the red-hued rock was used up during the capitol's construction. Today, the town is a small, forested community without a centralized downtown. The drive along CO 78 that leads to Beulah is a compacted dirt-and-gravel road that cuts directly through the heart of the Wet Mountains. Driving here during wet or wintry conditions can be hazardous, but when the weather is in your favor, this detour is worth the bumpy ride. Views of evergreens and wildlife along the roadside envelop visitors for the entire trip. It's also a way to cut the byway in two, should you prefer to skip the southern leg and head toward I-25.

Mile Marker 13 (CO 165) — Bishop's Castle: The passion of Jim Bishop, a creative, and perhaps odd, individual, has left its indelible mark along the byway at Mile Marker 13. Since 1969, Jim has been constructing a castle of sorts. While not meant to be a livable structure, the castle is more of a tribute to one man's passion and hard work. In his own words, painted in white on a faded sheet of metal, Jim states his ef-

Jim Bishop at Bishop's Castle

forts best: "Jim Bishop is creating — by the help of God with his mind and body this monumental art form. For the good of all. Open always on a true donation basis." He's promised to only consider the castle complete when he no longer has the strength to carry rocks in its construction. Only then will his artistic architectural gem be finished. This rock, steel, and mortar structure peeks through the pine trees that nearly engulf it. The fire-breathing dragon, castle walls, and castle turret were all constructed with stones found in the San Isabel National Forest — a fact that once pitted the National Forest Service against Bishop for usage rights to the rocks. Needless to say, Jim is still building.

Mile Marker 19 (CO 165)—Lake Isabel: The National Forest Service, during a campaign to promote recreation in national forests during the early 1900s, built a few cabins near Lake Isabel. While the cabins are no longer in use, visitors to the **Lodge at San Isabel** can see their nearly intact remains. When the lake was created by the construction of Lake Isabel Dam in 1936, hundreds of visitors flocked to its shores to enjoy the new recreation area. It is still popular among locals, especially those inclined toward trout fishing; self- or wind-propelled boats are also allowed on its 40 surface acres. Camping is available at La Vista, St. Charles, Ponderosa, Spruce, and South Side Campgrounds. Consider a foray into the Wet Mountain Range along the **Cisneros Trailhead,** which is open to motorized vehicles. As with any high-mountain trail, it's a good idea to be wary of late-afternoon thunderstorms.

Mile Marker 29 (CO 165)—Rye: The town of Rye, established in 1870, was originally founded as Table Top Mountain, a reference to the flat-top butte found nearby. The name was changed, so the story goes, because the U.S. Postal Service complained the name was too long to fit its circular cancellation stamps. Residents of the town made their living harvesting sturdy pine from the surrounding San Isabel National Forest, which made their reserves nearly limitless. With the relative decline in timber interests, the town still sustains itself through its natural surroundings. In the 1960s, Arkansas River Colorado greenback cutthroat trout—a species thought extinct—were found in a nearby stream. Scientists were quick to reintroduce the fish into their other natural waterways in hopes of repopulating the state. Cutthroats are still raised at the Rye Trout Farm at Mile Marker 29. Though the fish still struggle to sustain themselves, they are slowly making a comeback. If you hook one of these fish, be sure to release it back into the stream. Thanks to its formerly remote location, the town was also used in the 1800s as a quarantine area for local miners with smallpox and tuberculosis. Visitors need not worry today, as that chapter in Rye's history has long since closed. Accommodation options are extremely limited here, but nearby Colorado City and Walsenburg pick up the slack nicely. Continue on CO 165 toward I-25 to access Colorado City. Walsenburg is found a few miles south on I-25, and is your next stop.

Mile Marker 50 (I-25)—Walsenburg: Located along the I-25 corridor, Walsenburg is a frequent stopping point for travelers seeking a place to stay, eat, or fill

Spanish Peaks view from Westcliffe

up. Originally settled by Spanish farmers as Plaza de los Leones in the 19th century, it was renamed in 1873 after Fred Walsen, a profitable merchant who opened the first coal mine. Coal quickly became the main industry here; it became the best-producing coal town in Huerfano County. Truth be told, there aren't a great many attractions in this prairie town, so the town is used as more of a starting or ending point as opposed to a destination in itself. The **Walsenburg Mining Museum** hosts events from time to time, including its annual Christmas Bazaar. The town also has a modest water park (**Walsenburg Wild Waters**) where summer visitors can shoot down slides and escape the dry prairie air in chlorinated water. While sparse on diversions, the town does lay claim to one perennial favorite— **Lathrop State Park.**

Spanish Peaks. The Spanish Peaks are two mountain pinnacles clearly visible from the town of Walsenburg. Their lush sides led the Comanche, who long ago inhabited the area, to believe that they were the home of the rain gods and thus the source of life. In the 1500s, Spanish explorers made their way north and encountered the same mountains. Because the early-morning and late-afternoon light on their towering faces turned the mountains red, they named them the Sangre de Cristo, or the "Blood of Christ."

Lathrop State Park. Lathrop, accessed along US 160 about 3 miles west of downtown Walsenburg, is Colorado's first state park. It was the torchbearer for the now more than 40 parks found statewide. The list of activities available at the 1,594-acre park is impressive, and includes hiking, biking, waterskiing, boating, fishing, camping, golfing, hunting, and picnicking. **Martin's Lake,** open from Memorial Day to Labor Day, sports a beach designated solely for swimming, and it's a good place to let the kids play in the waveless water. The lake is also open to motorized boating and waterskiing, with a boat ramp accessing its 150 surface acres. For those that prefer wind- or self-propulsion, the 150-acre **Horseshoe Lake** is your best bet; be aware that it's closed after November for waterfowl hunting season. Golf is available on the park's **Walsenburg Golf Course.** The course is just hard enough to make it interesting, but don't expect a PGA-quality setup. Contact the golf course directly to schedule tee times. Hiking is limited to two trails. The **Hogback Nature Trail** is the shorter of the two, with a hikers-only 2 mile route that meanders up a ridge to provide views of the Sangre de Cristo Mountains to the west and the Wet Mountains to the northwest. **Cuerno Verde Trail** isn't much longer and is a 3 mile loop. The trail is open to both hikers and bikers and is wheelchair accessible.

Mile Marker 3 (CO 12)—La Veta: After getting on US 160 heading west for 8 miles, take CO 12 south to reach La Veta. Meaning "the vein" in Spanish, La Veta was once a major artery for travel and trade in the 1800s. Fur trappers heading into the nearby Spanish Peaks used this town as a resting and trading point for their profitable sojourns. The **Francisco Fort Museum** provides more information on the town's history. It's housed in the first structure within the Cuchara Valley, a fort constructed in 1862 by Colonel John Francisco and Judge Henry Daigre. It was originally built as a stronghold against possible American Indian attacks and as a center of commerce for traders. Golfers might want to drive, chip, and putt the **Grandote Peaks Golf Club,** a Tom Wieskopf-designed, 18-hole golf course in the center of town.

Mile Markers 6 to 8 (CO 12)—Cuchara Valley: At Mile Marker 6, in Cuchara Valley, is access to Indian Creek National Forest Road, which leads to **Sulphur Springs Ranch.** Just after Mile Marker 7, you start to leave the valley basin and enter the mountains. Your first indication of terrain change is a view of one of the short hogbacks, the foothills to the Spanish Peaks. Cottonwoods still surround the homes of this lush ranching community. At Mile Marker 8, if you look straight ahead and to your left, you'll notice an unusual type of exposed rock. It looks like a supremely brittle and thin butte. The dirt on the hogback has been naturally brushed away, revealing what appears to be the skeleton of a mountain. Below this delicate ochre and lichen-covered butte, a few head of cattle can often be seen grazing lazily. These cows are part of the valley's main industry: ranching.

Mile Marker 11 (CO 12) — Devil's Stair Steps: After Mile Marker 8, the road begins to dip and rise. More buttes, with their sandstone spines exposed by erosion, begin to appear on the roadside. Just after Mile Marker 11, on the right-hand side, are two signs. Each provides more information on these strange rock formations. One of the kiosks talks about **Profile Rock,** a radial dike similar to those you've been observing. This particular dike is found at Mile Marker 9.5. It's one of the hundreds of formations that radiate from the Spanish Peaks. Those with a sharp — or perhaps a creative — eye can discern the profiles of George Washington and Thomas Jefferson in Profile Rock's façade. It's said that a train on a trestle and a rearing horse or deer can also be made out.

This marker also details a legend of an American Indian tribe that once lived in the area. The tribe consisted of giants who once roamed around Wahatoya (one of the Spanish Peaks). These giants were perpetually quarrelsome, and used boulders as weapons to wage incessant war among them. The gods of Wahatoya watched with disgust as the tribe fought. The gods eventually grew angry and withheld rain from the area. When water became scarce, the giants ended their war and spread out over the land in search of better-hydrated areas. They left behind a single warrior to watch over the valley. Tired from his years of vigilance, this lone warrior finally sat to rest. The gods of Wahatoya respected his dedication to his post and turned him into a monument of stone, a testament to his duty. Visitors can now see this "frozen giant" as **Goemmer's Butte.**

A sign entitled GEOLOGY provides information about the **Devil's Stair Steps** located directly behind you ("radial dikes" is their official name). These are the same formations you saw about 1 mile earlier, where cattle graze. More than five hundred of these dikes radiate out of the surrounding peaks, like spokes on a wheel. In addition to the dikes, the kiosk explains the geology behind the peaks, which were formed from plate tectonics, not volcanic activity as many are led to believe from the area's volcano-shaped domes. But it's the legend that captures the most attention. It tells of the devil escaping from hell, eons ago, to survey the world. He used the radial dikes to reach this verdant valley from the depths of hell. As he viewed the beauty of Cuchara Valley, he began to formulate a plan for world domination. God learned of his desires and banished the devil from the valley. The devil retreated down the steps and, according to legend, never re-turned.

At Mile Marker 12, the road is flat but winds considerably, and leads you around even more radial dikes, which erupt from the ground every few hundred feet. You cross over the Cucharas River at Mile Marker 13. The Cuchuras River is the body of water whose touch turns the entire valley green. It's a meandering river, and hardly ever picks a straight line through the land. It takes the path of least resistance, as though trying to spend as much time in this beautiful area as possible. It's no more than 10 feet wide in sections, and is often surrounded by thirsty cottonwood trees.

After Mile Marker 14, you'll begin to see evergreens as the dogwoods give way. Aspen show themselves as well, a few dozen at a time. But it's the pine trees that give you the first inclination that you are beginning to rise in altitude. The soil around here is nearly crimson; look to the right side of the road for rust-colored soil after Mile Marker 15, an area where pine trees almost completely engulf the road. Notice the **Yellow Pine Guest Ranch** on your left. It has a yellow main of-fice and quaint red cabins just before Mile Marker 16. There are a few old, brightly colored ads, seemingly from a 1950s *Good Housekeeping* magazine, painted on the sides of old structures in the area. They look as if a local resident makes it his or her hobby to repaint them from time to time: Their colors are as vibrant as the day their first coat of paint was laid on the timber.

Mile Marker 16 (CO 12)—Cuchara: You now enter the town of Cuchara, a small homestead community for ranchers and farmers. This strip of valley is filled with lush grass, cottonwoods, aspens, and a wealth of evergreens. This tiny foothills town has a few amenities for travelers. The **Cuchara Inn** greets you on the left as you enter the town boundary; you can't miss it—look for a giant log structure near the **Timber's Restaurant.** On the left as you enter town sits a tiny park, com-plete with a children's play area and a few tennis courts. And just before Mile Marker 17, a small trailhead cuts into the forest.

You enter the lush **San Isabel National Forest** on the southwestern termi-nus of town. On your right after Mile Marker 18 is **Cuchara Mountain Resort,** a little-known ski resort—even to Coloradoans. At Mile Marker 19, you round a bend and hit a straightaway. The part of the valley that exposes itself after this bend is blanketed with quaking aspen, adding a lighter shade of green to the equally abundant dark-green pines. RV camping and a hiking trail can be found on Forest Road 422 (FR 422) at Mile Marker 20; it's a well-packed dirt road that leads deep into the San Isabel National Forest—established by President Theodore Roosevelt in 1902. It's open to cars, dirt bikes, and, in the winter, snow-mobiles. Pit toilets and parking are available at the trailhead. The parking area even has a trail map that provides more information on the **Cucharas River Recreation Area.** At 3.5 miles down car-ready FR 422 is Blue Lake, and 1 mile past that is Bear Lake. Bear Lake has a gloomy tale behind its name. In 1907 a black bear was killing livestock and hurting the bottom line for area ranchers. Asa Arnold, the first forest ranger for the San Isabel National Forest, set traps to catch the nuisance bear, and his efforts paid off. Unfortunately, the bear dragged the trap, and the tree to which it was attached, to a nearby lake. The weight of the trap and the injuries sustained by the bear caused it to drown in the lake. Bear Lake thus earned its name. Closer to the trailhead at Mile Marker 20 are the spruce-covered shores of Blue Lake, named for its distinguishing azure color, a much happier namesake.

The cliffs after Mile Marker 20 are sheared away from time to time, showing how red the soil beneath the surface is. After the recreation area, the road begins a steep incline and is surrounded almost exclusively by aspens; it's ideal for fall aspen viewing. You then run into the intersection with County Route 46 (CR 46). Continue along CO 12 and travel straight over Cucharas Pass. As you crest the hill soon after the intersection, you leave San Isabel National Forest and enter the Spanish Peaks/Purgatory River Conservation District. The pass is at Mile Marker 22, at an altitude of 9,941 feet.

Mile Marker 29 (CO 12)—North and Monument Lakes: At Mile Marker 29, you are greeted by **North Lake State Wildlife Area** on the left side of the road. Fishing is allowed, but with artificial lures only. A pullout just after Mile Marker 29 is perfect for a photo opportunity of the sloping and evergreen-lined reservoir. A kiosk at this stop speaks about the area's settlers and wildlife. It advises travelers to look for coyote, black bear, and golden eagles—the largest eagle in North America. It also speaks about Tom Tobin, a whiskey seller, trapper, scout, and bounty hunter from St. Louis who, in 1863, was awarded a buckskin suit for killing and bringing back the heads of two wanted murderers responsible for innumer-

The town of Stonewall

able cold-blooded deaths—even though he was promised much more before attempting the feat.

The road makes a hairpin turn around the lake and follows the opposite bank. There are handicapped accessible toilets on the right, just before that sharp turn. On the left of the road, across from the bathroom, is a turnoff to the lake. The road is in bad condition, but is short and leads directly to the shore and boat ramp. The lake is stocked on a regular basis, and a number of trout species can be plucked from the waters. At Mile Marker 30, another scenic pullout looks down onto the lake and valley in which you are currently driving, making for a pseudo-aerial photo opportunity of North Lake. A few bends in the road later, on the left-hand side, look for an elaborate stone entryway that marks the access point to **Monument Lake.** This lake is roughly the same size as North Lake, and is separated from its neighbor by a small ridge. A welcome center for Monument Lake can be found at Mile Marker 33. There are also cabin rentals available within the boundaries of this lake. Check in at the welcome center for details on renting. At Mile Marker 36, you bottom out from Cucharas Pass and enter a moderately sized valley. You are again introduced to radial dikes and grazing land dotted with cottonwoods.

Mile Marker 37 (CO 12)—Stonewall: This small cattle-ranching community is notable for its clapboard, log, and adobe homes. The downtown area, though small and rustic, does sport a restaurant and RV park with full hook-ups and high-speed Internet access. Look for it as soon as you enter town. The homes here are set within surrounding trees; in fact, their yards look like mini-forests. The **Wall of Legends Guest Ranch RV and Cabins,** complete with a café, can also be found in town—look for what appears to be an old barnlike structure. The town is quite small, as it begins at Mile Marker 37 and ends roughly at Mile Marker 39. **Picketwire Lodge and Store** at the intersection of Terceo and Road 13.0 is on your right, marking the end of tourist-ready stops in this tiny town.

Just past Mile Marker 41 on the right is New Elk Mine, a coal plant. Note its high cement tower connected by a webbing of metal tubes, which carry coal to a processing plant. Take a quick right over a cattle guard and down a dirt road to enter **Bosque del Oso State Wildlife Area** (Forest of the Bear), a popular big-game hunting area found just before Mile Marker 45. At Mile Marker 43, the Devil's Stair Steps–type scenery gives way to juniper-covered rolling hills as you drive east.

Mile Marker 48 (CO 12)—Weston, Segundo, and Valdez: Weston is a working community with nothing much to offer visitors. Unless you're a resident, it's best to blow on through. The town does offer you another entrance to Bosque del Oso State Wildlife Area. It's located on your right at Mile Marker 49.

At Mile Marker 52, the land begins to take on the look of the high-altitude desert of the Colorado Plateau. Access to **Spanish Peaks State Wildlife Area** is on your left at Mile Marker 54. At Mile Marker 56, you enter the town of Segundo. A small bar and one-pump gas station mark the entry to town. This is another working town, which still depends on coal mining. At Mile Marker 57, you enter the town of Valdez. It's hard to tell when one town ends and the other begins, though Valdez's convenience store and gas station is larger, newer, and easier to access.

The exposed walls on either side of the road evidence how prolific coal mining is here. Striations of pure coal appear nearly everywhere you care to look, making this area a veritable coal bonanza. Parts of the town even smell like a beach cookout—evidence of the plethora of coal in the ground. Strip mines, where the earth is removed to access the fuel, are common here. Off on the horizon, a giant butte looms. It has a blue hue to it, akin to the most opaque part of the ocean.

At Mile Marker 61 is an entrance to **Trinidad Lake State Park** and **Longs Canyon,** home to a wildlife viewing area and campground.

Mile Marker 62 (CO 12)—Cokedale: Giant mounds of coal (a slag pile) can be seen just after Mile Marker 62 once you crest a small hill. These slags are so immense they look like black sand dunes. Look for them on the left as you enter the **Cokedale National Historic District.** You can access Trinidad Lake State Park, Reeley Canyon, and Spanish Peaks State Wildlife Area to your right. Looking right, down Reeley Canyon, is a 20th-century ruin, the **Cokedale Coke Ovens.** They are composed of parallel rows of nearly innumerable boxlike concrete structures. They are no longer in use, and time and the elements have begun to chisel away at their frames. The coke ovens are on private property, so climbing in and around them is discouraged, but you'll be able to view them unencumbered from the dirt road itself. Coke ovens are used to refine and smelt iron from coal. It involves a process where the coal is subjected to extreme heat and, via a chemical reaction, is turned into coke, an iron-rich element most commonly used to harden steel.

Before the sand dune–like mounds of coal is a plaque dedicated to the many nationalities that came to labor, and die, in the area's coal mines. The descendents of these original workers still live in the small towns in this area. The plaque also provides more information on how the coke ovens worked.

The Cokedale coke ovens

The town of Cokedale at Mile Marker 62 is tiny with a few historic buildings, including the **Cokedale Mining Museum.** If you're looking for a place to stay, moving on to Trinidad is your best bet. As you turn left into the town of Cokedale, look left to see even more remnants of the mining operation, including an abandoned silo and a cement trestle. Take your immediate left, crossing a small stream to enter the very small, very quaint town of Cokedale. The roads are dirt and the buildings are a bit dilapidated, with a few historic buildings dispersed throughout town. Informational signs explain the stories behind a handful of these historic buildings.

Mile Marker 65 (CO 12)—Trinidad Lake State Park: The pinyon- and juniper-covered Trinidad Lake State Park is easy to access, making it an extremely popular weekend hangout for both visitors and locals. Anglers and boaters are the main enthusiasts drawn to the park, and with good reason. Rainbow trout, brown trout, catfish, largemouth bass, crappie, bluegill, and walleye can all be caught in these warm waters. But even if you don't like to bait a hook, you can still skim across the surface of the water on Jet-Skis or a boat, as boat ramps are available for the nautically inclined. If terrestrial pursuits fit your needs better than getting wet, Trinidad Lake State Park crisscrosses with a number of hiking trails The 0.5-mile **Carpios Cove Trail** is the park's shortest. It leads hikers up a slow incline to a picnic area. Camping is ample and a year-round activity. There are 63 sites total, though roughly half of these are closed during the winter months. Many sites have full RV hook-ups, but are still suitable for the tent camper.

Mile Marker 14 (I-25)—Trinidad: Trinidad sits at the confluence of two scenic and historic byways, Frontier Pathways and the Santa Fe Trail. Its history as a crossroads town is synonymous with its identity. A sandstone sculpture of a pioneer woman scouting the plains, with a child in the fold of one arm and a rifle in the other, stands near the **Colorado Welcome Center** at Trinidad. It's a tribute to those brave souls who traversed the Santa Fe Trail from Missouri to modern-day New Mexico (then part of Mexico). The visitors center where the statue stands is ideal for talking with locals and gathering as much free printed material about the area as you like.

Originally settled by the Spanish as part of New Mexico, the Trinidad of today still carries heavy evidence of its roots. Trinidad's historic downtown area, known as El Corazón de Trinidad or "The Heart of Trinidad," is a testament to this fact.

Downtown Trinidad

It's also a must-see for history-minded travelers interested in Spanish and American pioneers. Purchase a walking tour from the Santa Fe Trail Museum. It directs visitors to a number of historical markers indicating various locations and aspects of the town's storied past.

The **Trinidad History Museum,** located in the heart of El Corazón at 300 East Main Street, has procured and relocated to its grounds three historic buildings: the Baca House, Bloom Mansion, and Santa Fe Trail Museum. The **Baca House**—Trinidad's oldest standing structure—was originally the home of a successful farming and ranching family. Felipe Baca was elected to the territorial legislature in 1870 and was one of the most vocal opponents of Colorado's statehood. He feared, some say rightly, that statehood would mean the marginalization of the area's heavily Latino population.

The neighboring **Bloom Mansion** is an example of a Victorian mansion. The home was once the property of Frank Bloom, a man who made his fortune as a cattle baron in the 1800s. Many of the mansion's furnishings are original pieces, and those that couldn't be found were replaced with period reproductions. While the interior, with opulent drapery and wallpaper, is a testament to the wealth of the owner, it's the home's verdant Victorian garden that garners the most praise.

If you want to stay in an immaculate Victorian room of your own overnight, try the **Tarabino Inn,** an incredibly well-preserved Victorian offering different sizes and styles of rooms, each fully furnished in the Victorian style. In the morning, proprietors Kevin and Teresa will offer you sumptuous breakfasts that you can't find anywhere else, such as spelt blue corn pancakes and Spanish tortillas. For a one-of-a-kind dinner, visit **Rino's Italian Restaurant,** an Italian and new American eatery that is world-renowned for its singing waiters.

The **Santa Fe Trail Museum** abuts these two homes, but is starkly different from either of the two. Its adobe walls contain displays on the town's life as a trading post erected for trappers headed to and from the heights of the nearby Rocky Mountains, as well as the pioneers who heeded the call of manifest destiny to populate the West. The coup de grace of the museum is the original buckskin coat worn by legendary frontiersman Kit Carson.

Between Trinidad and Aguilar (I-25) — Ludlow Monument: From Trinidad, head north on I-25 to exit 27, and travel west on CO 44 for 1 mile to access Ludlow Monument. Chain-link fence surrounds the site of one of the most heinous acts ever visited upon the people of Colorado.

We all know of the honeycombing of mines throughout Colorado and the riches many of them divulged, but few realize the harsh conditions miners were forced to endure to extract the precious material. Long days, no benefits, and extremely dangerous work sites were just a few of the slew of problems facing the veritable army of mine workers. In the early 1900s, workers began to vocalize their discontent. Many groups found their voices through the power of unions, which served to galvanize their cause and gave them the courage to stand up to mine owners and demand better treatment. Mine owners were adamant about rejecting their workers' requests and wanted to keep the status quo. Many of the miners went on strike, including those at Ludlow Station, just north of Trinidad in the fall of 1913. Striking miners erected tent cities near the mines to discourage nonunion scabs from taking their places. Faced with losing skilled workers and millions of dollars due to the strike, owners turned to the state government for help. On April 20, 1914, a skirmish erupted between the Colorado state militia and the miners—who were now solidified under the UMW (United Mine Workers)—as the militia attempted to evict the strikers from their tent city. During the ensuing fight, one militia member was killed, along with five miners. The most disheartening human toll were the deaths of eleven children and one woman, who were found charred after the fight in the tent city, which was razed during the conflict.

This incident touched off an all-out war between the miners and owners, one that raged until December of that same year. President Woodrow Wilson was provoked to send the U.S. Army into the fray to quiet the blows. Finally, a tentative agreement was reached between both interests: The miners were allowed a union, and the owners were provided with control over the organization. While seen by many outside the fray as a grand compromise, many miners, even to this day, feel that they did not receive adequate recompense.

Today, a lone marble monument stands near the foothills of the Rocky Mountains, carved and erected as a tribute to the miners who let their voices be heard despite great opposition and threats to personal safety. Amenities at the monument include a covered picnic area adjoining the fenced-in monument and primitive restroom facilities.

After this final stop, your byway adventure ends. The town of Walsenburg (found north along I-25) and Trinidad (found south along I-25) are the largest towns nearby should you need to find accommodations, food, or facilities.

IN THE AREA

PUEBLO

Attractions and Recreation

Bighorn Archery Range, 600 Reservoir Rd. Call 719-561-5300.

El Pueblo History Museum, 301 N. Union Ave. Call 719-583-0453.

Lake Pueblo State Park, 640 Pueblo Reservoir Rd. Call 719-561-9320.

Pueblo City Park, 800 Goodnight Ave. Call 719-553-2790.

Pueblo Zoo, 3455 Nuckolls Ave. Call 719-561-1452.

WETMORE

Attractions and Recreation

Wet Mountain Goods General Store, 24644 CO 96. Call 719-784-4989.

Wetmore General Store, 758 CR 395. Call 719-784-6149.

SILVER CLIFF

Attractions and Recreation

Silver Cliff Museum, 606 Main St. Call 719-783-2615.

Westcliff Schoolhouse, 610 Main St. Call 719-783-2837.

A view of Trinidad

RYE

Accommodations

Lodge at San Isabel, 59 CR 371. Call 719-489-2280.

WALSENBURG

Attractions and Recreation

Lathrop State Park, 70 CR 502. Call 719-738-2376.

Walsenburg Golf Course, 1399 CR 502. Call 719-738-2730.

Walsenburg Mining Museum, 112 W. Fifth St. Call 719-738-0629.

Walsenburg Wild Waters, 700 W. Seventh St. Call 719-738-2628.

LA VETA

Accommodations

Sulphur Springs Ranch, 5218 CR 421. Call 719-742-5111.

Attractions and Recreation

Francisco Fort Museum, 123 W. Francisco St. Call 719-742-5501.

Grandote Peaks Golf Club, 5540 CO 12. Call 1-800-457-9986.

CUCHARA

Accommodations

Cuchara Inn, 73 E. Cuchara Ave. Call 719-742-3685.

Cuchara Mountain Resort, 946 Panadero Ave. Call 719-742-3013.

Yellow Pine Guest Ranch, 15880 CO 12. Call 719-742-3528.

Dining/Drinks

Timber's Restaurant, 23 Cucharas St. Call 719-742-3838.

WESTON

Accommodations

Picketwire Lodge and Store, 7600 CO 12. Call 719-868-2265.

Wall of Legends Guest Ranch RV and Cabins, 6878 CO 12. Call 719-868-3049.

COKEDALE

Attractions and Recreation

Cokedale Mining Museum, 7 miles west of Trinidad on CO 12. Call 719-846-7428.

TRINIDAD

Accommodations

Tarabino Inn, 310 E. Second St. Call 719-846-2115.

Attractions and Recreation

Colorado Welcome Center at Trinidad, 309 Nevada Ave. Call 719-846-9512.

Trinidad History Museum, 300 E. Main St. Call 719-846-7217.

Trinidad Lake State Park, 32610 CO 12. Call 719-846-6951 or 1-800-678-2267.

Dining/Drinks

Rino's Italian Restaurant, 400 E. Main St. Call 719-845-0949.

INDEX